THE PRESIDENT AS CHIEF ADMINISTRATOR

A Study of Franklin D. Roosevelt

By A. J. WANN

Public Affairs Press, Washington, D. C.

TO MY WIFE ANNELIESE

PREFACE

One of the major Constitutional responsibilities and most important functions of the President of the United States is to serve as the Chief Administrator of the administrative organization of the executive branch. Because of the vast growth in the size and activities of the national government and the increased complexity of the administrative problems resulting from that growth, the task of supervising and coordinating the administrative conduct of the executive branch constitutes one of a President's most laborious, troublesome, and time consuming duties. How well he is able to meet his administrative responsibilities has a significant bearing upon how successful he can be in leading his subordinates in the government to carry through his programs and translate his policies into effective action.

In view of the manifest importance of the President's administrative duties, it is somewhat surprising that they have been accorded such a relatively small amount of attention. The writing of this book grew out of a belief that additional study of the administrative aspects of the President's job is needed and that it would be of value in this regard to describe the efforts which were made by President Franklin D. Roosevelt in trying to meet his administrative responsibilities.

During Roosevelt's tenure in the White House there was a general tendency to describe his administrative conduct in predominantly negative terms, to dismiss his administrative record as essentially one of failure, and to conclude that his weaknesses in the administrative sphere detracted from his over-all presidential performance and his almost universally conceded abilities as a political leader.

From surveying Roosevelt's career, however, it seemed to this writer that a President who had handled the administrative challenges to the government during the country's most serious economic depression and its greatest war, who had seen the size of the administrative organization more than doubled during the time he was President, who had established the President's Committee on Administrative Management and vigorously supported its recommendations for governmental reorganization, who had created the Executive Office of the President and greatly expanded and institutionalized the White House Office, and who had developed the Bureau of the Budget into a major instrument of administrative management — it seemed that the administrative record of a President who had done these things at least warranted a more detailed examination and assessment.

Consequently, through the study of many of Roosevelt's speeches, press conferences, executive orders, official and unofficial statements, and letters, as well as many of the detailed accounts written by those who were closely associated with him, an attempt has been made to present a summary of what Roosevelt thought and did concerning some of the more important aspects of his role as chief administrator.

It should be emphasized that this study makes no pretence of being a definitive treatment of its subject, nor is it even intended to be a comprehensive one as there are several important matters concerning Roosevelt's performance as an administrator which are not dealt with at all. It is hoped, however, that within its limited objectives, this book will make at least a small contribution toward a better understanding of the administrative role of the President and of Franklin D. Roosevelt's record in fulfilling that role.

Like the authors of most books, I am indebted to a number of people without whose help this work could not have been written.

The idea for a study of the administrative conduct of President Roosevelt was initially sparked in one of the graduate seminars which I had a good many years ago at the Johns Hopkins University with the late Professor V. O. Key. In subsequent conversations and correspondence, Professor Key generously encouraged such an undertaking and made a number of helpful suggestions.

Deepest gratitude is owed to Professor Martin L. Faust of the Department of Political Science, University of Missouri, whose thoughtful advice and criticisms contributed much to the development of the manuscript. Sincere thanks are also expressed to Professor Lloyd M. Wells, another friend and former colleague at the University of Missouri, for his careful reading of the manuscript and beneficial comments, especially concerning the final chapter.

Gratitude for encouragement and support is also acknowledged to another friend and former colleague, President R. W. Fleming of the University of Michigan. While serving as Director of the University of Illinois Institute of Labor and Industrial Relations, he arranged a faculty leave of absence for me at a time when it was most needed for some of my research.

Recognition of contributions of a somewhat different kind should be recorded here for the late Frances Perkins, Secretary of Labor throughout Roosevelt's twelve years in the White House, and Louis Brownlow, Chairman of the President's Committee on Administrative Management. Both were greatly interested in the plans for this book and in long, informative conversations both drew on their years of close personal association with Roosevelt to provide many valuable facts and insights.

Thanks are also expressed to Anice Duncan, Ellen Sanders, and Elaine Armstrong for their invaluable services in typing various drafts of the manuscript.

Lastly, gratitude of still another kind is here formally acknowledged to my wife, Anneliese, and daughters, Lotti Ann and Kristin Kay, especially for their tolerance and forbearance during the sometimes disagreeable period in which this study was being written.

All errors of either commission or omission should, of course, be ascribed entirely to the author and not to any of the above.

A. J. WANN

Columbus, Ohio

CONTENTS

About the Author

A member of the faculty of the Ohio State University since 1964, A. J. Wann is Professor in the College of Administrative Science and Director of the Labor Education and Research Service. He previously was on the faculties of the University of Illinois, the University of Wisconsin, and the College of William and Mary. A native of Missouri, he obtained the A.B. in 1940 from Drury College, did graduate work in 1941-1942 at Johns Hopkins University and in 1948-1951 at the University of Missouri where he received the Ph.D. in political science.

Dr. Wann is the author of numerous articles in the fields of political science and labor relations and co-author of *The Philosophy and Policies of Woodrow Wilson* and *The American Federation of Labor and International Affairs*.

Chapter I

INTRODUCTION

The President of the United States has to perform four fundamental and diverse types of duties: first are those incumbent upon him as *Chief of State*, or the titular and ceremonial head of the government, and its principal representative and spokesman in both national and international affairs; second are his duties as *Commander in Chief* of the armed services of the country which make especially heavy demands during periods of national emergency and war; third are his duties as *Political Leader*, which involve his activities as legislative leader of the Congress, and as the principal political figure of his party and of the nation; and fourth are his duties as *Chief Administrator* of the ramified administrative organization which comes under his authority as the head of the executive branch of the government. This study is chiefly concerned with certain aspects of what President Franklin D. Roosevelt did regarding the last of these duties.

It is exceedingly difficult to isolate a President's role as chief administrator from his three other roles. This is especially true when his duties as commander in chief become inextricably involved with both administration and politics during wartime. But at all times, whether in war or peace, it is virtually impossible to draw a well-defined line of demarcation between a President's performance of his administrative functions and his political functions.

Almost all administrative acts of a President necessarily have some political significance. As one leading student of administration has observed, "It is especially hard in the United States to draw a clear line, at high levels, between the administrator and the politician. . . ."[1] Certainly administration at the President's level always takes place in a strongly political context. To try to divorce administration from politics is to attempt an arbitrary distinction not actually found in the conduct of the President's business. Therefore, in making a study such as this, one cannot disregard the fact that political considerations often play a vital role in determining a President's administrative decisions. In discussing this point, a former administrative assistant to President Roosevelt has said, "One must never forget that the President, besides being the chief executive of the federal government, is the head of his party and the political leader to whom the people look most frequently and most eagerly. . . . It is . . . important to keep in mind the paramount fact that all government operates essentially on the political rather than the administrative plane." [2]

In the popular mind a President is undoubtedly thought of most often in his role as political leader; he is judged primarily according to the policies which he advocates and the political skill he demonstrates in furthering those policies. He is exposed most clearly to public view as the leader of his party and of Congress, and as the one national leader who has to get elected to his position by the voters of the entire country. It is certainly not so common for a President to be thought of principally in his role as chief administrator. "For the most part," Louis Brownlow has written, "we think of him only as a national political leader, and we judge him to be right or wrong in the terms of the policies he pursues and the course of action that he espouses. We but seldom think of him as the chief administrator, as the manager-in-chief, as the occupant of the Presidency, which is our only Constitutional means of coordinating the vast and complex structure of the Executive Branch of the government. . . . We are predisposed to elevate the political consideration, the *what* to do, above the administrative consideration of *how* to do it." [3]

Despite this, there has undoubtedly been an increasing public awareness of the tremendous expansion which has taken place in the President's administrative burdens. This expansion has not been brought about by any basic changes in the Constitution whereby new functions were assigned to the President. Under the Constitution, Presidents have always been vested with complete responsibility for the administrative conduct of the government. Rather, the expansion has come from the great growth and increased complexity of the country itself and the enlarged role of the national government which has resulted. Although the President's Constitutional mandate as the government's chief executive has not been altered since 1789, far-reaching economic, technological, social, and political developments have made it necessary for him to perform many new tasks if he is to carry out that mandate. The increase in the functions of the government, with its corresponding growth in the obligations of the President, has been taking place throughout the country's history. It has been most pronounced, however, in the years of the twentieth century, resulting especially from the heavy stresses placed on the government by two major wars and a prolonged economic depression.

From the outset, the duties of the President have been extensive and taxing upon the time and energy of those occupying the office. In the summer of 1789, within a few months of his inaugural as the first President, George Washington complained that he had "no time to read or answer the many dispatches that poured in" on him; by June of the following year he wrote to a friend, "These public meetings with reference to and from different Departments . . . is as much, if not more, than I am able to undergo." [4] By the time he entered upon his second term, he wrote that he did so "with feelings not unlike those of a culprit who is, going to the place of execution." [5] If Washington's Presidential duties seemed oppressive, one cannot help but wonder what he would think of all the additional functions which have fallen upon the shoulders of Presidents in more recent times. The marked contrast between the Presidency in Washington's day and the present has been aptly summarized by the following statement:

"In George Washington's administration the President did not have to deal with international organizations, he did not have to draft legislation in detail, he did not have to submit a correlated executive budget, he did not have to coordinate great programs for the conservation of natural resources, he did not have to issue elaborate rules governing a competitive civil service, he did not have to supervise a large White House office staff, he did not have to address the people by radio, he did not conduct press conferences, he did not perform many of the ceremonial acts which now require presidential participation and relatively few of the statutory obligations were in existence." [6]

Although the work of the twentieth century Presidents has increased greatly in regard to all four of the major types of duties which a President must perform, the largest increase has probably occurred in the President's administrative functions. It is also likely that duties of an administrative nature have normally accounted, day by day, for more total expenditure of time and effort by recent Presidents than any of their other duties, though admittedly it is impossible to make a quantitative separation of presidential functions into hard and fast categories. In any case, the administrative organization which the President heads has grown to Gargantuan proportions in terms of people employed, diversity of activities performed, and services rendered. Under the Constitution, however, responsibility for the operation and conduct of the entire administrative organization must remain with the President, no matter how large that administrative organization becomes. Of course, sheer physical and mental limitations make it necessary for a President to delegate many of his administrative duties to others, but in so doing he cannot delegate any of the responsibility which the Constitution places upon him. He alone must bear final responsibility for directing and coordinating the many diverse parts of the administrative organization so that policies get translated into action; he alone must bear the final responsibility for seeing that the administrative work of the government gets done. The provision of the Constitution vesting all executive power in the President makes him automatically the chief administrator over the entire administrative organization of the government.

In spite of the fact that the President is probably more often thought of in his role of political leader, there is undeniably a general feeling on the part of the public that he should supervise and control the activities of all the administrative agencies of the national government. As Brownlow has said, "The expectancy is that the President will be the general manager of the entire machinery of government."[7] Although a large proportion of the public probably does not have a very clear or realistic conception of how the President functions as the administrative head of the government, or precisely what he can or cannot do to exercise authority over the administrative organization, it does expect him to keep control of how the government operates. This can be seen most clearly from the fact that if anything goes seriously amiss in the administrative workings of the government, the President is almost surely to be blamed. Harold Laski once contrasted this to England where "if things go wrong, or a mistake is made, an anonymous entity, 'the Government,' is blamed; in the United States it is the President who is blamed."[8] The extent to which the public holds the President responsible for the conduct of the administrative organization has been emphasized by Charles Hyneman in the following passage:

"The entire construction of his office as founded in the Constitution and shaped by experience presumes that the President will answer directly to the people for what the administrative branch of the government does. . . . It is extremely unlikely, their assumptions about administration being what they are, that the American people will consistently excuse the President for what they believe to be serious misconduct in administration."[9]

Although the writers of the Constitution fixed the responsibility upon the President for managing the administrative affairs of the government, they were exceedingly vague in providing an administrative organization for him to manage. The accounts of their debates leave no doubt about the fact that the members of the Constitutional Convention definitely meant that the various activities of the government should be performed by departments; yet, except for the rather indefinite usage of the word "department" in three different places in the Constitution,[10] nothing was done by the Convention to establish any administrative organization. It has been inferred, however, that the members of the Convention intended not only that departments should be established but that they should function under presidential supervision because of two specific provisions of the Constitution pertaining to the duties of the President. The first states that the President "may require the opinion, in writing, of the principal officers in each of the executive departments, upon any subject relating to the duties of their respective offices. . . ."[11] The second is the provision which requires that the President "shall take care that the laws be faithfully executed. . . ."[12] Both James Madison and Alexander Hamilton later confirmed that it was the Convention's intention to make the President responsible for the departments, Madison holding that it was the duty of the President to "inspect and control" all subordinate executive officers and Hamilton stating that "the President should exercise superintendence" over all administration.[13] Writing in *The Federalist*, Hamilton said, "The true test of a good government is its aptitude and tendency to produce a good administration," and he made it clear that it would be the first duty of the President to manage the government in such a way as to produce this "good administration."[14]

Although the above provisions of the Constitution place the responsibility for supervising the executive departments upon the President, the Convention left the power to determine the number and form of such departments entirely in the hands of Congress. Under the Constitution, as Don Price has said, "The President is responsible for the administration of the executive branch, but the Congress may to any degree it likes determine the organization and procedures of the executive branch."[15] Because of this Constitutional ambiguity, it is of basic importance to keep in mind that the President is in no way free to determine the structure of the administrative organization which he is expected to supervise. To carry out his administrative responsibilities, he must work through whatever departments and agencies Congress establishes; he may alter those departments and agencies only within the limitations Congress prescribes; he may re-organize the administrative organization only under such authority as Congress grants to him.

The President, of course, is not without influence in shaping what Congress may do concerning these matters. As with all other questions of public policy, he has the right to recommend appropriate legislation and to resort to all of the substantial resources at his command to secure its enactment. Indeed, it is a matter of record that a preponderant number of the changes which have been made in the administrative organization during the twentieth century have resulted from such Presidential initiative rather than from the initiative of Congress. And the President always has the power to use his Constitutional prerogative of veto if Congress passes a measure altering the administrative structure in a way he does not like. In order to change the administrative organization as he wishes, however, the fact remains that a President must secure the necessary authority to do so from Congress. His success or failure in obtaining such authority will frequently depend not alone on the administrative merits of his proposals but on factors that are highly political in nature. Consequently, administrative organization usually becomes a political matter as well as an administrative one. In assessing the record of a President in regard to administrative organization, one needs to look at the proposals for administrative change which he recommended to Congress, what authority he was able to get from Congress, and what improvement he was able to accomplish within that authority.

The administrative leadership which a President is able to provide depends greatly on the degree to which he can control the administrative organization which he has under him. The sheer size and complexity of governmental administration make it impossible for any person to perform the President's responsibilities single-handed. As all other mortals, the President has but twenty-four hours in his day and he must divide his time among the many tasks incident to all four types of essential duties which he has to perform. Because of the wide range of his obligations, the President must ordinarily confine his administrative role to that of providing general supervision and co-ordination. He has to depend upon the departments and agencies under him for the actual performance of the vast bulk of his administrative functions. Yet, in the limited time at his disposal, he must be able to control what goes on in the administrative organization if he is to make sure that the laws are being "faithfully executed." Under our system, "the reality of responsible government," Paul Appleby has said, "is dependent upon the ability of the President to control the executive branch." [16]

It is certainly not easy for the President to exercise this control. Some students of the subject have even despaired of his ever being able to do so: "The weakness in the President's control of administration is not lack of authority, but the impossibility of one man's handling the job. Time, physical strength, and the mammoth character of the task would veto the efforts of a superman if he had nothing else to do, and if the administrative machine was better organized to facilitate his control." [17] A President, however, must do his best to control the administrative organization in spite of these handicaps, unless he is to abdicate one of his major duties. It is incumbent upon him to try to get the government organized in such a way that he can manage it as effectively and efficiently as possible. For unless he has an administrative organization which he can manage adequately, he cannot ensure that it will be responsive to the new needs which will inevitably arise from changing circumstances, or that it will put into effect the improvements in administrative methods and procedures which experience indicates to be desirable.

The fact that a President ordinarily finds it possible to exercise only a general, top-level control of administration makes it necessary for him to parcel out much of his authority among a multitude of subordinates in the many departments and agencies of the executive branch. As a result, the President's most important and time-consuming job relating to the administrative organization is usually that of providing the over-all coordination of the many activities his subordinates are performing under his authority, and for which he is responsible. [18] "It is the President's supreme administrative task to coordinate the work of the departments and divisions of the Executive Branch," as Louis Brownlow has said. [19]

The departments and agencies are set up on a basis of specialization, each charged with the obligation of administering only a share of the President's authority. It is the President's problem to bring about a sufficient degree of team-work among them so that they will work together efficiently and in relative harmony. To do this, he often has to overcome very strong separatist tendencies which develop in most agencies as a result of their highly specialized functions and clientele. He also has to minimize the frictions which inevitably develop from conflicting temperaments and viewpoints among his

subordinates. Jurisdictional disputes and disagreements over inter-
pretations of policies are almost certain to occur between agencies
and these must be settled, or at least reconciled temporarily, if the
government's work is to be accomplished. In matters of this kind, the
President often finds it necessary to intervene directly. Unfortunately,
parties to such controversies know that both the ultimate authority
and ultimate responsibility for settling their disputes belong to the
President and they often will not accept a decision other than his
as final. Thus, a large part of the job of coordination inevitably falls
upon the President personally. The fact that it is usually difficult for
him to devote sufficient time and effort to this task, considering the
pressure of the many other things he has to do, has led Marshall
Dimock to observe:

"Inadequate coordination is the greatest administrative defect
in American National Government. . . . Our chief organizational weakness is that the President, in the nature of things, cannot provide
the coordinating attention which the world's largest governmental
structure requires. His time is preempted with too many other essential duties. . . ." [20]

If, as Dimock believes, the President cannot perform the function
of coordination adequately, he is obligated, nevertheless, to try to
do so. To make the task somewhat easier, he may attempt to
integrate and combine component parts of the administrative organization in such a way that some of the need for coordinative action will
be obviated. The degree to which he can do this, however, is often
sharply limited by provisions of legislation and political pressures.
He may try to supervise and control the departments and agencies
by such detailed and clear-cut directions and assignments of responsibility that jurisdictional disputes requiring his intervention will
be minimized. Once again, however, limitations imposed by legislation, plus the size, diversity, and complexity of the administrative
organization make it very difficult for a President to reduce the need
for coordination in this way.

By delegating some of his authority, a President may try to make
it possible for some of his chief subordinates to settle many disputes
satisfactorily before they have to be brought to him. In addition,
he may try to devise new and different kinds of coordinative machinery to act for him whenever such appears feasible. Lastly, he may
try to organize adequate staff assistance to help him secure the
information he needs to settle those disputes he has to settle himself

with as little expenditure of his own time and effort as possible. But whatever he does, the final responsibility for coordination always remains with the President. His success or failure as an administrative leader will depend very greatly on the degree to which he succeeds or fails as a coordinator. Consequently, in studying the record of a President in regard to administrative organization, one of the subjects which should be considered most prominently is what the President did, or did not do, concerning coordination.

This study of Franklin D. Roosevelt and the administrative organization of the executive branch which follows deals only with those aspects of Roosevelt's record which relate to the subjects discussed in this introductory chapter. It should perhaps be specifically noted at the outset that the account presented here in no way purports to offer a complete summary and evaluation of Roosevelt's total record as an administrator. Many of the tremendous war-time administrative problems with which he had to contend are not included within this study's purview, nor are other important aspects of his administrative performance, such as his appointments and removals of administrative subordinates and his conduct pertaining to government personnel matters generally.[m] In short, the limited purpose of this study is to present what Roosevelt thought and did in regard to reorganizing and coordinating the administrative organization of the executive branch. To achieve that purpose, an effort will be made in each of the succeeding chapters to answer one of the following questions:

What views on the need for improving the administrative organization had Roosevelt developed before he became President?

What changes in the administrative organization did Roosevelt bring about during his first term?

What methods did Roosevelt use in trying to coordinate the diverse parts of the administrative organization?

What new administrative machinery for coordination did Roosevelt devise?

What efforts did Roosevelt make to try to get Congress to provide for comprehensive reorganization of the administrative organization?

What authority to reorganize the administrative organization did Roosevelt get from Congress during his second term, and what was he able to accomplish within the limits of that authority?

What did Roosevelt do to develop the administrative organization to meet the expanding needs of national defense in its planning stage?

What did Roosevelt do to develop the administrative organization to meet the expanding needs of national defense in its operating stage?

Finally, what were some of the enduring effects which Roosevelt had upon the role of the President as the Chief administrator of the executive branch?

CHAPTER II

ROOSEVELT'S VIEWS BEFORE HE BECAME PRESIDENT

When Franklin D. Roosevelt entered upon his duties as President in March, 1933, questions of administrative organization were not his primary concern. Because of both the urgent necessities of the time and his personal views on the nature of the Presidency, his attention was concentrated mainly on the determination of policies to be pursued and the political methods needed to put those policies into effect. As he saw it, his paramount problem at that time was to take steps to meet the economic crisis then gripping the nation. In addition, his underlying attitude toward the Presidency subordinated the administrative aspects of the position to what he regarded as the more fundamental aspects of political leadership. This attitude can be seen clearly from a statement which he made in a newspaper interview during September, 1932:

"The Presidency is not merely an administrative office. That is the least part of it. It is more than an engineering job, efficient or inefficient. It is pre-eminently a place of moral leadership." [1]

In spite of this statement, it should not be concluded that Roosevelt was uninterested in matters concerning administrative organization or that he did not realize the importance of the administrative duties of a President. Raymond Moley has noted that Roosevelt once remarked to him, while discussing the appointment of his first Cabinet members, that "a Cabinet officer may get along without much administrative ability but a President cannot." [2] And according to Moley, Roosevelt well realized that the Presidency would involve the most grinding administrative work in the world. Actually, Roosevelt had developed a wide knowledge of administrative matters through his previous service in governmental positions, and he had been greatly interested in problems of administrative organization for years.

The seven and a half years which Roosevelt spent as Assistant Secretary of the Navy while Woodrow Wilson was President were particularly significant in developing his administrative background and in shaping his views concerning administrative organization. [3] Through his service in this position, he had an unexcelled opportunity early in his career to see first-hand how the national administrative organization operates and to participate in an important way in the actual conduct of governmental affairs.

The administrative burdens which fell on the shoulders of the young Roosevelt during those years were extremely heavy, particularly during the period of World War I.[4] According to all accounts, Secretary of the Navy Josephus Daniels depended on Roosevelt very greatly for the supervision of most of the administrative work of the department. In accordance with their mutually agreed upon division of labor, Daniels concentrated almost exclusively upon the political aspects of the department's affairs and upon the conduct of the major operations of the Navy, while delegating to Roosevelt the main responsibility for administration. Thus, Roosevelt's primary job was that of managing the routine, day-to-day conduct of the department's business. In performing this role, however, he managed to make his scope of activities quite extensive. While he gave first priority to those matters which the Secretary assigned to him, Roosevelt's interests in everything concerning the Navy were so far-reaching that it seems he tried to have something to do with almost all aspects of the department's operations. Secretary Daniels was to write many years later that he had often been asked what part of naval activities Roosevelt had been most interested in. The real answer, he said, lay in a remark Roosevelt used to make, "I get my fingers into about everything and there's no law against it." [5]

Daniels seems to have given Roosevelt considerably more power and responsibility than that usually delegated to individual Assistant Secretaries in other departments. Partially this may have been due to the fact that there were usually several Assistant Secretaries in other departments, but Roosevelt was the only one in the Navy. In any case, the wide range of administrative activities which came directly under Roosevelt's jurisdiction included supervision of civilian personnel, procurement of supplies and equipment, negotiation of contracts, management of navy yards, operation of docks and harbors, construction of camps, the conduct of labor relations and the setting of wage rates, and much of the work in preparing the department's annual budget.

Even before World War I broke out in Europe in 1914, Roosevelt devoted himself with great enthusiasm to trying to build up the preparedness of the Navy and the general administrative efficiency of the Navy Department. By inclination, he was a strong advocate of a

"Big Navy" and he did everything he could to achieve expansion of the naval forces. Although both Secretary Daniels and President Wilson also favored naval expansion, Roosevelt often vented feelings of frustration at what he regarded as their excessive slowness in accomplishing the objectives he thought necessary. He tried to overcome this procrastination of his superiors by taking vigorous action within the sphere of matters for which he was directly responsible. One of the things he concentrated upon particularly was trying to reorganize the administrative practices of the docks, harbors, and naval yards and renovate their facilities. He was quite successful in his efforts, and this probably constituted his major contribution to the improvement of the Navy before the war.[6]

After war actually started in Europe, Roosevelt worked with renewed vigor to try to get the Navy in a maximum state of readiness for the eventuality of United States' participation. Relatively early in the war, he came to regard it as almost inevitable that the United States would be directly involved, sooner or later. Because of this, he turned his attention in 1915 to the problem of the over-all administrative organization of the government's preparedness program and the increasing need for better top-level coordination. He became one of the first to urge a comprehensive scheme for supervision of all phases of industrial mobilization and in a personal interview in September, 1915, he urged President Wilson to create a Council of National Defense to coordinate the entire preparedness effort. Soon after, Roosevelt reported to a friend that the Prsident was interested in the suggestion and that he believed Wilson would see fit to establish such a Council "in time." He added, however, that the President did not wish to take such a step precipitously because he did not want to do anything which could be construed as "rattling the sword." Consequently, the matter was not acted upon during the winter of 1915-1916. Roosevelt was irritated at Wilson's delay in creating such an organization and he continued to agitate for it unofficially in Washington.

Finally, as events in the European war developed and as opinion within the Administration and in the whole nation crystallized against Germany, Wilson decided the time had come to bring such an agency into being, and authorization for a Council of National Defense along the lines Roosevelt had urged was approved by Congress in August, 1967.[7] It is interesting to note that in May 1940, Roosevelt was to rely on this same statute, which still remained on the books, to reconstitute a Council of National Defense (and an Advisory Commission of the Council, for which the act also provided) as the first important defense agency which he organized in preparing for World War II.[8] Also, it seems reasonable to assume that recollections of his experience in trying to get an agency established to provide over-all coordination of the national defense effort in 1915-1916 may well have influenced Roosevelt to include for this purpose an Office for Emergency Management in the Executive Office of the President when he set it up under the authority granted him by the Reorganization Act of 1939.[9]

After the United States entered the war in April, 1917, the burden of Roosevelt's administrative tasks grew enormously. Among the matters for which he was primarily responsible, that of procurement of supplies and equipment became especially important in view of the rapid expansion which the Navy was undergoing. Apparently Roosevelt handled this part of his job so effectively that not long after war was declared he was summoned to the White House. There he found himself confronted by the Chief of Staff of the Army and President Wilson, who told him, "Mr. Secretary, it seems that you have cornered the market on supplies. I'm sorry, but you will have to divide up with the Army." [10] This may have been Roosevelt's most spectacular success as a war-time administrator, but it was by no means unique. The general consensus of opinion among those familiar with his record during the war has been expressed by George Fort Milton: "The Navy's efficient procurement, supply and administration during the war was to a considerable degree the result of his endeavors." [11]

Not everything went smoothly in the Navy Department, however. Roosevelt was particularly disturbed by what he regarded as the faulty organization and obsolete administrative methods of the Navy. At one point in the summer of 1917, when a British officer informed him that Samuel Pepys had reorganized the Royal Navy in the Restoration period and that its administrative methods had not changed since, Roosevelt is reported to have replied that those of the United States Navy "had not changed since Christopher Columbus." Shortly after, he wrote to a friend that "The old machine is creaking horribly under the additional burden and, unless scissors are applied to the red tape and better organization started pretty soon, I fear there will be a great deal of justifiable criticism before we get through." [12] Roosevelt tried to do what he could to improve the organization and he sometimes cut red tape almost to the point of insubordination. Under the pressure of the war effort, however, he had to concentrate on the many things which needed to be done day-by-day rather than upon trying to get the department reorganized. Soon after the war, though, he was to return to this subject by outlining forcefully to a Congressional committee steps which he thought should be taken to reorganize and improve the Navy Department.

Roosevelt's experiences during the First World War undoubtedly had very great influence in developing his abilities as an administrator and did much to determine his later attitude toward administrative organization. Playing an important part in the detailed management of a large government department during time of war provided him with an excellent preparation for the administrative duties he was to face later as President. "The war years," James M. Burns has written, "had a maturing effect on Roosevelt. Long hours, tough decisions, endless conferences, exhausting trips, hard bargaining with powerful officials in Washington and abroad turned him into a seasoned politician-administrator." [13]

The war years also afforded Roosevelt an opportunity to become familiar with the operation of practically all parts of the administrative organization of the government. Although he occupied only a secondary position in the Wilson Administration, he represented the Navy Department on so many interdepartmental committees and in so many diverse activities relating to the various special war agencies that he got to know at firsthand how almost all of the administrative divisions of the government were organized and how they carried on their business. As Frances Perkins has testified, "The knowledge gained as a subordinate administrator was invaluable to him . . . as President. He had to think constantly about government as a system, and he gained a sense of its form and structure . . . which few people equaled." [14]

In later years, Roosevelt was to reveal in many statements that he had been a very close student of Woodrow Wilson's political and administrative methods. Although he was sometimes impatient with what he regarded as undue caution on Wilson's part, he was greatly impressed by the leadership and direction which Wilson provided for the war-time administration, and his close observation of Wilson undoubtedly affected his own conduct as President. Wilson's influence on Roosevelt extended even to relatively minor matters of administrative detail. For example, Louis Brownlow reports that once when he was at the White House discussing the administrative work of the President, Roosevelt said to him: "I learned a trick from Wilson. He once told me: 'If you want your memorandum read, put it on one page.' So I, when I came here, issued a similar decree, if you want to call it that." [15] As Frank Freidel has phrased it, Roosevelt "in a very real sense" spent over seven years "in Professor Wilson's school of public administration." [16]

During these years in Washington, Roosevelt formulated some definite ideas regarding the need for improvement in the organization and management of the whole national administration, as well as in the Navy Department. In the period just after the war, in fact, his greatest interest seems to have been the desire to get the government on a better organized, more efficient, and more businesslike basis. He took advantage of many opportunities to state his views on this subject. Of special significance in revealing his ideas along these lines was his testimony in 1919 before a House committee considering the establishment of a Bureau of the Budget, which would prepare an annual budget for the entire government. In his testimony, Roosevelt strongly endorsed the establishment of such a national budget system under the President's direction. He then went on to advocate a much greater centralization of authority in handling the financial affairs of the Navy Department and the government generally. He urged that the Secretary of the Navy should be given complete authority in all matters over the bureau chiefs of the department, and that the Secretary should be responsible to the President for the department's financial management and the President, in turn, should be responsible to Congress through the annual budget. Centralizing all authority for the administration of the department in the Secretary, Roosevelt stated, would lead to more efficient management. [17] He then proceeded to testify that in his opinion the President, like the Secretary of the Navy, badly needed better machinery to help him coordinate the work of all the departments and agencies. He believed that the President should have a special agency to inspect the activities of each department, to help him coordinate their financial estimates and control their expenditures, and to assist him in directing the personnel policies of the government. [18]

Roosevelt emphasized this theme of the need for better organization and management in the government in several speeches during 1919 and 1920. In one, he said that although the government was the largest business in the country, it was managed the worst, due to the archaic methods under which it functioned. He added that Congress was running the government "in such a way that if it was a private business it would be in the hands of a receiver in a week." In another speech, he stated that the organization of the government was "just about 100 years behind modern American conditions." And in an address at Harvard in 1920, he stressed that "Throughout the executive branch of the government, there must be re-organization and re-apportionment of work . . . along lines of simple business sense." [19] James Burns has summarized Roosevelt's views at this time in the following passage:

"The image Roosevelt presented to the world during the immediate postwar period was that of the brisk young executive. . . . He now became highly interested in improving the organization and administration of the federal government. Showing a keen grasp of the political context of public administration, he repeatedly urged that the President be given more control of budget-making, that Congress put its own houses in order by consolidating its appropriations activities in one general committee, that promotion be based on efficiency rather than length of service, that existing agencies be reorganized and functions redistributed, and that heads of executive departments be given more authority." [20]

Roosevelt continued his advocacy of governmental reorganization and better management during his campaign for the Vice Presidency in 1920. In the speech in which he accepted the nomination, he said: "Two great problems will confront the next administration, our relations with the world and the pressing need of organized progress at home." While devoting major attention to the number one question then before the country—whether the United States should become a member of the League of Nations—Roosevelt used part of his speech to spell out his belief that "organized progress" in domestic affairs meant "better organized, more efficient government." "There is no reason," he added, "why the effectiveness of the National Government should not at least approximate that of well-conducted private business." [21] He was to state similar views in numerous other speeches during the campaign.

Following Roosevelt's severe attack of infantile paralysis in 1921, which left him unable to walk without assistance for the rest of his life, he was forced to remain almost totally inactive in public life for many years. During this period, however, he followed governmental and political affairs very closely and continued to demonstrate his interest in securing better organization and increased efficiency in the government. About 1922 or 1923, as a matter of fact, he went so far as to plan to write a book dealing with these subjects under the title "The Machinery of Government." According to his plans, the volume was to be an analysis of the practical workings of the government, with major sections on "The Crying Need of a National Budget," "A Revision of Departmental Functions," and "Make Government Service Attractive." Unfortunately, he never completed more than a preface of a dozen pages.[22] About the same time, he did manage to finish an article setting forth his views on these matters, and sent it to the editor of the *Saturday Evening Post*, George Horace Lorimer, for possible publication. Lorimer, however, declined to publish it.[23]

Roosevelt was finally able to return to active participation in politics in 1928 when he was elected Governor of New York. The four years he spent in that office prior to his election as President were, of course, important ones in further developing his administrative background and his views on problems of administrative organization.[24] Probably no other experience could have given him such valuable administrative preparation for the Presidency. It has long been generally recognized that under the American system of government, serving as a state governor provides probably the best possible training for a future President. As Woodrow Wilson wrote many years ago, "The Presidency is very much like a big governorship. Training in the duties of the one fits for the duties of the other . . . . This is the only avenue of subordinate place through which the highest place can be naturally reached . . . ."[25]

The Governorship of New York is probably the country's largest and most difficult executive job, next to the Presidency. This is due not only to the size and importance of the state, but also to the fact that the direction of the administrative machinery of the state government is vested in the Governor in New York to an extent not yet realized in most other states. This administrative supremacy of the Governor resulted principally from the governmental reorganization measures effected by Roosevelt's predecessor, Governor Alfred E. Smith, whereby practically all of the state's administrative system was centralized under the Governor's control. After trying for several years, Smith had finally succeeded in getting the legislature to consolidate the 187 agencies of the state government, many of which had been virtually independent, into only 18 administrative departments responsible to the Governor.[26] Following this reorganization, there were only two state elective officials other than the Governor with administrative duties: the Attorney General and the Comptroller. Practically all other administrative personnel came under Roosevelt's supervision as Governor.[27] The only significant exception was the New York educational system which operated under the direction of a twelve-member Board of Regents. Under the reorganization, appointment of the regents had been left in the hands of the state legislature on the somewhat surprising grounds that legislative appointment would keep them and the educational system out of partisan politics.[28]

This extensive administrative reorganization had gone into effect only two years before Roosevelt became Governor. He referred to it prominently in the speech in which he accepted the nomination for the Governorship, and reiterated the views which he had expressed earlier concerning the importance of efficiency in government:

"We rejoice in the fact that the reorganization and consolidation of the administrative machinery at Albany is a thing done; but we must pay close attention to its actual operation and be prepared to improve it further in the interest of good business and clearly defined responsibility. I want to live to see the day when the business men of the Nation as well as political leaders will look to Albany as a model for business efficiency, which, in line with the most advanced modern thought, takes into consideration the human element as well as mere dollars and cents." [29]

In several of his 1928 campaign speeches, Roosevelt praised "the practical reorganization of State Government, of which we are so proud . . ." and contrasted what Governor Smith, then the Democratic candidate for President, had achieved in New York with the failure of Presidents Harding and Coolidge to do anything in the national government to bring about the badly needed "consolidation and reorganization of this governmental machinery." [30]

Certainly the reorganization which Smith had accomplished was of inestimable help in enabling Roosevelt to run the state government efficiently. In addition, serving as Governor under such a reorganized system strengthened the views he had already developed on administrative organization. Through personal, first-hand experience, he was able to see the advantages of a centralized, well-integrated administrative organization in actual operation.

In his campaign for the Presidency in 1932, Roosevelt talked about questions of administrative organization primarily in terms of the economies which could be brought about through comprehensive reorganization. Just before his nomination, he had wired an old acquaintance from his Groton school days, Colonel Robert R. Mc-Cormick of the Chicago *Tribune,* "Preliminary survey leads me to believe federal expenditures can be cut twenty percent by eliminating many functions not absolutely essential and by complete reorganization of many departments." [31]   He developed this theme at some length in several speeches during the campaign, but he discussed it most fully in the speech he delivered on the federal budget at Pittsburgh on Octobr 19, 1932. On this occasion, he stressed that reorganization was badly needed as the major means of reducing governmental expenditures. In his remarks, which in retrospect were to be singled out by his critics as probably the most significant of the entire campaign, Roosevelt pledged his allegiance to the provision in the Democratic platform calling for a 25 percent reduction in the cost of government operations, for, he said, "the first and most important and necessitous step in balancing our Federal budget is to reduce expense." [32]   To accomplish this reduction, he continued:

". . . we can make savings by reorganization of existing departments, by eliminating functions, by abolishing many of those innumerable boards and those commissions which, over a long period of years, have grown up as a fungus growth on American Government. These savings can properly be made to total many hundreds and thousands of dollars a year.

"Of course that means a complete realignment of the unprecedented bureaucracy that has assembled in Washington in the past four years.

"Now, I am going to disclose to you a definite personal conclusion which I reached the day after I was nominated in Chicago . . . . Before any man enters my Cabinet he must give me a two-fold pledge:

"1. Absolute loyalty to the Democratic platform and especially to its economy plank.

"2. Complete cooperation with me, looking to economy and reorganization in his Department.

"I regard reduction in Federal spending as one of the most important issues of this campaign. In my opinion it is the most direct and effective contribution that Government can make to business." [33]

The tremendous increase in Federal spending and the rapid creation of many new governmental agencies during Roosevelt's first years as

President led many to charge him with having been insincere in this Pittsburgh speech. The importance which he had consistently attached to the need for administrative reorganization since his days as Assistant Secretary of the Navy and his long and vigorous advocacy of efficiency and economy in government seem to belie this charge. The evidence indicates that while Roosevelt may have been both naive and extravagant in what he said, he was undoubtedly sincere.[34] The urgent economic and political problems growing out of the worsening depression were to claim almost all of his attention during his first years in the White House and were to cause him to pursue quite different paths of action than those outlined in the Pittsburgh speech.[35] The comprehensive administrative reorganization which Roosevelt wished was delayed—but it was not forgotten.[36]

CHAPTER III

CHANGES DURING THE EARLY THIRTIES

In spite of Roosevelt's early-developed views on the need for reorganizing the national administrative organization and his wide background of administrative experience, he did not devote major attention to administrative improvement during his first few years as President. These were primarily years of economic and social reform; the question of improving the administrative organization was for the most part neglected. Nevertheless, Roosevelt did bring about some substantial changes in the administrative organization early in his first term. These resulted mainly from the creation of a multitude of new agencies, some of which Congress established at Roosevelt's request and others of which Roosevelt established himself through authority granted him by Congressional delegation. To a comparatively lesser extent, some additional changes were brought about by a number of reorganization measures which Roosevelt put into effect in 1933 and 1934.

When Roosevelt came into the Presidency he possessed more authority from Congress to reorganize the government than had any preceding peace-time President. This was, in part, due to the efforts of his predecessor, Herbert Hoover, who was one of the most consistent and conscientious advocates of extensive executive reorganization. Since his days as Secretary of Commerce in the Harding Cabinet, Hoover's orderly engineer's mind had been appalled by the inefficiency and waste of the national government. In his annual messages to Congress on December 3, 1929, and December 8, 1931, and in a special message on February 17, 1932, he had emphasized that the administrative organization should be reconstituted along more efficient lines.

After repeated urging by Hoover, the House of Representatives finally created a special Economy Committee on February 23, 1932. It was directed to make recommendations on the organization of the government, and on possible economies that might be effected in governmental operations. The subsequent proposals of the Economy Committee were eventually enacted into law as Part II of the Legislative Appropriations Act, approved June 30, 1932.[1] The act itself made a number of minor transfers and consolidations of government agencies and functions, but its most important section gave the President wide authority to make additional changes and transfers by executive order. Congress placed no time limit on this grant of power; thus the possibility of continuous reorganization by Presidential action was provided. Nevertheless, the act was not without limitations, for it stated that either house of Congress could veto an executive order by adopting a resolution of disapproval within 60 days after the issuance of the order by the President.

On July 16, 1932, barely two weeks after approving the act, Congress adjourned. Consequently, it was not available to act upon any reorganization proposals until the new session began in December, 1932. Immediately after Congress reconvened, President Hoover transmitted to it Executive Orders 5959-5969, providing for a number of far-reaching changes in the executive branch. Among the most significant of these proposals were the following: all public works agencies and all educational, health, and recreational agencies were to be consolidated under the Department of the Interior; the General Land Office was to be transferred from the Department of the Interior to the Department of Agriculture; the Weather Bureau was to be transferred from the Department of Agriculture to the Department of Commerce; and the Bureau of Efficiency and all the accounting functions of the General Accounting Office were to be transferred to the Bureau of the Budget. In the month before he had issued the above executive orders, however, Hoover had been overwhelmingly defeated in his bid for reelection by Roosevelt. As a result, the Democratic-controlled House of Representatives showed no inclination to approve Hoover's recommendations. Instead, the House Democrats wished to give the opportunity of instituting changes to the new President-elect, who was to assume his duties the following March. In January, 1933, consequently, the House voted a resolution to disapprove all of the Hoover proposals.[2]

Later in the same session in which it defeated Hoover's executive orders, Congress saw fit to pass some amendments to the Legislative Appropriations Act which had the contradictory effect of both expanding and modifying the reorganization authority possessed by Roosevelt when he came into office. These new changes were approved on March 3, 1933, the day before Roosevelt's inaugural.[3] First of all, the President's power was expanded greatly by a provision which permitted him to abolish the whole or any part of an executive agency and any of its functions, except for the sole limitation that he could not abolish an entire department. A second significant increase in executive power resulted from the fact that the previous provision allowing a veto by either house of Congress was completely omitted.

Of course, Congress could still effectively kill any of the President's executive orders by the enactment of regular legislation. Such legislation, however, also requires the approval of the President, and if he should veto a bill disapproving one of his reorganization proposals, it would then take a two-thirds vote in each house to overcome his veto. This actually meant, therefore, that the President's reorganization plans would go into effect unless at least two-thirds of the members of both houses of Congress should be opposed. On the other hand, the amendments modified the President's power to carry through continuous reorganization as set forth in the original act by providing that the President's reorganization authority should expire at the end of two years.[4]

On March 20, 1933, a further amendment to the Legislative Appropriations Act which affected the President's reorganization powers was enacted by Congress at Roosevelt's request. It provided that organizational changes included in an executive order would become effective 60 days after the issuance of the order, whether Congress remained in session at that time or not.[5]

All in all, the wide authority given to Roosevelt under the above legislation constitutes the most extensive grant of powers to effect administrative reorganization ever entrusted to a President by Congress in peace-time. It is one of only three examples in which Congress has limited its own authority over reorganization matters to such an extent that it could only prevent changes proposed by the President from taking effect by enacting regular legislation which, in turn, the President could veto. The two other examples were the Overman Act of 1918 [6] and the First War Powers Act of 1941,[7] both passed in time of war. These three measures provide a marked deviation from the usual pattern which has been followed in other reorganization legislation. Normally, Congress has required the President to submit specific reorganization plans to it; these have then been subject to final disapproval through the adoption of resolutions by either one house (as in the original Legislative Appropriations Act of 1932) or both houses of Congress (as in the Reorganization Act of 1939), with the President having no right to veto such resolutions.[8]

Acting under this authority, Roosevelt proceeded to make a substantial number of organizational changes during 1933 and 1934.

Among the most important were the following: the creation of an Office of National Parks, Buildings, and Reservations in the Department of the Interior in order to consolidate all functions of administering public buildings and reservations, national parks, national monuments, and national cemeteries; the creation of divisions of Disbursement and Procurement in the Treasury Department to handle all of the government's disbursement and procurement activities; the abolition of the United States Shipping Board and the transfer of its functions and those of its subsidiary Fleet Corporation to the Department of Commerce; the consolidation of the separate Bureaus of Immigration and Naturalization into an Immigration and Naturalization Service in the Department of Labor; the transfer of the functions of the Federal Board for Vocational Education to the Interior Department, where they were assigned to the Office of Education;[9] the consolidation of all the government's agricultural credit agencies in a newly created Farm Credit Administration;[10] the transfer of the Office of the Alien Property Custodian and its functions to the Department of Justice;[11] the abolition of the Board of Indian Commissioners and the transfer of its functions to the Department of the Interior;[12] and the creation of a Division of Territories and Insular Possessions in the Department of the Interior to consolidate all the government's functions pertaining to territorial matters.[13]

In accordance with the two-year limitation provision, the President's authority to make executive reorganizations lapsed on March 3, 1935. As can be seen above, Roosevelt had made extensive use of his authority. He had not, however, taken advantage of the broad powers conferred upon him by Congress to put into effect the sort of comprehensive reorganization which he had long advocated. Certainly, there was still need for much to be done, particularly in view of the vast growth of governmental activities and agencies which had been taking place during the first two years of the New Deal administration. In the period between March, 1933, and the end of 1934, over sixty new agencies had been added to the national administrative organization.[14]

The establishment of these so-called "alphabet agencies" had, in almost all instances, been proposed and actively sponsored by Roosevelt, especially during the famous "Hundred Days" following his inauguration.[15] This period had been filled with feverish executive efforts to combat the depression and rebuild the confidence of the people in the government, in the economic system,[16] and in the future.

Roosevelt had built up tremendous popular support throughout the country by his energetic Presidential campaign, his confident inaugural address with its "Let me assert my firm belief that the only thing we have to fear is fear itself, ..."[17] and by his numerous "Fireside Chats" in which he explained the need for bold and positive action. His vigorous and skillful use of this popular support, combined with the gravity of the crisis confronting the nation, had led Congress to accede to almost every request Roosevelt made for new agencies and new powers with which to "wage a war against the emergency."[18]

Organizationally, in dealing with the depression, it was Roosevelt's general policy to assign new, emergency functions to newly created agencies, rather than to already existing departments.[19] His preference for this method was based on a combination of reasons.[20] First, he thought the departments already had enough to do in performing their usual duties under the difficult circumstances resulting from the economic crisis. Because of this, he did not want to over-burden the departments' regular personnel by holding them responsible for additional functions. Second, he thought that a new agency created to do a specific task would be able to give its full attention to that task. An existing department, on the other hand, would have to perform the new function in conjunction with all of its normal, routine activities. In the resulting competition for attention within the department, Roosevelt thought it probable that the new function would be the most likely to suffer.

A third factor which influenced Roosevelt was his belief that when an emergency ended, temporary functions needed only during the emergency could be terminated more easily and rapidly if they were vested in a special agency rather than in a permanent department. Special agencies created purely for the purpose of meeting crisis conditions expect to be ended when the crisis is over. The termination of any function assigned to a regular department, however, is almost certain to meet staunch resistance from within the department itself, and from the department's friends and supporters in Congress and among special interest groups. Fourth, Roosevelt thought that he could recruit more talented and expert administrative personnel to deal with specific problems by providing them with special agencies in which to operate rather than by placing them under the heads of existing departments and bureaus. He also believed that such able administrators, given relatively free rein in new organizations, would demonstrate more drive and energy in getting things accomplished than they would be able to do if placed in subordinate positions in the regular departments.

A fifth important factor which may well have encouraged Roosevelt to establish new agencies rather than working through the existing departments was the desire to fill a large number of government jobs by political appointees rather than through the established channels of the Civil Service, which was the prescribed practice for regular departments. It had been twelve long years since the Democratic party had been in control of the national government. The pressure for political jobs from the Democrats who had endured the long patronage drouth while three Republican Presidents occupied the White House was exceedingly intense. Many politicians throughout the country expected to be rewarded for their loyalty and devotion during the party's lean years. In addition, Roosevelt and his chief patronage dispenser, Democratic National Chairman James A. Farley, had many outstanding political debts to repay for services rendered prior to and at the 1932 nominating convention and during the subsequent campaign.

Because of the extremely high level of unemployment and the privation and misery being experienced by the jobless throughout the land when Roosevelt assumed the Presidency, the usually strong clamor for jobs on the government payroll which accompanies a change of national administrations from one party to the other was magnified to truly gigantic proportions. Farley, in his book *Behind the Ballots,* has provided a detailed, sometimes amusing, sometimes pathetic account of the enterprising efforts of unemployed Democrats to secure government employment during the first year or so after Roosevelt came into office.[21]

By creating the numerous new emergency agencies out from under the Civil Service system, Roosevelt was able to get many of these people into jobs much faster than he could possibly have done through adherence to the Civil Service rules. For Roosevelt's purposes of organizing rapidly to meet the economic crisis and at the same time getting substantial numbers of unemployed Democrats into patronage positions on the public payroll, the Civil Service system was too slow and cumbersome. Beset with inadequate appropriations and staff, the Civil Service Commission was simply not prepared to move as quickly and with the degree of flexibility which the emergency conditions required; jobs needed to be filled much faster than the Civil Service Commission was equipped to fill them.[22] Also, many of those found on the Civil Service eligibility register for higher level positions had been put there during the Republican years and could reasonably be expected to reflect the prevailingly Republican views of the professional and business groups from which most of them came. Staffing the agencies charged with carrying through the New Deal programs through the Civil Service system would run the serious risk of filling many key positions with those holding anti-New Deal sentiments.[23]

For all of these reasons it is not surprising that Roosevelt and the Democratic Congress saw fit to vest most of the emergency programs in newly-created agencies outside the regular departments and to exempt most of them from the requirements of the Civil Service Act. That Congress also had a strong desire to have new positions filled on the basis of political patronage can be seen from the fact that under the Emergency Relief Appropriations Acts passed in the early years of the New Deal, Congress exempted from Civil Service appointment all employees drawing salaries of $5,000 or more in the new emergency agencies by requiring them to have Senatorial confirmation. Thus, the new "alphabet agencies," with the joint blessing of Roosevelt and Congress, almost completely bypassed the Civil Service system and turned instead to the efficient employment service developed by Farley and his right-hand man, Emil Hurja, under the auspices of the Democratic National Committee. During Roosevelt's first two years as President, some 300,000 politically appointed workers were employed by the newly created agencies concerned with the emergency programs and the percentage of federal employees under the merit system sank to a low ebb.

By late 1935, the continued avoidance of the Civil Service system had become so disturbing to the Civil Service Assembly of the United States and Canada that it addressed a resolution to Roosevelt as follows:

"It is a matter of serious regret on the part of all those people who hope for continued improvement in public personnel administration that so many positions have been exempted from provisions of the Civil Service Laws either by legislative enactment or by executive order. . . . The explanation that an emergency exists is no longer a valid reason for excepting these positions from the classified service; and . . . the continued exclusion of such positions is a concession to the exponents of the spoils system and a neglect of governmental efficiency." [24]

Roosevelt, who had been a continuous and conscientious member of the New York Civil Service Reform Association since joining it in 1907 at the age of twenty-five, replied to the resolution immediately, emphasizing a number of extensions of the merit system which he had already made and stating that he intended to extend the merit system further in the future. Justifying his Civil Service record, he wrote:

"At the beginning of my Administration many of the eligible registers of the Civil Service Commission were several years old. Old registers had been extended in lieu of announcing new examinations. Hundreds of thousands of well-qualified persons who had lost their positions during the depression had been given no opportunity to qualify through open competitive examinations for Government employment. The appropriation of the Civil Service Commission had been greatly reduced and because of this fact and the widespread unemployment which resulted in excessive competition in civil service examinations the Commission was not in a position to supply immediately the personnel required by the recovery agencies. It was obvious that these agencies, if they were to be effective, would have to begin operations at once.

"One of the early acts of my Administration was to secure for the Civil Service Commission a deficiency appropriation for the purpose of replenishing its registers to provide qualified personnel for the regular Government agencies."[25]

Pointing out that "Civil Service requirements have been applied either by Act of Congress or by Executive Order, to the majority of positions in . . . The Securities and Exchange Commission, The Federal Communications Commission, The Railroad Retirement Board, and The Farm Credit Administration," and that "The Guffey Coal Regulation Act, the Motor Carrier Act, the Social Security Act, the Labor Relations Act, and the Public Utilities Act contain provision for the employment of personnel in accordance with the Civil Service Law and Rules," Roosevelt concluded:

"The merit system has been and will continue to be extended during my Administration. . . . The Civil Service Commission advises me that progress is being made in replenishing its registers and I hope that within the near future the Civil Service Law and Rules may be applied to agencies that are now excepted from civil service requirements. . . ."[26]

That Roosevelt later fulfilled this pledge during his second term has

been attested in vigorous terms by Professor Leonard D. White who
served as a Republican member of the Civil Service Commission from
1934-1937:

"No president made greater contributions to the public service than
Franklin D. Roosevelt. To him the country owes the greatest extension of the merit system ever made by any president, and even
more to him is due the realization—only partial as yet—of the true
functions and full purpose of personnel management in a vast public
service irrevocably vested with substantial power.

"His interest in a better public service, sometimes apparently sub-
merged under the pressure of events, was constant, and flowered
in four extraordinary years of constructive effort from 1937 to 1940."[27]

Undoubtedly, Roosevelt's method of creating new agencies to perform the new emergency functions did bring great vigor and enthusiasm into the conduct of administration. At the same time, however,
it developed an exceedingly disorderly, if not chaotic, organizational
structure which did considerable violence to the integrated "unity of
command" pattern generally admired by public administration authorities. Nevertheless, in the initial stages of dealing with the manifold difficulties of the depression, this organizational disorder had its
desirable aspects, for it encouraged the bold experimentation and freedom of administrative initiative which the critical circumstances demanded, and it brought, in general, the beneficial results which Roosevelt was seeking. In commenting on this aspect of the early days
of Roosevelt's administration, George Fort Milton aptly observed:
"This genius in disorder, with its disregard of the rules of the copybook gods, was among the chief of his assets in the chaotic weeks in
which a dozen or more major experiments were shaped." [28]

From studying the early New Deal years, one receives the un-
mistakable impression that at that time Roosevelt was more concerned with *what* was being done than he was with *how* it was being
done; administrative means were definitely subordinated to political
ends. It should not be inferred from this, however, that Roosevelt was
completely oblivious to the need for better administrative organization
during this period. He did put into effect a number of important
reorganization measures, although he certainly did not use to the
fullest possible extent the great reorganization powers which had
been delegated to him by Congress.

The evidence seems to indicate that in his first hectic years as
President, Roosevelt thought he could not divert his time and effort

from his duties of political and legislative leadership sufficiently to try to devise and put through a truly thorough reorganization of the administrative organization. He stated this view clearly in a message to Congress transmitting one of his early reorganization orders when he said: "The very urgent demands of the public business, both legislative and administrative, . . . have made it literally impossible to complete the study of consolidation. . . . Executive Order 6166 only affects such reorganizations as could be determined upon within the limited . . . time available for study." [29] Several years later, in describing the emergency years of 1933 and 1934, he was to write, "The times were such, that speed rather than administrative planning was the most important consideration in launching these social-economic programs." [30]

Raymond Moley has reported that he once asked Roosevelt toward the middle of the first term why he did not take a breathing spell "to stop innovations and improve the quality of the administration, men, and machinery of government." Roosevelt replied that "the time had not yet come for that." [31] This apparently continued to be his view until near the end of 1935; then, as shall be discussed in Chapter VI, he began to make plans for a comprehensive reorganization of the administrative organization such as he had advocated in the years before he became President.

CHAPTER IV

COORDINATING THE ADMINISTRATIVE ORGANIZATION

As discussed in Chapter I, perhaps the supreme task facing a President in regard to the administrative organization of the government is that of coordination. As the responsible head of the executive branch, he must utilize coordinative methods and devise administrative machinery which will weld together the many disparate parts of the administrative organization to a sufficient degree that they will work in relative harmony toward common over-all purposes. It is the President's job to see to it that the administrative organization will not be rent asunder by violent internal dissensions and the pursuit of conflicting specialized interests.

It was perhaps inevitable that Roosevelt's creation of a large number of new agencies outside the regular departments would result in numerous jurisdictional conflicts and a considerable amount of duplication of administrative effort. "New agencies burgeoned so fast," Raymond Moley has written, "that there was unlimited overlapping." [1] Because of this, the function of top-level coordination was especially important. Insofar as it was humanly possible for one man to do so, Roosevelt tried to furnish such coordination personally by keeping his hand in almost every important aspect of administration. He made the heads of practically all of the new agencies responsible directly to the President and did not require them to report through any Cabinet-level intermediaries. Consequently, he was faced with the burdensome task of dealing personally with a tremendous array of subordinate administrators. His administrative "span of attention" was constantly stretched to an exceedingly wide degree, but Roosevelt apparently preferred it that way. For this enabled him to keep informed concerning the many things which were being done within the administration. It also allowed him to make most of the important decisions himself. As a result, however, a terrific amount of administrative detail found its way to his office, and he had to spend an awesome number of hours in personal conferences with officials of the many agencies.

In part, Roosevelt's large number of personal conferences may have stemmed not only from the necessity of dealing with such a large number of agencies, but also from his natural tendency to handle his administrative work to the maximum extent possible through direct, face-to-face contacts rather than through written communications. Although the amount of paper work which he had to do was impressive, he was never inclined to be a "paper administrator." Instead, he might well be called an "administrator by conversation." It was his general practice to perform his coordinative functions mainly by bringing the people concerned with a given problem to his office to talk things over. In this way, he tried to arrive at agreements which were mutually satisfactory to all parties. Many times, of course, this did not happen and Roosevelt then had to make a final arbitrary ruling to settle the matter. However, he usually wanted to do this only as a last resort. He had great faith in his ability to persuade people to agree if he could get them to sit down and talk things through with him.

Roosevelt's normal routine work schedule at the White House, which he followed with great regularity, reflects very clearly his penchant for doing his administrative business directly by personal contact.[2] From the time when he woke up in the morning, he spent most of his day-time hours talking to people. It was the regular custom for his secretaries and other immediate personal staff members to go to his bedroom as he was finishing his breakfast in bed to discuss plans for the day's work, and he sometimes requested Cabinet members and others to confer with him at this time as well. In his diary, Secretary of the Interior Harold Ickes noted many such morning conferences with Roosevelt in his bedroom. On one occasion, Ickes wrote:

"When I got up to his study, his valet ushered me into his bedroom telling me that the President was shaving. He waved toward the bathroom and the President called out to me to come in. There he was, sitting before a mirror in front of the washstand, shaving. He invited me to sit on the toilet seat while we talked. When he was through shaving he was wheeled back to his room where he reclined on his bed again while his valet proceeded to help him dress. . . . I was struck all over again with the unaffected simplicity and personal charm of the man. He was President of the United States but he was also a plain human being, talking over with a friend matters of mutual interest while he shaved and dressed with the help of his valet. His disability didn't seem to concern him in the slightest degree or to disturb his urbanity."[3]

Roosevelt was customarily wheeled to his office about 10:00 a.m. and began a long list of appointments, normally scheduled at 15-minute intervals, which usually lasted until mid-afternoon. He almost invariably ate lunch about 1:00 p.m. at his desk together with some one with whom he was conferring. Many of his appointments, of course, were with political leaders, in Congress and out, and with other individuals whom he wished to see, or who wished to see him, for many kinds of reasons. But a very substantial number of his office conferences were with officials of governmental agencies with whom he discussed administrative matters.

The accounts which have been written by various Cabinet members and Roosevelt's other close administrative associates indicate the large amount of time which they spent in his office and the wide gamut of administrative problems with which he dealt personally. Roosevelt preferred to take care of his necessary paper work in the late afternoon and at night; it was then that he read his correspondence and dictated replies, considered the numerous memoranda and reports submitted to him, and worked on his speeches and other public statements.[4] It has been estimated that Roosevelt's normal working day as President averaged about fourteen hours.[5] Of this total, he usually spent, prior to World War II, from four to six hours in handling the ten to fifteen appointments which he generally averaged each day.[6] In addition, he spent a lot of time talking to people by telephone; one estimate is that he probably spent as much as a quarter of his average working day on the telephone.[7]

The large amount of his time which Roosevelt spent in talking with people resulted partially from his desire to keep himself fully informed about everything that was going on in the government. One of his closest associates, Samuel I. Rosenman, has observed that "He generally preferred to get his information orally; he could interrupt and ask questions; it was easy for him to get the gist right away."[8] He seemed to be interested in practically everything the government was doing in any field, often down to the minutest details, and he tried hard to keep abreast of virtually all actions which his subordinates were taking in his name.

Another strong personality factor which undoubtedly influenced the manner in which Roosevelt did his administrative work was the sheer enjoyment which he seemed to get from contacts with people. This appears to have been a natural characteristic which demonstrated itself early in his governmental career. Commenting that Roosevelt seemed "to stimulate himself by new contacts with new people," Frances Perkins has recounted that Newton D. Baker, Wilson's Secretary of War, once said to her during World War I, "Young Roosevelt is very promising, but I should think he'd wear himself out in the promiscuous and extended contacts he maintains with people. But as I have observed him, he seems to clarify his ideas and teach himself as he goes along by that very conversational method." Perkins went on to say, "As one saw him do the same thing in later life, both as Governor and as President, one realized how important for him were these varied and manifold points of contact. . . . He talked himself and his visitor into an understanding of the specific problem and the principles underlying it—an approach he certainly didn't have at the beginning of the conversation." [9]

Partially, at least, Roosevelt's enjoyment of dealing with people may have been attributable to his own enthusiasm for talking. Late in his life, while explaining to a group of newly-elected Congressmen why he was no longer able to see as many members of the House and Senate during the war as he had done previously, Roosevelt made the following candid statement:

"I think that part of it is my fault, so my secretaries tell me. When somebody comes in on a ten-minute apointment, I start to do the talking. I get enthusiastic, and the result is that at the end of ten or fifteen minutes my visitor hasn't had a chance to get in a word edge-wise. And that is something I am trying to school myself to omit, to try to let the other fellow talk, instead of my doing it. And that is about the hardest thing I have to do in this life, because as some of you who have been here before know, I love to talk. It's an unfortunate characteristic. So I say, please bear with me, and if you do come in, say to me quite frankly, 'Now listen, before you talk, Mr. President, let me have my say.' I think it would be a grand thing." [10]

Practically everyone ever associated with Roosevelt has attested to the correctness of his admission that "I love to talk." Almost without exception, all of the accounts which have been written by those who worked closely with him have mentioned his loquaciousness as one of his most pronounced characteristics. That Roosevelt's talkative nature was sometimes a source of amusement as well as irritation to his colleagues is indicated by the following story related by Cordell Hull:

"One day, grinning broadly, he entered the Cabinet meeting some-what late. He said he had just been the victim of a bit of impertinence

on the part of a member of his family. This relative had told him:
'Sir, you talk so much we never have a chance to say anything.' The
President laughed as he recounted the episode, then turned to me
and said: 'Cordell, do you agree with that?'

"I replied: 'Well, Mr. President, just before I came over for the
meeting today, some newspapermen met me at the State Department and said to me:

" 'Mr. Secretary, there's a a rumor going about the White House
food is very poor. We'd like to know what you think about it.'

" 'I never eat the White House food,' I answered.

" 'What!' they exclaimed. 'We know you go frequently to the
White House for luncheon or dinner.'

" 'That,' I said, 'is true enough. But I always eat luncheon or
dinner before I go over there. Then, while the President is eating, I
have a chance to do a little talking.'

"The President joined in the general laugh." [11]

Roosevelt's talkativeness may have had its desirable aspects, as
Perkins and others have said, for he often seemed able to develop and
crystallize his views on a problem most effectively by talking about
it at length, in a way which suggested that he was actually doing his
thinking "out loud." To some degree, however, his fondness for talking
undoubtedly complicated the accomplishment of his administrative
work by often leading him to spend more time in personal conferences
than might have been necessary — time which he might have used
to better advantage in doing other work.[12] The stories are legion as
to how he almost invariably ran behind in his appointment schedule
because he practically never finished a conference in the time allotted
for it. This was mainly due to the full and detailed way in which he
discoursed upon virtually any question which came before him and
to his almost insatiable curiosity which led him to make all sorts of
searching inquiries about relatively minor administrative matters.
According to several accounts, Roosevelt almost drove his appointments secretaries, Marvin McIntyre and Major General Edward
Watson, to despair by chronically disrupting their carefully laid out
schedules, and there were a good many occasions when they finally
had to break into a conference to usher out a visitor with Roosevelt
still vigorously expounding a final point as the person was shoved
through the door.[13]

In addition to these more apparent effects of Roosevelt's personal
characteristics upon his administrative methods, the evidence seems

to indicate that his strong tendency toward maintaining wide personal contacts with his subordinate administrators may also have resulted from either a conscious judgment or an intuitive feeling on his part that a President's effectiveness as an administrative leader may depend a great deal upon the degree to which he is able to give his subordinates the impression that he is in personal touch with them. Or, to phrase it another way, Roosevelt seems to have felt that a President's administrative success may well be influenced by the proportion of people whom he is attempting to direct and control with whom he can remain in direct personal contact, either by face-to-face conversation or by the telephone.

He realized, of course, that he could not possibly know all of the problems and difficulties which were certain to arise in all the departments and agencies under his jurisdiction. Accordingly, it was obvious that he would not be able to make all of the important administrative decisions himself, no matter how badly he wished to do so or how hard he tried; numerous matters of significance to the success or failure of his administration would have to be decided by his subordinates without ever being brought to his attention. Because of this, it seemed important for him to try to have enough face-to-face contact with the specific administrator in direct charge of affairs in a particular department or agency to give that person a sufficiently strong impression of Roosevelt's general outlook, his approach to problems, and his personality in making decisions so that the administrator's conduct would continue to be guided by Roosevelt not only in dealing with the matter immediately at hand which had brought him to the President's office, but also in dealing with all subsequent problems of a similar nature which might arise in the agency, and for which explicit Presidential decisions would not be forthcoming or solicited. In this connection, Roosevelt's recognition of the importance of his efforts to maintain a constant awareness throughout the administrative organization that he was in touch with what was going on in all the departments and agencies seems clearly implied in some informal extemporaneous remarks which he made to a group of government employees in New Jersey on January 18, 1936, when he said:

"In the course of the average day in Washington I suppose I come in contact with the representatives of about half of all the Federal agencies that there are, personally, or by telephone, or by correspondence. I try to keep in touch with the coordinating of all our work as much as is humanly possible." [34]

Although Roosevelt tried hard to do his job of coordination to the maximum degree, his time and attention were limited, and the large number of administrative subordinates heading the departments and the new agencies made it impossible for him to deal with all of them by himself. Consequently, he tried to utilize some additional methods, both formal and informal, to help him perform his task of coordination. One of his main approaches to the problem was that of using several close personal assistants, or special agents, to do some of his necessary coordinative chores for him. Their work was usually done on a highly informal basis, with Roosevelt relying on them for a lot of the behind-the-scenes tasks involved in gathering information, talking to the parties concerned in a given dispute, trying to find possible grounds for agreement, and formulating alternative courses of action which he might pursue.

Almost invariably, however, Roosevelt retained the authority to make final decisions in his own hands and did not delegate it to these special assistants. They were asked to do particular jobs for him as the need arose and there was little organized system in the whole procedure. These men were assignd to all sorts of tasks, both administrative and political, and Roosevelt does not seem to have developed any definite pattern in determining which particular person would be asked to do what job. If circumstances had not made it necessary, he probably would have preferred not to use them at all but to do himself the things he asked them to do. As his personal secretary, Grace Tully, has written "his own determination to fight out each problem and decision was more than ordinary. He knew that intermediaries are never popular and his own inclination was toward direct contact." [15] Certainly, Roosevelt did not give any one of these special assistants sufficient authority, or use him in such a systematic way, that he could be regarded as an "assistant President" or "chief of staff." [16]

Among the principal persons who served Roosevelt in this "trouble shooter" capacity during his first years in office were the three Columbia University professors, Raymond Moley, Rexford Tugwell, and Adolf Berle, who had formed the core of his so-called "brain trust" during the 1932 campaign. Another was Frank C. Walker, a close political friend of Roosevelt's who had been a Montana lawyer and businessman and Treasurer of the Democratic National Committee.[17] Beginning in 1934, Roosevelt also started to use two young government lawyers, Thomas G. Corcoran and Benjamin V. Cohen, in this capacity. Corcoran was brought to his attention by his old friend, Professor Felix Frankfurter of the Harvard Law School, where Corcoran had been a student.[18] Cohen had been brought to Washington from Chicago by Secretary of the Interior Ickes, to work in the new Public Works Administration.[19]

It was perhaps natural for Roosevelt to turn to members of the "brain trust" for assistance in view of the great help which they had been to him in the campaign and in the period between his election and inauguration.[20] Overcoming some serious objections that this would be an unwise use of the "brain trust" members,[21] Roosevelt appointed them to various administrative positions in the departments and agencies, but with the end in view that they would also serve as personal assistants for him in the White House.[22] That they did provide valuable assistance to Roosevelt in a wide variety of activities during his first two years in office can be seen clearly from Moley's detailed account of this period.[23]

Gradually, however, for reasons too numerous and detailed to enumerate here, Roosevelt's use of the "brain trusters" as trouble shooters declined. Moley, whom Roosevelt had used most in this capacity, slowly dropped out of the White House inner circle after several major differences developed between him and Roosevelt. By the second term he had become an embittered critic of many of Roosevelt's activities.[24] Tugwell was to remain in government service much longer, but after the first two years or so, he was called upon to serve Roosevelt less frequently in any kind of personal coordinative role. Because of Louis Howe's illness and the decline in Moley's influence by 1934, Corcoran and his colleague Cohen came to be used much more by Roosevelt in this capacity.[25] Beginning in 1934-1935, they were to become increasingly important in such work until near the end of Roosevelt's second term.[26] Samuel Rosenman was to write of them:

". . . gradually they became two of the most important handymen and trouble shooters the President had. . . . For four years—from 1936 to 1940—I would say that they were as intimate and important a part of the Administration as any Cabinet officer or Presidential advisor—and much more so than most of them. . . . These two men, working together during the second term, took many burdens from Roosevelt's shoulders." [27]

In summary, it appears that Roosevelt used these special assistants in an unofficial, informal, irregular, and sometimes haphazard manner to aid him in maintaining contacts with his subordinate administrators, to find out for him specific information he wanted about administrative activities, and to help him work out agreements and better relationships among the representatives of the various agencies. He seems to have regarded them as a sort of extension of himself; they were to do some of the things which he did not have time to do for himself. He did not conceive of them as "coordinators" who could make binding decisions and take final actions for him. These functions he reserved to himself. Nevertheless, though their authority was limited, these men performed many badly-needed services.

Before 1939, it should be remembered, Roosevelt did not have any institutionalized, regularly provided assistance of this nature within the White House staff. When he entered the Presidency, the only immediate assistants provided for a President by legislation were three secretaries.[28] By utilizing these special assistants as he did, Roosevelt was filling in a large gap which existed in the organization of the President's office—a gap which was made particularly serious by the establishment in 1933 and 1934 of so many new administrative agencies for the President to supervise. It was this deficiency which Roosevelt sought to correct in 1937 in his request to Congress, finally approved in 1939, for authorization to appoint six administrative assistants to the President.[29] Under the terms of the Reorganization Act of 1939, the jobs which men like Moley, Tugwell, Corcoran, and Cohen had performed were formally provided within the White House Office. His actual experience in using such special assistants during the years 1933-1936 had doubtless influenced Roosevelt's decision to make such a request. His unofficial special assistants of the 1930's were in many ways the prototypes of the official administrative assistants who were to serve him, and his successors, in the White House after 1939.

When Roosevelt became President, one institutional agency did exist to aid him in his functions of administrative management and coordination. This was the Bureau of the Budget which had been established by the Budget and Accounting Act of 1921. In a way which was reminiscent of his testimony before a Congressional committee in 1919 on the need for a national budget system,[30] which has been referred to in Chapter II, Roosevelt began his first term by placing considerable reliance on the Budget Bureau for assistance. Although he had not been completely satisfied with the system provided by the Budget and Accounting Act as it was finally passed,[31] he set out to revitalize the work of the Bureau of the Budget as a Presidential staff agency. He called upon the Bureau for help in the more positive aspects of administration which are involved in coordinating the activities of the governmental agencies, rather than relying upon it strictly for the more negative aspects—holding down governmental expenditures—which had been almost its sole function under his predecessors.

The increased role which Roosevelt gave to the Bureau of the Budget probably came not only from his views on the importance of the budgeting process, which Rexford Tugwell has called his "constant preoccupation with budget matters," [32] but also in part from his high initial regard and liking for the man he appointed as his first Budget Director, Lewie W. Douglas. Roosevelt thought the position of Director of the Budget should be one of the most important in his new administration, and he had prevailed upon Douglas to resign from his seat in Congress to take the post. The prestige which he gave to the position and to Douglas is evidenced by the fact that he asked Douglas to attend all Cabinet meetings. In addition, Douglas had a standing appointment, along with Moley, in Roosevelt's bedroom each morning between 9:00 and 9:30 to discuss the business of the day. [33]

One of the major ways in which Roosevelt used the Bureau of the Budget as a coordinating device was the requirement he laid down shortly after taking office that all executive orders prepared by the various departments and agencies for his consideration and signature should be submitted to him through the Budget Bureau. [34] Since several different agencies might be affected by an executive order originating in one particular agency, the Budget Director was assigned the coordinating responsibility of clearing such orders through all interested agencies, including in all cases the Attorney General for advice on legality, before transmitting the order to the President for action.

Of course, executive orders always had to be signed by the President before going into effect so that Roosevelt in any case would have been in a position to review them as they came before him. However, the great mass of such orders which the departments and agencies deemed it necessary for him to issue in accomplishing their emergency missions very quickly made it a crushing administrative job for Roosevelt. [35] He realized that more than the mere cursory Presidential review which he had time to provide was needed if unity of policy was to be guaranteed and overlapping and duplication in administration prevented. Thus, he called upon the Bureau of the Budget to do part of his job of coordination, in effect by obtaining the views of all agencies concerned with a proposed executive order and then advising him as to the consistency and feasibility of the order. In addition, the provision for clearance through all interested agencies was designed to insure that each agency would be fully informed about what the President was authorizing other agencies to do in regard to any particular problem.[36]

In addition to this coordinating function regarding executive orders, Roosevelt also expanded the Bureau's authority in 1933 to include clearance of many of the proposals from agencies of the administration for new legislation. It had been customary under Roosevelt's predecessors for heads of departments to take legislative proposals directly to the President personally without reference to the Budget Bureau. Late in 1933, Roosevelt issued an order to all agencies requiring them to clear all bills "carrying appropriation measures" through the Bureau of the Budget for presentation to the President.[37]

Not long afterward, Roosevelt also began to use the Bureau increasingly for the clearance of so-called enrolled bills, i.e., bills which had been approved by both houses of Congress and sent to the President for approval or veto. Previously only those enrolled bills which pertained specifically to appropriations had been referred by the White House to the Budget Bureau for study and recommendation. Roosevelt, however, started sending all relief bills involving an expenditure of funds to the Bureau in 1934, asking it to circularize the interested agencies and to return their recommendations, along with those of the Bureau itself, to him for action.[38] During the next three years, he gradually expanded this practice to include more and more types of legislation so that by 1938, he was sending virtually all bills to the Bureau for this purpose.

In addition to these increased coordinating functions of a formal nature which Roosevelt delegated to the Bureau of the Budget, evidence that he relied upon Douglas for a wide range of administrative services during his first few months in office is provided by the accounts of many of those associated with the government at that time, such as Ickes, Moley, and Perkins.[39] Nevertheless, this did not mean that the Budget was destined to play anything like as important a role in administrative management and coordination during Roosevelt's first few years as President as it was to play after 1939. Unfortunately, there were several factors which limited the effectiveness of the Bureau and which restricted the use Roosevelt made of it.

The gradual estrangement which developed between Roosevelt and Douglas was probably the most serious of these limitations, in view of Roosevelt's strong tendency to view administrative matters largely in terms of the personalities involved, and to delegate authority, in the main, only to those for whom he felt a personal affinity and regard. Roosevelt's early enthusiasm for Douglas was slowly to turn into a lack of confidence and even mistrust, and these feelings came to be shared by Douglas regarding Roosevelt. Their differences arose primarily over the economic and fiscal policies Roosevelt pursued to combat the depression.

Reflecting his background as a banker and businessman, Douglas advocated a much more conservative course of action than Roosevelt thought desirable. Roosevelt's Pittsburgh speech on the Federal budget and some of his other campaign utterances on the need for reducing expenditures in government and for a balanced budget had been taken quite literally by Douglas. As Budget Director, he tried hard to hold Roosevelt and the rest of the administration inflexibly to those principles. For example, he was strongly opposed to large-scale public works and tried to use his influence to prevent the inauguration of any government relief program which would do more than "provide subsistence relief in the cheapest possible terms for citizens out of work and without funds," as Perkins described his attitude.[40] He also thought that some of Roosevelt's fiscal policies, such as the decision to go off the gold standard, were dangerously radical.[41]

As the gulf on policies between the two men continued to widen, Roosevelt came to be suspicious of Douglas's loyalty. He mentioned to Ickes on several occasions that he was convinced Douglas was preparing elaborate memoranda about all matters upon which they differed so that there would be a written record to justify Douglas's own actions if things went wrong, and that he was greatly disturbed by this display of "bad faith."[42] Inevitably, of course, such feelings seriously affected the degree to which Roosevelt relied upon Douglas and he began to call on him and the Budget Bureau less and less for assistance. Finding himself increasingly out of sympathy with Roosevelt's program and feeling that his usefulness was at an end, Douglas eventually resigned in August, 1934.

By this time, considerable harm had already been done regarding the use which Roosevelt made of the Budget Bureau. He had devised

by then other administrative patterns which minimized the role of
the Budget Director, and he had developed the habit of relying upon
other people to do some of the tasks involved in coordination and
administrative management which the Budget Director might better
have performed. This is reflected to some degree by the fact that
Roosevelt did not deem it necessary to name a person of major public
stature as a full-time Director of the Budget to succeed Douglas.
Instead, at the suggestion of Secretary of the Treasury Henry Morgenthau, he appointed Daniel Bell, a Treasury Department career man
who had first gone to work as a bookkeeper in that department in
1911.[43] Bell became the Acting Director of the Budget and continued
in that status until 1939.[44] Throughout this time, he also held office
as Assistant to the Secretary of the Treasury in charge of fiscal and
auditing matters. Although Bell proved to be competent enough in
running the routine affairs of the Bureau, he was not called upon for
assistance by Roosevelt to anything like the same degree that Douglas
had been in 1933, or as his successor, Harold Smith, was to be after
the administrative reorganization of 1939. He was not asked, as a
rule, to attend Cabinet meetings, and there is no doubt but that the
prestige of the Budget Bureau declined somewhat because of the fact
that Roosevelt saw fit to have it headed for five years by an Acting
Director who also held an appointment as a subordinate aide to the
Secretary of the Treasury.

In addition to these important consequences of Roosevelt's split
with Douglas, there were several other factors of an even more fundamental nature which limited the Bureau's usefulness during Roosevelt's first years in office. First of all, the Bureau itself was not organized internally in such a way that it could provide very much help
in matters of general management and coordination and in organizational improvement. The purposes behind the establishment of the
Bureau of the Budget had been to bring greater economy and efficiency in the government. However, the main emphasis of the Bureau
had been centered almost exclusively upon the first of these objectives
and not much attention had been given to the latter.

Previous Budget Directors had operated on the theory that if
economy is enforced stringently enough, increased efficiency is certain
to follow. As a result, they had concentrated almost exclusively upon
holding down the requests for appropriations so that a balanced
budget could be achieved. Although this was an admirable purpose, to
be sure, which they had performed quite well, they had neglected

almost entirely the more positive aspects of the budgeting process. They had made practically no attempt at investigating the operations of the administrative organization to ascertain improvements which needed to be made. The Budget and Accounting Act of 1921 had specifically authorized the Bureau to make detailed studies of the administrative organization for the purpose of advising the President as to changes that should be made in organization and methods and in the grouping of services. This authority, however, had been almost unused and the Bureau's potential as a vehicle for the improvement and reorganization of the government remained virtually dormant. As Harold Smith was later to write, the Bureau had achieved a reputation "as an economy-minded, restrictive agency, skilled only in saying 'No'." [45] But it had done little to serve as a staff arm of the President in helping him to perform his functions of over-all management and coordination, or to aid him in trying to better the administrative organization.

The Bureau had "practiced what it preached" regarding frugality to such a degree in regard to its own operations that it was seriously understaffed and functioned on a very small and inadequate internal budget. Prior to 1938, the Bureau's average number of personnel ranged from 38 to 42,[46] certainly an inadequate staff to accomplish all of the duties assigned to it by the Budget and Accounting Act and to enable it to be of maximum assistance to the President. Describing the earlier activities of the Bureau, Harold Smith wrote in 1941:

". . . it tried to set an example of economy to the point of making itself virtually impotent, at least in the light of its potentialities. . . . The experience of nearly two decades shows that the principle of a central bureau of the budget is a sound one, but that the machinery set up in the Bureau has been too restricted in size and scope to enable it to fulfill its responsibilities completely." [47]

Another factor which probably had a limiting influence on the effectiveness with which the Bureau of the Budget could serve as a managerial and coordinating agent of the President was the fact that the Bureau was set up as a part of the Treasury Department. Although the Director and Assistant Director were appointed by the President without need for Senatorial confirmation and were responsible directly to him, the fact that they were located in the Treasury Department remained the cause of confusion and misunderstanding as to the relative relationships and levels of authority between the President, the Budget Director, the Secretary of the Treasury, and the other department and agency heads. Concerning this point, the first Director of the Budget, General Charles G. Dawes, had written: "The effectiveness of the Budget machinery depends upon its independence of departments and its complete dependence upon the President. . . . The Budget Bureau really should not be a Treasury bureau, since it operates directly under the President. . . ." [48]

The Bureau was designed to be a Presidential staff agency, but the Budget Director was in some ways a subordinate of the Secretary of the Treasury. Consequently, when dealing with the Budget Director, other agency heads were sometimes not clear as to whether they were dealing with the President or the Department of the Treasury. Roosevelt undoubtedly complicated this ambiguity further by appointing an Acting Director of the Budget who also continued to serve as Assistant to the Secretary of the Treasury. [49] This quite naturally had a tendency to weaken the prestige and influence of the Budget Director in his dealings with the heads of the other agencies. All in all, it may be concluded that although Roosevelt did utilize the Budget Bureau to a considerable degree for assistance in coordinating the administrative organization, it was not nearly as much help to him prior to 1939 as it could have been had the limiting factors mentioned above not been present.

As many other Presidents, Roosevelt made little use of his Cabinet in any kind of formal or institutional way as a coordinating mechanism. Although the Cabinet has long been popularly regarded as a coordinating instrumentality of the President, it has rarely served such a function. Most students of national administration would agree with Pendleton Herring's observation that "The cabinet . . . has failed to function as an institution for the . . . coordination of federal activities." [50] The way in which the Cabinet is constituted is, in itself, not conducive to making it an effective agency to assist the President in his coordinative functions. The members of the Cabinet are, above all, the operating heads of large and important individual departments; they have no collective responsibility and cannot properly be regarded as a single entity except when the President calls them together into a collective group. As department heads, it is only natural that they should think primarily in terms of the specific interests of their respective departments rather than of the interests of the administrative organization as a whole.

Because each deals with a specialized clientele, department heads often become the chief governmental spokesmen for specialized and competing private interest groups. As a result, Cabinet members are often more competitive than cooperative in their dealings with each other and in their relationships to the President. They are competitors for appropriations, for increased authority and prestige, and for the President's confidence and support. This inevitably leads to the outbreak of interdepartmental feuds and conflicts of interest which the President has to try to settle. Consequently, as Louis Brownlow has said, "the President all too frequently finds the Cabinet, which is deemed to be his principal help, actually operating as the principal hindrance to him in carrying out his task of over-all coordination and management." [51] Or, as Paul Appleby has put it, "Department heads . . . throw into the Presidential lap a very great many more differences than they prevent from landing there." [52]

Under Roosevelt, certainly, the Cabinet's coordinative contribution was very slight. He usually held Cabinet meetings regularly every Friday, but he used them very little as a device for shaping the over-all administrative conduct of the government, or for trying to iron out disagreements and jurisdictional disputes. According to Frances Perkins, one of the two members of his original Cabinet who served throughout his twelve years in office,[53] Cabinet meetings under Roosevelt were always very casual, informal, and unplanned affairs.[54] No formal agenda was ever prepared in advance of meetings, and Roosevelt never called upon the group to make any collective decisions on specific questions. Perkins recalls that she asked the members to vote on a matter on only one occasion, and then he prefaced his request with a remark that he would not feel bound by the result of the vote but wanted it merely as an expression of opinion.[55]

Normally, Roosevelt proceeded at Cabinet meetings by going around the table and asking the members if they had anything which they wished to report. There was complete freedom to bring up anything one wished, according to Perkins, and Roosevelt never tried to restrict the subjects discussed. He often introduced matters himself, asked quite a lot of questions, and in general did a good bit of the talking at meetings.[56]

In the early days of the first term, Perkins remembers, Roosevelt encouraged some very searching inquiries and lengthy discussions, participated in by practically all of the Cabinet members, concerning plans for some of the New Deal programs, such as public works and relief. But as affairs settled down somewhat, Cabinet meetings tended to fall into a routine pattern of members reporting upon activities within their departments which they believed might be of interest to the President. Such reports, however, were often not of much interest or importance to the other members of the Cabinet who were mainly preoccupied with the problems and responsibilities of their own departments. "Roosevelt's cabinet administration," according to Perkins, "came to be like most previous ones—a direct relationship between a particular cabinet officer and the President in regard to his special field, with little or no participation or even information from other cabinet members. Certainly almost no 'cabinet agreements' were reached." [57] Another of the most influential of Roosevelt's Cabinet members, Jesse Jones, has confirmed this evaluation:

"Matters of high governmental policy were seldom discussed at Cabinet meetings. . . . My principal reason for not having a great deal to say at Cabinet meetings was that there was no one at the table who could be of any particular help to me except the President, and when I needed to consult him I did not choose a Cabinet meeting to do it. I made no suggestions to other Cabinet members about their departments and asked none from them." [58]

Another significant factor developed early in the first term to deter both Cabinet members and Roosevelt from airing their problems and expressing their views frankly in Cabinet meetings. Premature "leaks" of confidential information to newspapermen, members of Congress, and others began to occur with considerable frequency and this naturally had an inhibiting effect on the discussions. [59] Also, in view of the rivalries which had developed very quickly between some of the members of the Cabinet, they were increasingly reluctant to bring up matters of importance before their colleagues but much preferred to discuss them privately with the President. Because of the circumstances, Roosevelt seems not only to have condoned this practice but to have encouraged it. He almost invariably remained in the Cabinet room after meetings ended so that those individual members who wished to do so could talk to him alone. And of course he saw many of them in his office on other occasions throughout the week.

Roosevelt made almost no use of Cabinet meetings to settle disputes between the heads of two or more departments; he felt that such meetings were an inappropriate and ineffective place to try to iron out conflicts. He much preferred to try to arrive at agreements by getting the parties together to talk things over with him, or by talking to them individually, or in some cases, by having one of his special assistants represent him in trying to find grounds for an acceptable compromise. Thus, insofar as members of the Cabinet were concerned, Roosevelt's function of coordination was exercised almost exclusively by dealing with them in their separate capacities as heads of the departments rather than in their collective capacity as a Cabinet. In fact, for all practical purposes, their collective capacity was virtually non-existent. How little Roosevelt made use of the Cabinet as a top-level collegial body for coordination is summarized very clearly by a candid passage which Harold L. Lckes confided to his diary early in 1935, after he had attended a particularly dull Cabinet meeting:

". . . only the barest routine matters were discussed. All of which leads me to set down what has been running in my mind for a long time and that is just what use the Cabinet is under this Administration. The cold fact is that on important matters we are seldom called upon for advice. We never discuss exhaustively any policy of Government or question of political strategy. The President makes all of his own decisions and, so far at least as the Cabinet is concerned, without taking counsel with a group of advisers. On particular questions he will call into his office persons directly interested, but it is fair to say that the Cabinet is not a general council upon whose advice the President relies or the opinions of which, on important matters, he calls for. Our Cabinet meetings are pleasant affairs, but we only skim the surface of things on routine matters. As a matter of fact, I never think of bringing up even a serious departmental issue at Cabinet meeting, and apparently the other members follow the same policy, at least to a considerable extent." [60]

CHAPTER V

DEVISING NEW COORDINATIVE MACHINERY

Despite Roosevelt's failure to use his Cabinet as a coordinating agency, he did make use of the individual Cabinet members in some new coordinative machinery which he devised early in his first term. Since most of the work of the government in dealing with the problems of the depression was being done by the new specialized "alphabet agencies," Roosevelt thought it important to establish a formal, top-level coordinating council which would encompass both the heads of the new agencies and the heads of the regular departments. Apparently his first intention in forming such a council was to bring together the heads of the new agencies and the heads of only those Cabinet departments which were most directly concerned with the emergency program. Ickes reported in his diary on June 7, 1933, that in a conversation with him, Roosevelt "said it was his idea when the legislation now pending was passed to organize some sort of interdepartmental conference. This would be made up of those in charge of the big new public works and other projects authorized by legislation already passed or pending, together with the Secretaries of Labor, Agriculture, Commerce, and Interior." [1]

Before Roosevelt had established this new Executive Council on July 11, 1933, [2] however, he had decided to broaden the membership to include all of the members of the Cabinet, as well as the Director of the Budget, the Administrator of National Recovery, the Administrator of Agricultural Adjustment, the Administrator of Federal Emergency Relief, the Federal Coordinator of Transportation, the Governor of the Farm Credit Administration, the Chairman of the Board of the Reconstruction Finance Corporation, the Chairman of the Board of the Home Owners Loan Corporation, the Chairman of the Board of the Tennessee Valley Authority, the Director of Emergency Conservation Work, the Secretary to the President, the Assistant Secretary of the Treasury, and an Executive Secretary. [3]

The purposes of the Executive Council, according to the executive order creating it, were "to provide for the orderly presentation of business to the President, and to coordinate the inter-agency problems of organization and the work of the new governmental agencies established pursuant to the emergency legislation."[4] The Council's twenty-four members met each Tuesday afternoon in the Cabinet room at the White House with Roosevelt himself usually presiding. As temporary Executive Secretary, Roosevelt appointed his old friend and political adviser, Frank C. Walker, who was to carry out "such duties as may be prescribed him by the President."[5] Walker, however, was not made in any way the directing head of the Council's work, and it was provided that "in the absence of the President, the senior Cabinet Member present shall preside,"[6] rather than the Executive Secretary. It was clear that Roosevelt definitely intended to be the director of the Council himself, and that he did not regard the Executive Secretary as in any sense the "chief of staff" to the President.

Actually, the Executive Council functioned more or less as an enlarged Cabinet, with Roosevelt conducting the Council meetings in much the same way as he did those of the regular Cabinet. Although he may have originally intended that the Executive Council would serve as a broad coordinating agency, it did not function effectively in that way. The Council was not provided with a staff, nor did it have any formal power to coordinate the work of the departments and agencies other than that exercised by Roosevelt himself. The only coordinating function served by the Council was that of enabling the heads of the regular departments to meet once a week with the heads of the new emergency agencies and the President to exchange ideas and information on problems that were interdepartmental in scope. In itself, this was undoubtedly of considerable value in the early days of the New Deal, but neither the Council nor the Executive Secretary served in an important way to make decisions of a coordinative nature for the President. Such decisions were made by Roosevelt himself, with the Executive Council serving only as a source of information and advice. Walker's most valuable role continued to be that of an informal "trouble shooter" who served the President behind-the-scenes in trying to iron out difficulties and smooth ruffled feelings, rather than in his formal role as Executive Secretary of the Executive Council. Except insofar as it may have been valuable as a device for exchanging information and for enabling the heads of the departments and agencies to get to know each other better, the Council did not serve as an effective mechanism for coordination.

In November, 1933, Roosevelt thought it desirable to create an additional coordinating organization with a more limited membership than the Executive Council. This new National Emergency Council was assigned the specific purpose of "coordinating and making more efficient and productive the work of the numerous field agencies of the Government" which had been established under the three major emergency legislative enactments, namely the National Industrial Recovery Act, the Agricultural Adjustment Act, and the Federal Emergency Relief Act.[7]

By November, Roosevelt had been in office eight months. Much had been done in almost feverish haste to try to stem the tide of the economic depression, but no spectacular improvements had yet resulted. Although economic conditions were definitely better than in March, millions of people were still unemployed and in desperate need. As the fourth winter of the depression came on there was growing unrest and uneasiness throughout the country as the rapid recovery hoped for following Roosevelt's inauguration proved to be slow in materializing. As a matter of fact, the business revival which had taken place to some degree during the summer months had apparently ceased; the relief rolls which had been declining gradually since March had begun to rise again in October. Under the direction of Harry Hopkins, the Federal Emergency Relief Administration, in conjunction with state and local agencies, was providing direct relief to prevent starvation and the most extreme cases of hardship.

However, serious difficulties were being experienced in taking care of people in sufficient numbers to meet the pressing needs. Because of the speed and sense of urgency in launching the program, a considerable amount of administrative confusion and duplication had developed. Undoubtedly one of Roosevelt's major objectives in establishing the new National Emergency Council was to try to eliminate such conditions and to improve the relief program. As he later wrote, "That was the primary objective of the National Emergency Council —to see that we were not duplicating work, to see how in an administrative way we could improve the administrative machinery."[8] The National Emergency Council was thus regarded by Roosevelt as an important administrative move to bring greater efficiency into the relief program and the other emergency New Deal measures.

In establishing the National Emergency Council Roosevelt undoubtedly had some significant political motives as well. The creation of the Council, with its attendant publicity, dramatized to the public that efforts were being made to improve the emergency programs. It was designed to serve as something of a "shot in the arm" to both those in the administration carrying out the emergency programs and to the general public in encouraging increased support of the New Deal's efforts. Also in November at almost the same time that he was establishing the National Emergency Council, Roosevelt, at Hopkins' urging, was moving from a policy of providing mostly direct relief to the unemployed to one emphasizing the provision of work relief through the newly established Civil Works Administration.[9] Direct relief had served as an important stop-gap measure to alleviate the most serious conditions through the spring and summer of 1933, but it had not in any sense been sufficient to meet the nation's economic needs adequately. Roosevelt did not want to go through another winter relying largely upon an inadequate direct relief program for the millions of unemployed but wished instead to revitalize the government's efforts by providing extensive work opportunities for those on relief.

Originally, Roosevelt had established the Public Works Administration under the terms of Title II of the National Industrial Recovery Act[10] as the major agency to stimulate economic revival and renewed employment through large-scale public works projects. Although the PWA, under the supervision of Secretary of the Interior Harold Ickes, had begun to make some progress, it had gotten off to a very slow start. This was partly due to the absence of any previously made comprehensive plans for public works, which meant that planning had to be begun almost from scratch. It was also due in considerable degree to the extreme caution exercised by Ickes in spending the taxpayers' money. Though Roosevelt sympathized with Ickes' deliberate care in selecting projects and Ickes' insistence that the government should get its money's worth from each project, the President was faced with the disappointing fact that the PWA had not provided the needed stimulus to employment nearly as fast as originally hoped. Accordingly, he moved to set up the CWA to help provide a way for the unemployed to get through the winter until the PWA would get going in higher gear the following year. Because of this, a major purpose of the National Emergency Council was to help in keeping the jurisdictional lines straight between the CWA and the PWA and to try to avoid as much as possible the almost inevitable conflicts which seemed likely to develop between the two agencies and their highly volatile administrators, Hopkins and Ickes.

Another political factor which influenced Roosevelt in setting up the National Emergency Council was his belief that information was badly needed by the people throughout the country on the work of the relief program and of the other new emergency agencies. Roosevelt thought it was highly important that people should know what was taking place and should have a reasonably complete picture as to how the New Deal program was progressing. Accurate and comprehensive explanations of the various measures, Roosevelt felt, would build support from the public for what was being done. Consequently, he visualized the National Emergency Council and the subordinate state and county branches to be created under its jurisdiction as an unexcelled channel for the wide dissemination of information to the people. So a combination of reasons, administrative and political, motivated him to set up the new Council.

In constituting the National Emergency Council, Roosevelt returned to the original idea which he had expressed to Ickes in June, prior to the creation of the Executive Council. The new organization was composed only of the Secretary of the Interior, the Secretary of Agriculture, the Secretary of Commerce, and the Secretary of Labor from the Cabinet departments, and the Administrator of Agricultural Adjustment, the Administrator of Federal Emergency Relief, the Administrator for Industrial Recovery, the Chairman of the Home Owners Loan Corporation, the Governor of the Farm Credit Administration, and a representative of the Consumers' Council.[11] It was to be headed by an Executive Director who was "authorized to execute the functions and to perform the duties vested in the Council by the President."[12]

A statement issued by the White House on December 6, 1933, spelled out somewhat more specifically that the President was creating the new Council for the purpose of "consolidating, coordinating and making more efficient and productive the emergency activities of the Federal Government, and for the purpose of assisting in carrying into effect the provisions of the various emergency acts."[13] According to this statement, the Council was charged with the responsibility of providing temporary machinery "for the adjustment of such controversies as may arise from the operation of the National Industrial Recovery Act and the Agricultural Adjustment Act."

In addition, the Council was assigned the duty of setting up "in Washington a central information bureau for the purpose of conveying to the general public all factual information with reference to the various governmental agencies." Similar information bureaus were to be set up "throughout the various counties in the United States," and state directors and county councils for the National Emergency Council were to be appointed "in order that local activities may be linked directly and effectively with the Federal administrative power."[14] Frank Walker was asked by the President to perform the duties of the Executive Director of the National Emergency Council, along with his job as Executive Secretary of the Executive Council, until a permanent Executive Director should be appointed.

On December 19, Roosevelt issued an executive order augmenting the membership of the National Emergency Council to include the Director of the Budget, the Attorney General, and the Chairman of the Federal Trade Commission. In a statement issued with this executive order, he announced that the new Council was holding its first meeting that day, and that it and the Executive Council would meet thereafter on alternate Tuesdays.[15] At the first meeting, Roosevelt discussed some of his reasons for establishing the Council. He stated that when Congress was in session he had "probably on the average of between three or four hours a day of conferences with congressional leaders" and could not devote enough time to the administrative end of government. He then continued: "It is quite remarkable to me that we have not had more overlapping and clashes," but the time had come "when I have got to have somebody to act as sort of *alter ego* for me during the congressional session, going around and acting as my legs and ears and eyes and making certain—what might be called suggestions . . . working out these things in such a way that they will not come up to me during the session of Congress."[16]

Roosevelt intended that the National Emergency Council should assume those functions of the Executive Council which pertained to the emergency activities being pursued to meet the problems of the depression, while the Executive Council would continue to meet for the mutual exchange of information concerning those matters not directly affecting the emergency program. Because of the large degree of interlocking membership between the two Councils, however, a clear line of demarcation between their respective functions does not appear to have been maintained very rigidly, and by the autumn of 1934, Roosevelt decided that it was unnecessary to maintain both Councils. Accordingly, they were merged in October, 1934, by an executive order which appointed all of the members of the Executive Council to the National Emergency Council. The separate existence of the Executive Council was terminated, and all of its functions and duties were transferred to the National Emergency Council.[17]

One of Roosevelt's major purposes in establishing the National Emergency Council had been to coordinate not only the activities of the various emergency agencies in Washington but also to coordinate their field operations throughout the country. To that end, National Emergency Council directors were appointed in each of the states to establish closer coordination in the operations of the different Federal agencies working within the state, and also to coordinate Federal activities with those being undertaken by the states themselves in such fields as relief and public works. Much of the time and effort of the National Emergency Council staff in Washington and in the states was devoted to working out better federal-state relationships in the joint administration of the emergency programs. The Council also functioned as a centralized reporting agency, as the state directors were made responsible for consolidating information and submitting periodic reports to Washington on the work of all the Federal agencies operating within their jurisdictions, and also for reporting on the activities of the state agencies as well.

In addition, the Council was assigned the task of serving as a centralized agency to disseminate information and to provide guidance to the people of the country about how to make use of the various recovery and relief agencies. By making a single field organization under the National Emergency Council responsible for reporting and disseminating information, rather than allowing each agency to continue to do these things for itself, Roosevelt stated that he was trying to "wipe out all needless and costly duplication of personnel" and "make for a more effective administration."[18] In performing these functions, the Council did a competent job which contributed to the over-all effectiveness of the emergency programs. In the area of providing coordination between the heads of the various agencies in Washington, however, the Council proved rather early not to be a particularly valuable device. The Council itself was undoubtedly too large to act effectively as a coordinative agency, and the Executive Director was not given sufficient authority by Roosevelt to act for him in making final decisions. Along with problems of major importance, many petty difficulties were raised at the meetings, and a lot of time was undoubtedly wasted by the busy men who attended.[19]

By the summer of 1934, Roosevelt had come to realize the limitations of the National Emergency Council, at least to some degree, and he appointed a new and smaller committee from among the Emergency Council members "to coordinate the activities of the Administration affecting relief and unemployment and in general the activities under the various emergency recovery measures." [20] This new agency was given the name Industrial Emergency Committee and it was composed of the Secretary of the Interior, the Secretary of Labor, the Administrator of Federal Emergency Relief, the Administrator for Industrial Recovery, and a Director appointed by the President. Before the end of the summer, Roosevelt also appointed the Administrator of Agricultural Adjustment to be a member of the Committee. [21]

The President's appointment as Director of the new organization went to Donald R. Richberg, a former Chicago law partner of Ickes who had come to Washington in 1933 as General Counsel for the National Recovery Administration. Richberg was given a leave of absence from his duties with the NRA to take this new job. At the same time, he was appointed as Executive Director of the National Emergency Council and as Executive Secretary of the Executive Council to succeed Frank Walker, who left the government temporarily to attend to his private business affairs. [22] Regarding the purposes of this Committee, Roosevelt was later to write: "One primary reason for the creation of the Industrial Emergency Committee was to bring the NRA into line with a coordinated Government policy, to see to it that each of the major agencies or departments concerned with the recovery program was working in harmony with the objectives of the others and was following reasonably consistent general policies." [23]

Problems involving the administration of the NRA were the most pressing to be dealt with by the Committee and after General Hugh Johnson submitted his resignation as Administrator for Industrial Recovery in September, 1934, Roosevelt vested responsibility for the formulation and coordination of the general administrative policies of the NRA in the Committee. [24] In addition to this responsibility for the NRA, however, the Committee was looked to by Roosevelt much more than the larger National Emergency Council had previously been as a general coordinating agency for the major emergency programs. In describing the Committee's functions, Richberg later wrote: "For many weeks this small group met, first in a preliminary discussion and then with the President, for the formulation of policies fundamental to the operation of these major federal agencies of relief and recovery." [25]

When the National Emergency Council and the Executive Council were merged in October, 1934, the Industrial Emergency Committee was also made a part of the reconstituted National Emergency Council by the following provision of the executive order: "The Industrial Emergency Committee, as heretofore established, shall continue to exercise all the functions and duties heretofore imposed upon it and serve as a sub-committee of the National Emergency Council." [26]

In consolidating all three of these top-level coordinating bodies into the new 34 member National Emergency Council,[27] Roosevelt indicated that he expected the new organization to serve as a general coordinating medium for all the administrative activities of the executive branch, whether carried on by the regular departments or by the new emergency agencies. Public administration authorities at the time regarded this as a very encouraging development in bringing more order into the conduct of the New Deal administration, and one of them hailed the new Council as the "center of the whole mechanism of administrative coordination." [28] Certainly the purposes and duties of the organization as set forth in the executive order which established it were impressive and all-inclusive:

"It shall be the purpose of the National Emergency Council (a) to provide for the orderly presentation of business to the President; (b) to coordinate interagency problems of organization and activity of Federal agencies; (c) to coordinate and make more efficient and productive the work of the field agencies of the Federal Government; (d) to cooperate with any Federal agency in performing such activities as the President may direct; and (e) to serve in an advisory capacity to the President and the Executive Director of the National Emergency Council." [29]

The effectiveness of the new organiaztion would, of course, depend upon the degree to which Roosevelt would actually delegate authority to it, and the power which he would give the Executive Director to act for him. Certainly the language of the executive order was generous in vesting quite extensive authority in the Executive Director. He was "authorized to execute the functions and to perform the duties vested in the Council by the President," and subject to the approval of the President, was to prescribe "such rules and regulations as may be necessary to effectuate the purposes for which the Council is created." In addition, he was authorized to issue on his own "such rules and regulations as he may deem necessary to supplement, amplify, or carry out the purposes and intent" of the rules which had been issued with the President's approval.[30]

If Richberg, as Executive Director, was to carry out these responsibilities fully and make the National Emergency Council the "center of the whole mechanism of administrative coordination," it was necessary for him to be recognized clearly as the superior of the heads of the departments and agencies, either by the President's specific designation or by a definite informal understanding that this was the President's intention. It had to be clearly established that he was closer to the President than any other official, that he was in a position to know the President's wishes, that he could speak for the President, and that he would be assured of Presidential backing in case of conflicts. In view of the language setting forth his duties in the executive order, the press was quick to dub Richberg as the "Assistant President" and the "Number One Man" of the administration. Writing a year later, however, Richberg denied that he had thought of the job in such terms. In describing his functions, he said that it was

". . . the essence of my job . . . to reduce the number and complexity of controversies that could only be settled in the White House—and though I may not have merited the President's always generous encouragement, I certainly worked hard at that job—and it was never necessary to stir up any trouble in order to keep busy! . . . . my duties and responsibilities proceeded directly and solely from and to the President—a fact well understood and given much publicity by the press—even to the unfortunate extent of giving me the undeserved and undesirable nickname of "Assistant President." One of the constant embarrassments to a President and his subordinates is a public interest, which the newspapers naturally seek to satisfy, in identifying some one person as wielding the greatest influence in the administration.

"The fact is that the countless problems of our Chief Executive require him to rely on the specialized services of a large number of aides and at the same time to check their judgment by the opinions of many others. The creation of any secondary Pooh Bah or Grand Vizier would simply impair the President's ability to get the best services out of the responsible heads of government departments and agencies and would constantly interfere with his effort to get first-hand information essential to his decisions. The burdens of the President can be lightened by delegations of power and by having the drudgery and detail of supervision and coordination entrusted to administrative assistants; but the burden of an infinite variety of decisions affecting major policies and the manner of carrying them out cannot be shared. The President must meet these responsibilities alone, and no other person should be expected to know how he will act until his final decision is made." [31]

Apparently, however, some of Richberg's colleagues in the National Emergency Council did not believe these were Richberg's sentiments at the time, for they were disturbed by what they regarded as his efforts to live up to the "Assistant President" designation. Ickes, for example, wrote in his diary:

"The National Emergency Council held a meeting at two o'clock and it was evident that Richberg has been getting in some fine work. He is steadily building up his own power, and he acted today like the fair-haired boy of the Administraiton. He looked like the cat that had swallowed the canary. He is gathering under his control all of the various interdepartmental committees, although why the Director of an Emergency Council should have anything to do with committees that attach to the permanent branches of the government is more than I can undertsand." [32]

In another diary entry, Ickes makes it clear that Roosevelt, too, was bothered by the references to Richberg as the "Assistant President," and that he did not actually intend for the Executive Director to exercise the extensive authority over the departments and agencies which had apparently been assigned to him on paper:

"At Cabinet meeting the President referred to the stories that have appeared in the newspapers during the last few days, especially the one in *The New York Times* which, in a sensational manner, announced that Richberg is a sort of an Assistant President and outranks the whole Cabinet. These stories annoy the President very much indeed. He spoke of this matter Thursday night during the White House conference and he dwelt on it again at the Cabinet meeting. To listen to the President, one would never think that Richberg was more than an exalted messenger boy, but to read the newspapers, one would think that the President really shares his power with him. A good many people think that these news items exalting Richberg are being fed out by his own staff. There seems to be little doubt that Richberg is reaching out in every direction for all the power he can possibly gather unto himself. He is even talking about suggesting to the President a reorganization of the Departments. He is as busy as a bull pup in fly time. I discovered last night that Morgenthau does not like him and certainly Harry Hopkins feels about him as I do." [33]

In any case, it became obvious fairly soon that Richberg did not have the status and authority to act as the President's main coordinative assistant. Several officials of the administration continued to have more influence with Roosevelt than Richberg and many important administrative decisions were made by Roosevelt without Richberg's knowledge.[34] Many of the department and agency heads ignored Richberg consistently and carried their problems directly to Roosevelt instead.[35]

According to Richberg's account, he resigned as Executive Director in May, 1935, in order to help prepare and argue the government's presentation before the Supreme Court in the Schechter case, in which the constitutionality of the NRA was being tested.[36] According to Icke's diary, however, Roosevelt had already decided in April to remove Richberg:

"The President told me today that Frank Walker had agreed to come back. He will reinstate him as Director of the Emergency Council, dispossessing Richberg in that job. I didn't ask him what would happen to Richberg, who is now chairman of NRA, but it looks to me as if this will mean a distinct change in his status. Certainly he won't be entitled any longer to the characterization of 'Number One Man' or 'Assistant President.' It looks to me as if his usefulness in the Administration is practically at an end." [37]

Roosevelt had made it abundantly clear by the time of Richberg's resignation that he did not regard the Executive Director as his principal assistant, charged with the responsibility of coordinating all the administrative work of the executive branch. In returning Frank Walker to the position, he placed the organization in the hands of a man who, in Robert Sherwood's words, was "a quiet, gentle, trustworthy, unquenchably friendly man who was invaluable to Roosevelt through the years as spreader of oil on troubled, administrative waters." [38] Walker's unambitious and unostentatious nature would certainly never lead anyone to think of calling him the "Assistant President."

In addition to his dissatifaction with Richberg, one of Roosevelt's main reasons for requesting Walker to return as Executive Director was that he wished to assign him to the delicate job of serving as general coordinator and "peacemaker" in the new work relief program which Congress had approved early in 1935. Roosevelt created quite an elaborate and cumbersome administrative organization for the program. Walker became director of a new Division of Applications and Information in the National Emergency Council, which was to serve as a central clearing house to receive, study, and pass upon all suggested plans for the expenditure of funds for relief and public works. Ickes was named chairman of an Advisory Committee on Allotments, which would make recommendations as to the relative merits and priority of projects and submit them to the President for final approval. Finally, Harry Hopkins was appointed administrator of the Works Progress Administration, a new operating agency which was set up to execute the program "in such manner as to move from the relief rolls to work on projects or in private employment the maximum number of persons in the shortest time possible," and which was authorized to "recommend and carry on small useful projects designed to assure a maximum of employment in all localities." [39]

To Walker, Roosevelt entrusted the difficult task of settling the disputes which might arise between Ickes and Hopkins. "Under a plan suggested by the President," Ickes wrote in his diary, "when Hopkins and I cannot agree whether a project is PWA or WPA, Frank Walker is to act as umpire." [40] This role as "keeper of the peace between the two jarring New Dealers," [41] as Sherwood characterized it, must have been almost a fulltime job for Walker in itself, for although Ickes and Hopkins shared a grudging admiration and liking for each other personally, the rivalry between Ickes' PWA and Hopkins' WPA became an intense and often bitter one.

As Sherwood has described the situation, there were many conflicts between Ickes and Hopkins which "had to be referred to the harassed umpire, Frank Walker, who would usually render what Ickes has described as a 'Solomonian verdict,' giving half of the project to each agency." Since Walker's decisions often "satisfied neither contestant, the dispute would end with both Ickes and Hopkins executing sweeps around Walker's flanks to the President himself, and he would be forced to decide which of them would enjoy the prestige to be derived from laying the sewer pipes" used in the "modernization of the sewage system in Atlanta, Georgia." [42] By settling some of the disputes between Hopkins and Ickes, Walker was undoubtedly helpful to Roosevelt in keeping down the amount of friction in the relief program.

But in most of the more serious disagreements Roosevelt himself still had to serve as the coordinator. Ickes' diary reveals in many places the tremendous amount of time which Roosevelt devoted personally to the administrative affairs of the program. And Louis Brownlow, in describing what he called "the weird piece of machinery for administering the new Emergency Relief Appropriation Act," has written:

". . . the President did something that, I believe, shocked every student of public administration to the marrow of his bones. He set up a perfectly impossible plan which a good many of us at once dubbed the 'five-ring-circus'. . . . It confused nearly everybody and particularly the practitioners of orderly administration. But the confusion the experts then suffered was greatly to be compounded later on. The thing worked! . . . Perhaps this weird scheme would not have worked for any other man but Franklin D. Roosevelt. In fact, in my opinion, it could not have worked for any other person, and it would not have served his needs had he not personally undertaken the tremendous burden of the actual task of co-ordination." [43]

As the administrative pattern of the New Deal became somewhat more stabilized after the hectic days of 1933 and 1934, Roosevelt was to call the National Emergency Council together less and less as a group. Meetings were no longer held according to a regular schedule, and by the end of 1935 and early 1936, this "Super Cabinet" met quite infrequently. The Council finally held its last meeting as a separate organization on April 28, 1936.[44] In setting forth his views on the National Emergency Council in a later conversation with Louis Brownlow, Roosevelt said:

"The whole NEC was a wonderful essay in democracy. It was exactly like a New England town meeting. It gave everybody a chance to blow off. I learned many things there—many things that those who were reporting never suspected that I learned and some that they wouldn't have liked me to know anything about. They also learned a lot about each other. At the beginning it was a wonderful device for keeping up the morale of the whole team, as long as instant relief and recovery were the sole goals.

"But like a New England town meeting, it was too big to do much actual work. It had to be split up into committees and subcommittees until in the end I couldn't take it any more because I found myself making stump speeches to the council instead of listening to its members. The time came when I could get most out of it by just talking to Frank Walker alone, especially after the organization of the whole relief setup in the spring of '35."[45]

The administrative staff of the National Emergency Council was maintained long after the Council itself held its last meeting as the Washington office and the various field offices throughout the country continued to operate. As mentioned earlier, Roosevelt had assigned to the Council at the time of its establishment the responsibility of setting up "in Washington a central information bureau for the purpose of conveying to the general public all factual information with reference to the various governmental agencies," and to "set up similar bureaus throughout the various counties in the United States."[46] This function had been quickly developed into a centralized information service which issued general information concerning all phases of governmental activities. Included in this service was the task of answering questions submitted by the public about the organization and operations of the government; by 1938, over 100,000 such inquiries were handled annually by the Council.[47]

As part of its information service, the Council had also been instructed by Roosevelt to start publishing an annual *United States Government Manual*, to set forth in simplified form the organization and functions of all government agencies. Through its state and local offices, the Council also continued to serve as a centralized reporting agency for the coordination and transmission of information to the President concerning the progress and effects of the various agencies of the government in their field operations. In addition, the Council carried on a press clipping service which provided the President and other leading officials of the executive branch, as well as the members of Congress, with a comprehensive summary of what newspapers throughout the country were printing about governmental activities. And through its state offices, the Council continued to be responsible for coordinating the field work of the various agencies with each other, and with the state and local governments involved.

Since the Council itself, however, was no longer holding meetings or functioning as originally intended, Roosevelt decided to abolish it by the end of 1937, and distribute its main duties to other parts of the administration. This was also in keeping with a recommendation which had been made by the President's Committee on Administrative Management in the report which it had submitted the previous January. Accordingly, Roosevelt issued an executive order on September 16, 1937, which stated that the Council should be terminated in December of that year.[48] However, as Roosevelt later wrote, "By November of 1937, the 1937 economic recession had become widespread, and by December it had become quite acute."[49] Because of this, he decided to continue the Council in operation until June 30, 1938, with the view in mind that it might prove useful as a coordinating device in the 1937 economic situation if the government should have to undertake such a large-scale emergency program as that of 1933 to 1935. For the most part, however, Roosevelt's main use of the Council in 1938 was as an informational agency. Early that year, in order to build up its services along these lines, he appointed a former Washington newspaper editor, Lowell Mellett, as Executive Director.[50] Under Mellett's direction, the Council's functions as the government's centralized information agency were expanded and improved.[51]

As the deadline for the expiration of the Council once again approached, Roosevelt issued Executive Order 7906 on June 6, 1938, extending its life for still one more year, until June 30, 1939. Before the latter date, however, Roosevelt had finally abolished the Council and transferred its functions to the newly-created Executive Office of the President. This was done as part of his Reorganization Plan No. II, which he issued on May 9, 1939, under the authority he received from Congress in the Reorganization Act of 1939.[52] To carry on the functions of the Council, he established a new Office of Government Reports in the Executive Office of the President, and appointed Mellett as its director.[53]

Thus the long and checkered career of the National Emergency Council finally came to an end. Off and on through the years it had undoubtedly helped Roosevelt to meet his responsibilities for the coordination of the administrative organization. It provided him with a convenient, flexible device which he could use as he saw fit to meet new circumstances and new needs as they arose. Although he allowed the Council itself to become a completely quiescent body by early 1936, he had continued to rely on its administrative staff for important services. By the end of its existence, the Council was performing no significant function in coordinating the actual administrative operations of the government, but it had become an important coordinative agency for consolidating and unifying the government's informational and reporting activities. In this capacity, it was a valuable staff agency to Roosevelt. By providing him with regular informative reports about the operations of the various parts of the government, it aided him in his job of coordinating those operations.

Roosevelt emphasized the coordinating value of the Council in a statement which he issued at the time he transferred its functions to the Executive Office of the President: "Its usefulness as an actual Council, which met weekly under my chairmanship, was very great in the period of the emergency which then confronted the country, but, as time has gone on, it no longer operates as a Council but does continue to carry on important activities which are indispensable to the President of the United States. . . . The coordinating and reporting functions of the Council have to do with the presentation to the President of factual information, independently gathered, as to the progress and effect of our Governmental activities." [54] The Council, he continued, was "designed to give the President the information he requires from all parts of the country." [55]

Valuable as the National Emergency Council had been to Roosevelt in various ways, he had never actually used it as a powerful coordinating agency with broad authority to act for him, as had originally seemed to be his intention at the time of its establishment. The evidence indicates that he did not use the Council in such a way because he did not really wish to have very much coordination in the administrative organization other than that which he could provide himself. Roosevelt, as John Gunther said, "always saw to it that he himself was the last judge and arbiter." [56] As a result of this attitude, he had to devote a very great amount of his time to settling the disputes and arguments of his subordinates as it was virtually certain that a considerable amount of friction would develop within the New Deal administration between representatives of the various departments and agencies.

Many of the officials Roosevelt appointed to key administrative posts were ambitious men who were constantly seeking more power and influence and who were passionately devoted to furthering the particular programs for which they were responsible. As a result, there were many bitter conflicts and jurisdictional disputes within the administration almost from the very beginning. A surprising number of the accounts which have been written by Roosevelt's close associates document the extent and seriousness of these conflicts. Ickes' diary is particularly revealing in this regard for the combative and irritable Ickes was at the center of many of the troubles. At one time or another, he carried on serious feuds with Henry Morgenthau, Harry Hopkins, Hugh Johnson and Secretary of War Harry Woodring, among others, and he seems to have been engaged in an almost constant battle with Secretary of Agriculture Henry Wallace. As the accounts show, such conflicts always ended up squarely in

Roosevelt's lap for he gave no one else sufficient authority to settle them for him.

Although Roosevelt always publicly disapproved the outbreak of such disputes, several of his associates have observed that he sometimes seemed actually to have encouraged rivalries and jealousies between the heads of two or more agencies in the belief that such competition would keep them on their toes and would encourage more alert attention to duty on the part of all concerned. In this connection, Frances Perkins has written that Roosevelt said to her on one occasion:

"There is something to be said for having a little conflict between agencies. A little rivalry is stimulating, you know. It keeps everybody going to prove that he is a better fellow than the next man. It keeps them honest too. An awful lot of money is being handled. The fact that there is somebody else in the field who knows what you are doing is a strong incentive to strict honesty."[57]

The fact that Roosevelt often was not explicit or definite in delegating authority or in giving directions to his subordinates undoubtedly contributed to many of these jurisdictional conflicts. Raymond Moley has commented critically on this characteristic of Roosevelt's: "Subordinates often did not know for sure what they were to do, or what Roosevelt's answer was to a given problem. . . . His habit of giving vague assignments of authority brought about violent conflicts in his official family."[58]

Certainly Roosevelt sometimes delegated authority so loosely and established such indefinite jurisdictional lines that those working under him were almost certain to find themselves stepping on each other's toes. Quite often, he would even go so far as to ask two or more people to work on the same problem for him without letting them know that he had done so. As a result, according to Moley, his subordinates "sometimes thought they had an exclusive assignment till they ran into two or three others with the same assignment."[59] Even some of those who remained more friendly to Roosevelt than Moley were seriously disturbed by this habit. For example, Samuel I. Rosenman has written:

". . . Roosevelt had developed a habit of asking two different people to do the same thing for him at the same time. Sometimes he had forgotten that he had asked one person to do the job by the time he asked the second. Sometimes he did it, I am sure, in order to have one check on the other—without either knowing it. Invariably the two persons working on the same project would run into each other. Those who were unfamiliar with the President's method of working would get irritated; those who worked with him for any length of time grew accustomed to this strange and inefficient practice and did the best they could. Although the President was apologetic whenever it was called to his attention, he never fully dropped this habit."[60]

On numerous occasions, Roosevelt appointed men who differed greatly from each other in viewpoint and personality to work together in the same agency, or to do parts of the same job. By so doing, he almost seemed to be inviting the conflict and competition which inevitably resulted. For example, he divided authority in the NRA between the Administrator, Hugh Johnson, and the General Counsel, Donald Richberg, in a way which was pleasing to neither; he placed Moley and later Sumner Welles and Adolf Berle in the State Department and dealt with them directly on matters that were certain to infringe on the authority of the Secretary of State, Cordell Hull; as already indicated, he gave both Ickes and Hopkins control over aspects of the public works and relief program; both Ickes and Wallace were given jurisdiction over matters involving conservation; he kept Charles West and Oscar Chapman in the Department of the Interior against Ickes' wishes and used them for work which Ickes did not approve. Perhaps the most flagrant example of all was the retention in office for many months of Harry Woodring as Secretary of War and Louis Johnson as Assistant Secretary of War when the two men wouldn't even speak to each other. General George C. Marshall, who was Army Chief of Staff at the time, is reported to have described the situation between Woodring and Johnson as follows:

"I had to be chief of staff to a secretary of war and his first assistant who weren't speaking to each other. They not only didn't make any secret of how they hated and despised each other, they ran to the President behind each other's back. Then the Presidnt would send for me to get the facts. It was the most miserable experience of my life. If we hadn't been trying to prepare for a war I knew was coming, I don't think I could have stood it."[61]

Whenever Roosevelt would deal directly with those occupying subordinate positions in some of the departments, as he frequently did, resentment and irritation on the part of the department heads naturally resulted. On one occasion, after Roosevelt had called Assistant Secretary of the Interior Chapman directly to tell him to come to a meeting at the White House, Ickes complained to his diary:

"Just what I shall do in this situation I have not yet made up my mind. I want to be perfectly sure that I am doing the wise thing, but I have no disposition to submit to many incidents of this sort. At the very least I shall feel obligated to speak quite frankly to the President. He had no right to go over my head in my absence. It looks like disciplinary action. Neither do I think he has the right to do what he does so frequently, namely, calling in members of my staff for consultation on Department matters, without consulting me or advising with me."[62]

In the same vein, James Farley has reported the following from a conversation with Cordell Hull: " 'God, Jim,' Hull exploded with feeling, 'you don't know what troubles are. Roosevelt is going directly to Welles and Berle. . . . He's bypassing me. . . . He only discusses matters with me when he feels he is obliged to do so because of their importance.' "[63]

Partially, at least, this tendency to divide up authority and to encourage competition among his subordinates was probably due to the nature of Roosevelt's personality. He did not like to delegate too much of his authority to any one person, or to feel that he was too deeply committed to any individual. He always wished to be at the center of everything which was being done and to make the final decisions in all important matters, and even in many which weren't so important but in which he was interested. This method of administration helped to satisfy his insatiable curiosity about what was going on, for all the subordinates who got involved in squabbles would beat a hasty path to Roosevelt's office to tell him their version of the story. Perkins has said that Roosevelt used this technique because it provided him with "a kind of pipeline . . . to give him the vicarious experience of what was going on in an enterprise in which he was interested."[64]

In addition to providing him with information, his methods undoubtedly aided him in maintaining control of the administrative organization. Whenever he put two strong, competing people into the same agency, or gave them both authority over the same program, he made each of them, in effect, more dependent on him. Each had to turn to Roosevelt for support when the inevitable conflicts arose; each had to try to win Roosevelt as an indispensable ally if he was to succeed against his rival. For only Roosevelt had sufficient

authority to decide between them. As a result, final control over determining the course of action to be pursued remained clearly in
Roosevelt's hands. In discussing Roosevelt's division of authority in
this way, James Burns has observed that Roosevelt was "in effect,
adapting the old method of divide and conquer to his own purposes."[305]
And Gunther has aptly summarized this technique as follows:

"Sometimes it seemed that FDR positively loved a muddle, so that
in the end everybody would have to come back to him and say help-
lessly, '*You* fix it!' Over and over he distributed authority and established two or even three competing agencies, not only with conflicting
powers but set up so that each chief thought he alone had most—
with the result that ultimate responsibility remained where it had
been all along, on Mr. Roosevelt's desk. It was as if he were saying,
'Go ahead and have your fun; in the end return to me.' "[306]

Roosevelt tried very hard to keep maximum control over the administrative organization centered in himself because he thought that
was where it properly belonged. Under the Constitution, he was responsible for the work of the executive branch. Consequently, he
tried to control the conduct of his administrative subordinates in such
a way that his authority would be commensurate with his responsibility. His administrative methods, despite the confusion and conflict
which they caused in profusion, helped him to achieve that purpose,
and enabled him to impress his leadership to a very substantial degree upon the whole administrative organization. This fact has been
recognized by Herbert Simon, Donald Smithburg, and Victor Thompson in their book, *Public Administration:*

" 'Organization experts' have usually been rather harsh in their
treatment of Franklin D. Roosevelt because of his violations or apparent ignorance of 'sound canons of organization,' but it is at least
as good an hypothesis that President Roosevelt kept some control
over the development of policy in fields in which he was interested
by purposely refusing to define jurisdictions in sharp, clear, and mutually exclusive terms. Whether he did this consciously, it is unnecessary to argue. But certainly the lack of clarity in the assignment of
responsibilities during President Roosevelt's leadership of the Federal
bureaucracy gave his own personality a greater impact on the development of administrative policy than would have been the case had
the Federal bureaucracy been organized in accordance with the
dreams of a typical artist of organization charts."[307]

Roosevelt's method of fuzzy delegation of authority and the resulting rivalry which it engendered also stimulated many of his subordinates to greater achievement. To win Roosevelt's approbation and support, his competing administrators would each try to do a better job than the others. Each wished to impress Roosevelt with his own accomplishments so that the President would rely upon him more than upon his rivals. "He had a wonderful knack," John Gunther has said, "for playing one person against another so as to get the best out of both."[68] In the experimental, improvised, and somewhat hectic programs of the New Deal, such competition helped to develop the kind of administrative attributes Roosevelt was seeking: bold initiative, eagerness to try new methods, energy, flexibility, and ingenuity. These qualities were at a premium in meeting the tremendous problems of the depression, and Roosevelt encouraged his lieutenants to vie with each other in demonstrating such traits. Arthur Schlesinger, Jr. has described this aspect of Roosevelt's administrative methods as follows:

"F.D.R. prized liveliness, vitality, ideas. He surrounded himself with men who had these qualities. In an effort to test and develop their abilities, he even sometimes set them against each other, with an old free enterpriser's faith that competition is the life of government as well as of trade. The technique of indefinite jurisdiction was sloppy copybook administration; but it often provided a testing of initiative, competence and imagination which produced far better results than playing safe by the book."[69]

In summary, then, it can be said that Roosevelt went to considerable lengths early in his Presidency to try to devise new coordinative machinery, such as the Executive Council, the Industrial Emergency Committee, and the National Emergency Council, to aid him in meeting the need for Presidential coordination. These agencies, along with the Bureau of the Budget and a number of his personal assistants, were unquestionably of value in helping him to perform his coordinative functions. The evidence is abundantly clear, however, that he used them only as means to help him to coordinate, and not as effective coordinating devices in themselves. He delegated authority and controlled his subordinates in such a way that the power to make final coordinative decisions almost always remained in his own tight grip. It is accurate to say that Roosevelt himself was actually the only truly important coordinating instrumentality of the administrative organization prior to the establishment of the Executive Office of the President in 1939.

CHAPTER VI

THE MOVE FOR COMPREHENSIVE REORGANIZATION

By the autumn of 1935, as the need for new legislation to combat the depression began to subside, and as the work of the new emergency agencies gradually became somewhat more stabilized, Roosevelt decided that the time had come for him to devote attention to a comprehensive reorganization of the administrative organization of the government. Unfortunately, however, the broad authority to reorganize which Congress had granted to him in 1933 had expired on March 3, 1935. Roosevelt felt, as he later wrote, that "some progress was made in consolidating related functions"[1] during the two years in which that authority had been in effect. The pressure of events, however, had prevented him from making an attempt to take full advantage of his reorganization powers. He realized that the organizational changes which he had made in 1933-1934 fell far short of the comprehensive reorganization which he had advocated in the years before his election. He also realized that the need for such reorganization had been greatly increased by the large number of new agencies which he had established outside the jurisdiction of the regular departments. He later described the situation in the following manner:

"The joints of the federal machinery began to creak; sheer weight of numbers of units responsible to the President made the job of Chief Executive an almost unbearable task. It seemed evident that I had to be provided with expanded staff facilities to assist in the job of administrative management.[2]

"By 1935 I became convinced, . . . that it would take an overhauling of the entire administrative mechanism in order to make it run more efficiently and economically.

"It had become apparent that the government was becoming cluttered with a number of uncoordinated, independent units which did not fit into any organized plan. With the expansion of the fight for economic recovery and reform along many fronts, it was natural that many new agencies should be created. Aside from the Bureau of the Budget, I had no staff to assist in the managerial direction and control over the expanded governmental structure. It had become almost impossible for me to confer at sufficient length with so many department and commission heads; and it became quite obvious that some rearrangement of the system was essential.

"Accordingly, in October, 1935, I started preliminary conservations regarding a broad administrative survey, which I felt should cover such things as over-all administrative activities, and the elimination of conflicts in authority among the various agencies." [3]

One factor which might be singled out as perhaps having had special significance in speeding up Roosevelt's concern about the need for overhauling the administrative organization was the serious rebuff which he suffered in 1935 from the Supreme Court in the case of *Humphrey's Executor v. United States.*[4] On May 27, 1935, the same day the Court handed down the decision in the Schechter case which invalidated the NRA, the justices also agreed unanimously that Roosevelt did not have unlimited authority to remove from office a member of the Federal Trade Commission or of the other independent regulatory commissions. Roosevelt and his advisers had assumed the President did possess such authority on the basis of the 1926 decision in the case of *Myers v. United States,* written by Chief Justice William Howard Taft, in which President Wilson's removal of a postmaster had been unequivocally upheld by the Court.[5] It had been pointed out to Roosevelt by James Landis, a close associate who had served as law clerk for Justice Brandeis at the time of the Myers case, that Taft's opinion contained language which had been placed there deliberately and after discussion among the justices for the specific purpose of making sure that the decision in the Myers case would be applicable to the independent commissions.[6] Nevertheless, to Roosevelt's surprise and consternation, the Court had changed its mind in the nine intervening years and now ruled that he had acted illegally in arbitrarily removing Commissioner Humphrey without reference to any of the specific causes set forth as grounds for dismissal in the statute creating the commission, i.e., inefficiency, neglect of duty, or malfeasance in office.

Humphrey had been reappointed by President Hoover in 1931 to serve a second seven-year term on the Federal Trade Commission. In October 1933, Roosevelt requested his resignation, stating that "the aims and purposes of the Administration with respect to the work of the Commission can be carried out most effectively with personnel of my own selection," but not indicating any specific charges against Humphrey. After a brief time, when Humphrey failed to resign, Roosevelt wrote him again, expressing the hope that his resignation would soon be forthcoming, and adding, "You will, I know, realize that I do not feel that your mind and my mind go along together on either the policies or the administering of the Federal Trade Commission, and frankly, I think it is best for the people of this country that I should have a full confidence." When Humphrey still refused to resign, Roosevelt ordered him removed from office, whereupon Humphrey challenged the President's action in the courts. Before the final ruling on the case by the Supreme Court, however, Humphrey had died, but the case was continued by his executor who sought the accrued compensation allegedly owed to Humphrey's estate.

In its decision, written by Justice Sutherland, the Court distinguished the Humphrey case from the Myers case by holding that whereas the duties of a postmaster were purely executive and administrative in nature, and thus clearly under the President's jurisdiction, a Federal Trade Commissioner also exercises quasi-legislative and quasi-judicial powers which were not subject to the direction of the President, and which Congress had not intended to be under executive control. Therefore, the Court ruled, the President's authority to remove a Federal Trade Commissioner is limited to the causes which have been specifically set forth by Congress in the statute establishing the agency.[7]

Roosevelt was greatly chagrined by this decision and regretted that he had not proceeded originally by bringing charges directly against Humphrey, according to a statement which Harold Ickes recorded in his diary on June 4, 1935: "The President said that he had made a mistake in not preferring charges. He had actual proof of malfeasance in office, but he didn't want to file such charges against Humphrey, believing as he did that he could get rid of him by milder methods."[8]

With the Humphrey's decision thus limiting his direct authority over the personnel of the independent regulatory commissions, Roosevelt felt frustrated in his efforts to exercise the degree of direction and control which he thought desirable over their administrative policies and procedures. Thus, in addition to the other benefits which he thought would result, it was natural for him to look to administrative reorganization as a possible means of trying to integrate all of the separate independent agencies into major executive departments where they would clearly be subject to the President's administrative supervision.

According to Louis Brownlow's account, the first of the exploratory conversations concerning administrative reorganization which Roosevelt referred to in his statement above actually took place as early as the late spring or early summer of 1935 between the President and the members of the Advisory Committee to the National Resources Board.[9] This Advisory Committee had originally been established under the name National Planning Board as a part of the Public Works Administration. It consisted of the President's uncle, Frederic A. Delano, who was an internationally known authority on city planning, the Columbia University economist, Professor Wesley C. Mitchell, and the University of Chicago political scientist, Professor Charles E. Merriam.[10] During one of the conversations in October, 1935, the President requested Merriam to submit a memorandum on the subject of improving the "over-all administrative management or supervision" of the government. In preparing this document Merriam enlisted the assistance of Louis Brownlow, Director of the Public Administration Clearing House in Chicago, who had been in close consultation with the members of the Advisory Committee during their earlier discussions of the subject.

Following receipt of the Merriam-Brownlow memorandum,[11] Roosevelt continued to discuss the idea of appointing a special committee to make a thorough study of the administrative organization of the government on several other occasions with members of the Advisory Committee. His interest in having such a study undertaken continued to grow during the winter of 1935-1936, but because of questions of political timing, he did not wish to launch such a committee on its task until near the end of the Congressional session. In late February, Roosevelt agreed to a suggestion from Delano and Merriam that Brownlow be asked to prepare a more precise statement of the work which might be included in such a study. This was done, and after a series of three meetings with Brownlow during the first half of March to work out the necessary arrangements, Roosevelt, on March 22, 1936, officially announced the apointment of what subsequently came to be known as the President's Committee on Administrative Management. The statement announcing the appointment of the Committee stated that its purpose was "to make a careful study of the relation of the Emergency Agencies to the regular organization of the Executive branch of the Government." [12]

According to Brownlow, he and Roosevelt agreed that announcement of the Committee's appointment was to be a "spring board

... to say that the time had come to consider the new agencies created during the emergency, and, to the extent that they were to be made permanent, how to fit them into the regular establishment; that to do this adequately would require a study of the regular establishment itself and the relationships and lines of responsibility from the several agencies up to the President." This would in turn justify the Committee in dealing with what Roosevelt and Brownlow agreed to be the fundamental problem which "essentially . . . is how to implement the President with simple but effective machinery which will enable him to exercise managerial direction and control appropriate to the burden of responsibility imposed upon him by the Constitution." [13]

Originally Professor Merriam and his colleagues on the Advisory Committee of the National Resources Board had proposed that either the President or the National Resources Board itself might request a private, unofficial group outside the government, the Public Administration Committee of the Social Science Research Council, to make such a study. Louis Brownlow was then chairman of the Public Administration Committee which included most of the leading academic figures in the field of public administration. The study could have been supported by funds from the Rockefeller Foundation which had recently made some liberal grants to the Social Science Research activities of the Public Administration Committee. The idea of having the study financed by Rockefeller funds did not appeal to Roosevelt and at a meeting on February 20, 1936, he is quoted as having "reiterated his belief that politically the name of Rockefeller in connection with such a study would have a bad effect on the Hill." [14] Consequently, he concluded that it would not be politically expedient to use private funds for the purpose.

In addition, Roosevelt thought that the subject of the study was of such magnitude and importance that it should be undertaken by a committee which he would appoint, and which would have official governmental status and support in accomplishing its work. At first Roosevelt was inclined to set up the Committee as an adjunct to and financed by the National Resources Committee, but after discussions with Acting Director of the Budget Daniel Bell and Brownlow, he decided that the group should be an auxiliary of the National Emergency Council, which was already authorized by law to study the emergency agencies and how to fit them into the regular establishment. Accordingly the March 22nd announcement stated that "This committee will serve as an adjunct of the National Emergency Council which will provide the necessary office facilities and such personnel as the committee may require." [15]

In discussing the appointment of the President's Committee on Administrative Management, Clinton L. Rossiter has observed: "The immediate impulse . . . was Franklin D. Roosevelt's own candid recognition that an otherwise professional performance during his first term in the Presidency was being severely hampered by the sheer multiplicity and complexity of his duties and by the want of effective assistance in their discharge. . . . Mr. Roosevelt's solution was thoroughly in character. Never one to let an important national problem lie around unstudied by a special commission, he set wheels turning in early 1936 with the appointment of the President's Committee on Administrative Management." [16]

Although, as Rossiter says, there can be no doubt that Roosevelt was becoming increasingly concerned about improving the administrative organization in 1935, another factor which influenced him to appoint the President's Committee at that time may have been the fact that Congress was also showing increased evidence of concern about the problems of governmental administration. By early 1935, Congressional criticism of Roosevelt for establishing so many of the so-called "alphabet agencies" had become relatively widespread. Some Congressmen were concerned about the duplication and overlapping in the New Deal administration; some had developed a distrust of the methods of the top administrative personnel of some of the temporary agencies; some were perturbed at the waste of funds and the inefficiency which they observed in the emergncy programs.

In 1933 Congress had appropriated for the national recovery and public works program the then-tremendous sum of $3,000,000,000 to be used during the next two years with very few strings attached as to how the President could spend the money except that it should be used in ways to improve the depressed economic situation. This was the largest appropriation ever authorized by a Congress up to that time to be expended largely at Presidential discretion. Some of the uses to which Roosevelt and the new agencies put the funds were not viewed with great enthusiasm by many members of Congress and there were charges that money was being used by some agencies in ways which Congress had never intended.

Nevertheless, despite the Congressional outcries and wails of anguish about the spending, the waste, the inefficiency the leaf-raking and the "boondoggling" in the relief program, Congress decided once again in

1935 to make its appropriations for work relief and recovery in much the same lump sum fashion with the actual expenditure of the funds to be decided by the President. And instead of the program being curtailed, it was expanded with Congress voting the President a total of $4,800,000,000—a billion and a half dollars more than in 1933. In spite of this, however, Congressional criticisms of the New Deal administrative agencies continued to grow and there was considerable sentiment expressed in Congress for the elimination of some of the agencies and for incorporating others into the regular departments.

It was natural for Congress to prefer to have important activities of government vested in the regular departments where, both formally and informally, Congressional control and influence were easier to exert and where Congressional wishes were usually given more respectful attention than in the new temporary agencies. Through the years, close and confidential relationships had grown up between the senior members and staffs of Congressional committees and veteran staff members of the departments who dealt with the same subject-area or field of endeavor. Few such relationships existed with the emergency organizations. Once the crisis conditions which had seemed to justify creation of the new specialized agencies had improved substantially, there was strong feeling in Congress to try to get back to the more comfortable arrangements of the good old days when most of the government's administrative work had been done by the regular departments.

The Congressional leader in the movement toward administrative reorganization was Senator Harry F. Byrd of Virginia. Byrd had led a vigorous administrative reorganization movement for the Virginia government while serving as Governor of that state, and he was already becoming famous for his definite views on the subject of economy in government. In January, 1936, he had introduced a resolution in the Senate to create a special committee to investigate the executive agencies of the governmnt. This proposal rceived the approval of the Senate in February, 1936,[17] and as a result, a committee of five Senators was established for that purpose with Byrd as chairman. This committee, in turn, requested five private citizens, all trained and experienced in the field of public administration, to serve as an advisory committee, with Louis Brownlow as Chairman.[18] At Brownlow's suggestion, the Senate committee entered into a contract with the Brookings Institution under the terms of which that agency was to aid the committee by conducting an investigation into the national administrative organization and by preparing a factual report embodying recommendations regarding possible improvements.

At a meeting in his office on February 20, 1936, Roosevelt had "restated his intention to submit to the Congress a message near the end of the session in which no action would be requested, an informative message, as he described it—in which procedure for a study of Government reorganization or management would be explained to the Congress." [19] In view of the establishment of the Byrd Committee, however, Roosevelt decided to modify his original intention.

On the same day that he announced the appointment of the President's Committee on Administrative Management, he also addressed a letter to the Vice President (as President of the Senate) stating his intention of appointing such a group, and requesting "that the Senate, through its special committee, cooperate with me and with the committee which I shall name in making this study, in order that duplication of effort in the task of research may be avoided and to the end that it may be as fruitful as possible." [20] In a similar letter to the Speaker of the House of Representatives, he wrote: "I respectfully suggest that the House of Representativs also create a special committee of a similar character through which the House of Representatives could cooperate with me and with the committee that I shall name in making this study. . . ." [21] Following the President's suggestion, the House did eventually create the Select Committee to Investigate Executive Agencies with Representative James Paul Buchanan of Texas, chairman of the House Appropriations Committee, as chairman. [22] Like the Senate group, this Committee also utilized the Brookings Institution to assist in its investigations.

In his letters requesting the cooperation of the Senate and House, Roosevelt spelled out more fully the reasons which had led him to appoint the President's Committee on Administrative Management. "Many new agencies," he explained, "have been created during the emergency, some of which will, with the recovery, be dropped or greatly curtailed, while others, in order to meet the newly realized needs of the Nation, will have to be fitted into the permanent organization of the Executive branch. One object of such a study would be to determine the best way to fit the newly created agencies or such parts of them as may become more or less permanent into the regular organization. To do this adequately and to assure the proper administrative machinery for the sound management of the Executive branch, it is, in my opinion, necessary also to study as carefully as may be the existing regular organization. . . . I then determined to appoint a committee which would assist me in making such a study, with the primary purpose of considering the problem of administrative management." [23]

As chairman of the President's Committee on Administrative Management, Roosevelt selected his old friend, Louis Brownlow, who had already been named as chairman of the four-man advisory group for the Senate committee.[24] Another member of the Senate advisory group, Luther Gulick, was also apointed to the President's Committee, and the third member was Charles E. Merriam, who had been involved from the outset in the discussions with Roosevelt concerning plans for establishing such a committee.

Initially Roosevelt had been inclined to name a committee which would include all of the members of the Advisory Committee of the National Resources Committee, plus Brownlow and one or two others. Some time later, however, he had reached the conclusion that the committee should be very small and should consist of Brownlow, Merriam, and Frederic A. Delano. The latter felt, however, that he should not be a member because of his personal relationship as the President's uncle. Roosevelt, Merriam, and Brownlow were all anxious to get the former Republican Governor of Illinois, Frank O. Lowden, to serve on the committee. Lowden, then living in retirement, had carried through a thorough reorganization of the Illinois state government while governor in 1917. This had been a pioneer accomplishment in the field of administration, and Roosevelt and the others greatly valued Lowden's experience and views. Lowden's health was such that he felt he had to refuse the offer to serve on the committee. Because of the time factor, Brownlow then recommended that it might be better for Roosevelt to go ahead and name only Brownlow, Merriam, and Gulick so the work could get underway, and then others could be added later if it should be thought desirable. This was the final decision but Roosevelt never saw fit to appoint any additional members to supplement the original three.

The President's Committee, aided by a sizable staff and various technical consultants,[25] launched into an intensive study of the national administration, with primary attention focused on the problem of enabling the President to function more effectively as the chief administrator of the entire executive branch. The Committee divided its broad area of inquiry into several major fields and assigned each field to a specialized study committee of experts to analyze the deficiencies in the existing organization and to recommend proposals for improvement. The special studies which resulted were then submitted to the Committee for use in preparing its over-all report and recommendations to the President.[26]

As 1936 was a Presidential election year, Roosevelt and the Committee agreed that the Committee's work should be kept out of the political campaign and that no report should be rendered to the President until after the November election. Brownlow had a final meeting with the President on April 28 at which he reported in general terms as to how the Committee was getting started with its work. He also got the President's approval for the Committee to use officially the title "President's Committee on Administrative Management" which it had been using unofficially in its own discussions for some time.

Following the April 28th meeting, the Committee promised the President that it would not see him or communicate with him about the subject matter of the study until after the election. According to Brownlow, this pledge was scrupulously observed. The Committee had its first meeting with the President on November 14 following his overwhelming re-election on November 2. At this meeting, which Merriam was not able to attend, Brownlow and Gulick discussed at length all of their tentative recommendations with the President. Because of this, they were later criticized in some quarters for allowing Roosevelt to exert excessive influence upon their decisions. In this connection, Brownlow has written:

"The President's Committee has been severely criticized by Professor Lindsay Rogers and others . . . it being Mr. Rogers' contention that such a committee should have made up its own recommendations, put them on the President's table, and left to the President the responsibility for changes. This happens not to have been the conception of the task that the members of the Committee entertained. We had been apointed to an official committee by the President and we thought we should consult him, especially about his own office, inclining to the notion that he might know more about the Presidency than any or all of us. And finally, Professor Rogers does not seem to have taken into consideration the possibility that perhaps the president persuaded us to his own view." [27]

One particular example in which Roosevelt did exercise decisive influence upon the Committee concerned the question of setting up a group of administrative assistants in the White House to aid him in managing and coordinating the work of the departments and agencies.

Roosevelt was naturally very much interested in this matter, and had some definite ideas as to how he expected these assistants to function. As early as May 15, 1936, Harold Ickes reported the following in his diary concerning a conversation with Roosevelt:

"This led him to discuss the reorganization of the executive branch of the Government, which I think he really has very much at heart. Among other things he is developing in his own mind a theory of having two or three executive assistants each of whom could coordinate certain departments, take care of routine matters, and bring to him others for consideration. I told him I thought this would be a good plan, as it would save him a lot of time and trouble. As a matter of fast, as I have said on other occasions, I marvel at his ability to handle the mass of detail that he finds in his lap from day to day." [28]

After Brownlow and Gulick discussed this matter with the President on November 14, Gulick wrote a lengthy memorandum that day in which he recorded that Roosevelt described what he wanted the assistants to do as follows:

". . . 'Executive Assistant to the President' was the title he suggested for each of the members of the 'Secretariat.' He went on to outline their duties in these terms: 'There would be one for foreign affairs. He would go out in the morning and see Hull, and then go to the Treasury, to Agriculture, to Commerce, to the Federal Reserve, and find out what was up, touching foreign relations wherever it was. And he would come back and tell me. Another executive assistant would cover the business relations. A third would deal with financial affairs, and the fourth would handle welfare and conservation. . . .' Louis Brownlow came in with, 'That's all right, but you left one out.' 'What's that,' said the President and Brownie said, 'Planning and personnel.' " [29]

The Committee itself had at first been inclined to recommend the establishment of an administrative secretariat under the direction of one man, modeled somewhat on the example of the British Cabinet secretariat. This would have provided the President with an Executive Secretary designed to function as something of a formal chief of staff for administrative purposes. Brownlow has written, however, that "in our conversations with the President, the members of the Committee . . . found Mr. Roosevelt reluctant to set up any sort of secretariat under one person. After hearing him at length we agreed with him, and thus came to recommend a corps of administrative assistants instead of an administrative secretariat under a single head." [30]

According to the Gulick memorandum, Roosevelt said, "You can't have just one Executive Secretary. The damn columnists would never let him alone. They are always looking for the 'white haired boy.' Just now they are writing up Corcoran. Way back, it was Raymond Moley, and there was no truth in that either." Gulick's memorandum continues:

". . . Brownlow went on with the thought that there would be some confusion and lack of coordination and much waste time for four men reporting directly to the President, and that he could get just what he was after by adding a man for liaison with planning and personnel who would be tacitly placed by the President as 'primus inter pares.' FDR was enthusiastic and added, 'Yes, that's the fellow who never goes out'." [31]

Roosevelt had made it abundantly clear, however, that he did not wish to create an official "chief of staff," or "assistant President," and he convinced the Committee that it should formulate its report in conformity with his views.

The Committee had completed a draft of its report and was ready to submit it to the President by December 17, 1936, when Roosevelt returned to Washington from a trip to South America. Five days later Roosevelt presented the general provisions of the report to the Cabinet, as Ickes noted in his diary:

"The President brought to Cabinet with him the report of his Reorganization Committee and he gave us the outline of the plan. As he had already told me, it calls for the change of the name of this Department to that of Department of Conservation, and the addition of a Department on Public Works and one on Public Welfare. The duties of the departments are described in the broadest possible general terms, and it is contemplated that a continuing power will be given to the President to shift bureaus and agencies, subject to disapproval by Congress within a reasonable time. All of us approved the bill heartily in principle. . . . The President refused to discuss any details, insisting that he might do anything or nothing under the plan." [32]

Another member of the President's Cabinet, Frances Perkins, has criticized the way in which Roosevelt and the President's Committee "kept the report under wraps until just before it went to Congress." [33] Perkins thinks this was undoubtedly a mistake "which created a lot of antagonism on the part of many people." Roosevelt and the Committee should have publicized fully the changes contemplated in the report earlier than they did, according to Perkins, so that the purposes which the report was designed to accomplish would have been much better understood, both by those within the government and by the general public. By delaying the public release of the report until it was presented to Congress, Perkins believes Roosevelt missed an opportunity to build up popular support for his reorganization proposals which could have been very valuable in the struggle which eventually developed over the subject.[34] When this question was raised with Louis Brownlow, he emphasized that the report, including its important support documents, was not ready in final form much earlier than its release, and that the printed volumes were only completed during the first week of January, 1937. He was inclined to believe that an earlier public release of the report in advance of its transmittal to Congress would not have made much difference.[35]

On Sunday, January 3, Roosevelt spent over three hours with Brownlow going over the page proofs of the report. By the end of that session, according to Brownlow, "the President had thoroughly mastered the document and was able in his discussions to quote whole sentences, and sometimes three or four sentences together, verbatim." [36] On the following Friday, Roosevelt reviewed the report in considerable detail with the Cabinet, and on Sunday afternoon, January 10, he discussed the report at length with the Democratic leadership of both houses of Congress.[37] Roosevelt presented the entire report himself to the Congressional leaders, relying on the members of the President's Committee only occasionally to answer specific questions. In discussing this meeting, Brownlow has commented:

"The President knew the report in general and in detail as well as did either Merriam, Gulick, or I. The few questions he asked of us were only to bring out emphases rather than to make up for his lack of knowledge. He had done his homework superbly. He has not only the text but the implications of the recommendations at his tongue's end." [38]

The meeting started at two o'clock and ended at six after Roosevelt had ranged through virtually everything included in the report, emphasizing some parts which he thought would appeal to his audience and minimizing other parts which might arouse antagonism.[39] On the following day, Roosevelt held a lengthy press conference at which he went through the report to explain it section by section to the

Washington newspapermen. Then on January 12, 1937, he transmitted the report to Congress with his enthusiastic endorsement. In the message he presented to Congress along with the report, Roosevelt made a persuasive appeal for the adoption of the report's major recommendations.[40]

"Now that we are out of the trough of the depression, the time has come to set our house in order. The administrative management of the Government needs overhauling. . . . The Executive structure of the Government is sadly out of date. . . .

"In these troubled years of world history, a self-government cannot long survive unless that government is an effective and efficient agency to serve mankind and carry out the will of the Nation. A government without good management is a house builded on sand.

"Will it be said 'Democracy was a great dream, but it could not do the job?' Or shall we here and now, without further delay, make it our business to see that our American democracy is made efficient so that it will do the job that is required of it by the events of our time?

"I have examined this report carefully and thoughtfully, and am convinced that it is a great document of permanent importance. I think that the general program presented by the Committee is adequate, reasonable and practical, and that it furnishes the basis for immediate action.

"The Committee has not spared me; they say, what has been common knowledge for twenty years, that the President cannot adequately handle his responsibilities; that he is overworked; that it is humanly impossible, under the system which we have, for him fully to carry out his Constitutional duty as Chief Executive because he is overwhelmed with minor details and needless contacts arising directly from the bad organization and equipment of the Government. I can testify to this. With my predecessors who have said the same thing over and over again, I plead guilty.

"The plain fact is that the present organization and equipment of the Executive Branch of the Government defeat the Constitutional intent that there be a single responsible Chief Executive to coordinate and manage the departments and activities in accordance with the laws enacted by the Congress. Under these conditions the government cannot be thoroughly effective in working, under popular control, for the common good." [41]

Roosevelt incorporated into his message a brief statement in which the President's Committee had summarized its five-point program:

"1. Expand the White House staff so that the President may have a sufficient group of able assistants in his own office to keep in closer and easier touch with the widespread affairs of administration, and to make speedier the clearance of the knowledge needed for Executive decision;

"2. Strengthen and develop the managerial agencies of the Government, particularly those dealing with the budget and efficiency research, with personnel and with planning, as management-arms of the Chief Executive;

"3. Extend the merit system upward, outward, and downward to cover practically all non-policy-determining posts; reorganize the civil service system as a part of management under a single, responsible Administrator; create a citizen board to serve as the watchdog of the merit system; and increase the salaries of key posts throughout the service so that the Government may attract and hold in a career service men and women of ability and character;

"4. Overhaul the 100 independent agencies, administrations, authorities, boards, and commissions, and place them by Executive Order within one or the other of the following twelve major Executive departments: State, Treasury, War, Justice, Post Office, Navy, Conservation, Agriculture, Commerce, Labor, Social Welfare, and Public Works; and place upon the Executive continuing responsibility for the maintenance of effective organization;

5. Establish accountability of the Executive to the Congress by providing a genuine independent postaudit of all fiscal transactions by an Auditor General, and restore to the Executive complete responsibility for accounts and current transactions."[42]

Anticipating objections which might be advanced against his proposals, Roosevelt concluded his message as follows:

"In placing this program before you I realize that it will be said that I am recommending the increase of the powers of the Presidency. This is not true. The Presidency as established in the Constitution of the United States has all of the powers that are required. In spite of timid souls in 1787 who feared effective government the Presidency was established as a single, strong Chief Executive office in which was vested the entire Executive power of the national Government, even as the legislative power was placed in the Congress and the judicial in the Supreme Court and inferior courts. What I am placing before you is the request not for more power, but for the tools of management and the authority to distribute the work so that the President can effectively discharge those powers which the Constitution now places upon him. Unless we are prepared to abandon this important part of the Constitution, we must equip the President with authority commensurate with his responsibilities under the Constitution.

"I would not have you adopt this five-point program, however, without realizing that this represents an important step in American history. . . . But in so doing, we shall know that we are going back to the Constitution, and giving to the Executive Branch modern tools of management and an up-to-date organization which will enable the Government to go forward efficiently. We can prove to the world that American Government is both democratic and effective." [43]

Meanwhile, the Brookings Institution was continuing its investigations on behalf of the Congressional committees. It submitted from time to time, as they were completed, a series of fifteen functional reports dealing with various aspects of the administrative organization. All of these reports were eventually collected together and published in a single volume of over 1200 pages on August 16, 1937. [44]

In order to give more effective and time-saving consideration to the President's proposals and to those emanating from the Brookings group, and to the witnesses appearing for and against, the two houses of Congress, by a joint resolution approved February 3, 1937, created a Joint Committee on Government Organization. [45] This Committee was composed of nine members of the Senate and nine members of the House of Representatives, with Senator Joseph T. Robinson of Arkansas, then Senate Majority Leader, as chairman, and Representative John J. Cochran of Missouri, chairman of the House Committee on Government Operations, as co-chairman. Following Senator Robinson's sudden death on July 13, 1937, he was succeeded as chairman by Senator James F. Byrnes of South Carolina.

Roosevelt apparently had sufficient grounds to feel that the merit of his proposals and his impressive political strength would lead Congress to accept his recommendations. Just nine weeks before he submitted the report of the President's Committee to Congress, he had been re-elected by an overwhelming margin as he won the electoral votes of forty-six of the forty-eight states. Of a total popular vote of almost 45,000,000 Roosevelt received a total of 27,476,673 while his opponent, Governor Alfred M. Landon of Kansas, received only 16,679,583. Under his leadership, the Democratic party had also won unprecedented majorities in both houses of Congress. For the only time since the development of political parties in the United States,

one party had won more than two-thirds of the seats in both houses
of Congress, as the Democrats obtained 75 of the 96 seats in the Senate
and 333 of the 435 in the House. Roosevelt's great political victory
of 1936, however, was not to mean an equally great legislative victory
in 1937.

Numerous bills containing some of the proposals of both the President's Committee and the Brookings group were introduced in both
houses of Congress, and lengthy hearings were held by the Congressional Joint Committee during February, March, and April of
1937. Although almost all aspects of the recommendations of the
President's Committee were discussed during the hearings, a large
amount of the time was taken up by lengthy consideration of the
Committee's proposal to replace the Comptroller General with an
Auditor General who would be responsible to Congress for conducting
an independent postaudit of all of the government's fiscal transactions.
As proposed, however, the Auditor General would not have had any
power to make preaudits of government expenditures with the authority to disallow payments or refuse to approve contracts, as done
by the Comptroller General. The responsibility for these functions
was to be vested in the Secretary of the Treasury, who would operate
with the advice of the Attorney General as to the legality of the settle-
ment of public accounts. The Brookings Institution report also
recommended changing the title of Comptroller General to Auditor
General, but differed sharply from the President's Committee in
favoring the retention by the Auditor General of the Comptroller
General's preaudit authority to disallow payments and to disapprove
contracts.[46]

It was exceedingly unfortunate that the entire issue of administrative reorganization was soon overshadowed by (and in many ways,
disastrously intertwined with) the great controversy precipitated in
the halls of Congress over the proposals to reorganize the federal courts
which Roosevelt submitted on February 5, 1937. The two reorganization movements became almost inseparably linked in the thinking of
many people. Numerous Senators and Representatives who were
experiencing the new-found exhileration of reasserting Congressional
prestige by shouting "Attempted Dictatorship" at the court reorganization scheme, were quick to level the same intemperate charge at
the recommendations of the President's Committee.

The outbreak of Congressional hostility to Roosevelt's court reform
and administrative reorganization proposals came actually as a climax

to difficulties which had been developing gradually between Roosevelt and Congress for quite some time before. Acting with due deference to the seriousness of the economic crisis, to Roosevelt's great popularity and prestige, and to the positive leadership which he had demonstrated, Congress had gone along with practically all of Roosevelt's legislative proposals in the emergency days of 1933-1935.

By 1937, however, conditions had changed. During 1935 and 1936 many members of Congress had become increasingly restive under what they regarded as Roosevelt's high-handed and arrogant manner of dealing with Congress. Many resented the degree to which Roosevelt had been able to dominate the operations of the government and both his actions and his policies antagonized numerous Congressmen. Criticism was growing more vocal and sharper by 1937 and the court and administrative reorganization measures provided the sparks sufficient to touch off the explosion of a full-scale Congressional rebellion. These two proposals, and especially the one involving the sanctity of the federal courts, provided Roosevelt's growing opposition with the issues upon which they could take a strong stand for a show-down battle between President and Congress. Consequently, it was over these two issues that the first major head-on clash between Roosevelt and those opposed to him in Congress was to take place. Very soon after the introduction of the court plan, it was obvious that the extended four-year "honeymoon" between Roosevelt and Congress had definitely come to a jarring end.

In addition to the growing Congressional discontent which erupted to the surface over the court plan, there was a more specialized concern which bothered many Congressmen regarding the administrative reorganization proposals. At the heart of the matter was the basic question of who should control the determination of the administrative organization of the executive branch — Congress or the President? Should changes in the organization be made as they had usually been made in the past, by regular legislation enacted by Congress, or should they be made by the relatively new method of granting power to the President to issue reorganization orders which would automatically go into effect with the force of law unless disapproved by Congress? Congressional fears and suspicions of further Presidential aggrandizement were certainly not in the least allayed by the provision in Roosevelt's original proposal that the President's reorganization plans would go into effect unless disapproved by the same vote required to override a Presidential veto, i.e., a two-thirds majority in both houses of Congress.

The Constitution, of course, had left the entire subject of determining the administrative organization of the government to be dealt with by regular legislation. As a result, the organization of the departments, and that of bureaus, divisions, and the other administrative sub-divisions had normally been directly controlled by Congress. As Louis Brownlow has observed, "the leaders of the legislative branch . . . from the beginning of the government had considered themselves responsible for the control, confinement, bridling, and ultimate determination of the organization of all branches of the government." [47] As noted in previous chapters, there had been few exceptions to this rule.[48]

During World War I, Congress had passed the Overman Act which gave President Wilson the authority, as part of his war powers, to shift bureaus and divisions and to make certain other limited reorganizational changes in connection with the war program. Late in the administration of President Herbert Hoover, Congress had enacted a law authorizing the President to make some types of organizational changes which would be effective unless disapproved by Congress within sixty days. When Roosevelt became President, he had similar authority for two years and did, as discussed earlier, put into effect several reorganizational changes which were not disapproved by Congress. These three examples were the only exceptions to the longstanding practice that Congress would provide by legislation for the administrative organization of the government. In general, many Congressmen were not anxious to abandon this role by granting the President increased powers over the determination of organizational matters. More specifically, many were especially not anxious by 1937 to grant any additional powers of any kind to Roosevelt whom they were already accusing of having stretched the Presidential authority more widely than it had ever been extended before. So despite Roosevelt's tremendous electoral triumph of 1936, the atmosphere in the Congress when he introduced his administrative and court reorganization proposals was one of growing resentment and suspicion, increasingly hostile criticism, and incipient rebellion.

Because Congress was preoccupied with the raging fight over the courts throughout most of the 1937 session, very little positive action was accomplished in regard to reorganization. When Senator James F. Byrnes succeeded Joseph T. Robinson as chairman of the Committee on Government Organization in July, he reported to Roosevelt that, in view of the rancor created by the court fight, he thought it would be unwise to try to push through action on reorganization during the remainder of that session of Congress. He indicated, however, that if Roosevelt insisted, he would go ahead to do the best he could to get favorable action. As a result, Roosevelt sent the following letter to Byrnes on July 26, 1937:

"Dear Jimmy:

"It is now, I think, about six months since my message to the Congress recommending certain authority to effect a reorganization of the Administrative branch of the Government in order to put the departments and agencies on a business-like basis. It was well understood at the time by Senator Robinson and all of our friends that it would be better to do this at this session of the Congress rather than to have it drag along in the 1938 session.

"Now, six months later, the matter in the Senate seems to rest on the holding of open hearings.

"The legislation is just as necessary today as then—even more so and, of course, from my point of view as the responsible head of the Executive branch of the Government, I hope the legislation will be passed. However, 'you are the doctor.' All I can do is ask you to read again my message to the Congress in respect to reorganization.

"I understand that some of our friends feel that by passing a simple bill giving the President six Executive Assistants, the President will be satisfied by having these jobs to hand out. The President is not seeking any assistants for such a purpose—as a matter fact, I would hardly know what to do with six Executive Assistants if I do not have any authority to put the government as a whole on a business-like basis. It is a little like giving the President the envelope of the letter without any letter in it!

"I am sure you will see my predicament. The whole subject has been discussed backwards and forwards to my certain knowledge since the early days when you and I first came to Washington and I hope the Democratic party will accomplish something which so many previous Administrations and Congresses have failed to do at all.

"Do help out your country once more!" [49]

On August 12, 1937, as Congress rushed toward adjournment, the reorganization bill was finally brought to a vote in the House of Representatives where it passed by the surprisingly large margin of 283 votes to 75, a much greater majority than had been anticipated by anybody in view of the opposition which had been expressed and the antagonism engendered by the court fight. The Senate, however, did not take any definite action on the measure prior to the adjournment of Congress on August 21st. Consequently, the matter had to go over to the next session for any further action.

On October 12th, Roosevelt issued a proclamation calling for a special session of Congress to convene on November 15. That night, in a "Fireside Chat," he discussed the legislation with which he hoped Congress would deal in the special session. In emphasizing that Congress should enact his reorganization prososals, he said:

"To carry out any twentieth century program, we must give the Executive Branch of the Government twentieth century machinery to work with. I recognize that democratic processes are necessarily and rightly slower than dictatorial processes. But I refuse to believe that democratic processes need be dangerously slow.

"For many years we have all known that the executive and administrative departments of the Government in Washington are a higgledy-piggledy patchwork of duplicate responsibilities and overlapping powers. The reorganization of this vast government machinery which I proposed to the Congress last winter does not conflict with the principle of the democratic process, as some people say. It only makes that process work more efficiently."[50]

On the day the special session convened, Roosevelt sent to Congress a message in which he vigorously reasserted the need for reorganization and reiterated his strong endorsement of the five-point program proposed by the President's Committee. Then, in discussing the charge which had been made that his reorganization plan would not result in any substantial financial savings, he stated:

"The experience of states and municipalities definitely proves that reorganization of government along the lines of modern business administrative practice can increase efficiency, minimize error, duplication and waste, and raise the morale of the public service. But that experience does not prove, and no person conversant with the management of large private corporations or of governments honestly suggests, that reorganization of government machinery in the interest of efficiency is a method of making major savings in the cost of government.

"Large savings in the cost of government can be made only by cutting down or eliminating government functions. And to those who advocate such a course it is fair to put the question—which functions of government do you advocate cutting off?"[51]

In spite of Roosevelt's pleas, the special session did not act on his reorganization proposals, and it was not until February, 1938, that a reorganization bill embodying most of the recommendations of the President's Committee was taken up for action on the floor of the Senate. Almost immediately a renewed flood of "dictatorship" charges was advanced by many of the same groups who had opposed the court plan so vehemently. The anti-Administration forces, prominent among which were the radio orator, Father Coughlin, the National Committee to Uphold Constitutional Government, many Congressoinal lobbyists, a sizable segment of the press, and the Republican opposition in Congress, organized a most effective campaign to discredit the reorganization proposals. Because of their efforts, a barrage of telegrams descended upon the members of the Senate urging the defeat of the bill. Ickes described the situation in his diary as follows:

"During the last week or ten days there has been a perfectly tremendous amount of propaganda put out. Telegrams have poured in on the Senators literally by the thousands. Ordinary commercial business on Monday morning had to be set aside by the telegraph companies. Labor got into the fight and all the farm organizations. I am convinced that some Government people were in on it, but they kept under cover, doing their fighting behind such organizations as I have named." [52]

In spite of this opposition, the bill did squeeze by the Senate on March 28, 1938, by the narrow margin of 49 to 42.[53] When the bill moved to the House of Representatives, however, the avalanche of opposition quickly reached even greater proportions.

"I do not believe," Ickes wrote in his diary, "that I have seen so much hysteria over any proposed piece of legislation since the world war and the attempt of President Wilson to force the ratification of the League of Nations. I cannot believe that some of the men in public life and some of the newspapers which are bitterly denouncing this bill as an attempt to confer dictatorial powers upon the President can be sincere. Even the *Washington Star* last night, which usually is very sane and level-headed, had an editorial declaring that the passage of this bill would pave the way to sovietizing the United States. Hysteria has been stimulated and fanned, as I believe, by those individuals and interests who, starting with the Court fight, have determined to break the President at all costs and put an effective stop to the liberal movement in this country. Finances seem to be ample and the will to ruin unabated. Father Coughlin, the irresponsible and ignorant Catholic Priest, is again splitting the air by means of the radio, thun-

dering denunciations and anathemas and exhorting the people to defend their liberties from a threatened tyranny." [54]

At first, Roosevelt had been inclined to ignore the assertion of his
opponents that passage of the bill would give him dictatorial powers.
"The charge of dictator . . .," he later wrote, "at first seemed such a
flagrant violation of the facts as not to justify recognition." However,
because it was "soon conjured into a real fear in the minds of many
people," he decided that "a simple restatement of the purposes of the
bill would clear the air." [55] Accordingly, on March 29, 1938, he drafted
and made public his now-famous letter, addressed to an unnamed
recipient, in which he disavowed the dictatorship intentions which had
been attributed to him by his opponents. He wrote:

"Many thanks for your letter telling me that you are concerned over
the charges in several newspapers that the reorganization bill now
before the Congress, would make me a Dictator.

"1. As you well know I am as much opposed to American Dictatorship as you are, for three simple reasons.

"A: I have no inclination to be a dictator.

"B: I have none of the qualifications which would make me a
successful dictator.

"C: I have too much historical background and too much knowledge of existing dictatorships to make me desire any form of dictatorship for a democracy like the United States of America." [56]

Following this statement, Roosevelt then went ahead to assert once
again, in simplified terms, the desirable reasons for the enactment of
the reorganization measures which he had proposed.

In an effort to save the bill in the House, Roosevelt also began to
negotiate some concessions with Congressional leaders. In doing so,
he was perhaps thinking back of the charges that he had lost his court
fight because he had been willing to make compromises too little and
too late. He agreed to exempt the Office of Education, which had been
scheduled for transfer from the Department of the Interior to the New
Department of Social Welfare, because of the fear expressed by some
religious groups that the change would mean more federal control of
education. Because of the opposition of veterans' organizations, he
agreed to exempt the Veterans Bureau, and he indicated a willingness
to grant immunity to several other key agencies if the House leaders
thought it necessary to secure passage. Probably his most important
concession concerned the right of Congress to veto his reorganization
proposals. In the original bill, Congress had been given the power

to disapprove executive orders which made reorganizational changes only by a two-thirds majority in both houses of Congress. In his compromise move, Roosevelt agreed that only a simple majority should be required, which meant, of course, that his reorganization proposals would be far easier to defeat.[57]

All of Roosevelt's efforts proved to be of no avail. The combined resistance to several of the bill's provisions was too great and the House voted to send the measure back to committee by a close vote of 204 to 196 on April 8, 1938.[58] This constituted Roosevelt's second major legislative defeat since he had become President, following by less than a year his first serious rebuff over the court plan.

Some of the Congressional leaders who had led the fight for the bill told Ickes that the two main reasons it had been defeated were the provisions pertaining to the abolition of the Civil Service Commission and the creation of the new Department of Social Welfare. As Ickes noted in his diary:

"There has been a good deal of opposition right along to supplanting a bipartisan Civil Service Board of three by a single administrator. It seems that the opposition to the new Department of Public Welfare centered largely in the supposition that if it were set up, Harry Hopkins would be named Secretary. The opposition was headed up by the Catholic Church which fears Harry and some of his principal assistants because they have been social workers and are in favor of birth control and that sort of thing—or at least supposed to be. It had been thought, however, that the Catholics would be satisfied with the amendment that the House had already adopted preventing the removal of the Office of Education from the Department of the Interior." [59]

Another major source of opposition to the President's recommendations had developed from the plan to incorporate all of the independent regulatory commissions into the regular executive departments. As Louis Brownlow pointed out, "What most alarmed the regulatory agencies and the businesses and industries regulated by them was the proposal to put those agencies also under departmental supervision for all their activities except those quasi-judicial in character." [60]

It should be kept in mind that the independent commissions were constituency-serving agencies in which well-established relationships and clear understandings had gradually developed between the regulators and the regulated. The President's proposal meant a loss of independent status for the commissions which would mean that an almost inevitable change would take place in such relationships and understandings. It was Roosevelt's definite intention that the President, operating through the heads of the appropriate departments, should have overall control of the administrative procedures and practices of the commissions. This, in turn, was certain to have an effect on the way in which the agencies' regulatory policies would be carried out. Consequently, many business and industrial groups were greatly aroused by this threatened change as they much preferred to retain the status quo. And leaders of these groups were the kind of people who could mobilize and underwrite a major campaign to get large numbers of telegrams, letters, and postcards to descend on the Congress expressing opposition to the President's proposals.

Certainly the large-scale propaganda barrage carried on against the reorganization bill had undoubtedly contributed to the crystallization of Congressional opposition. In retrospect, the tremendous outpouring of violent and excessive denunciations which were prompted by the administrative reorganization measures seems almost unbelievable. The magnitude of the opposition's efforts can be seen from an entry Ickes made in his diary a few days after the bill's defeat:

"There is not the slightest doubt that this was the issue on which the most terrific propaganda on record was brought to bear. According to the papers this morning, 333,000 telegrams at a cost of approximately $150,000 were sent to Senators and Representatives in opposition to this bill. The great bulk of these came from two or three eastern states, principally New York. Many of them showed on their face that the senders not only had not read the bill but didn't understand its provisions. It has all been a very successful engagement in the campaign of hate that has been waged against the President almost without interruption since the organization of the Liberty League prior to the 1936 campaign."[61]

With the defeat of his reorganization proposals by such a narrow margin in the House, Roosevelt was placed in a dilemma. He had to decide, on the one hand, whether to accept the defeat, adopt a conciliatory attitude toward Congress in order to get his other legislation passed, and bide his time until he could attempt to get the reorganization bill through the next session of Congress, or whether, on the other hand, he should make an all-out effort to get the bill out of committee and back on the floor of the House for another vote. He received sharply conflicting advice from various of his associates. Some, such as Jim Farley, Press Secretary Stephen Early, and William C. Bullitt,[62] among others, counseled moderation and a conciliatory attitude toward Congress. Others, such as Ickes and Corcoran, urged an immediate all-out fight, which they thought would be successful. Corcoran declared that it was up to the President "now to show whether he was going out like Herbert Hoover or like Andrew Jackson," [63] and Ickes wrote of the conversation he had with Roosevelt the day after the bill's defeat:

"The President . . . didn't seem to have much fight left in him. . . . I have never talked to him as I did yesterday. I hit him with words telling him that he couldn't accept such a defeat; that if he did this Administration was through. I begged him to go along with the fight. . . . And then I said:

" 'Mr. President, if I were you I would call a special meeting of my Cabinet. I would say to them: "God Damn you, I am not going to be satisfied with lip service with respect to this bill. I want every one of you to get out and line up every vote you can. We have got to win this fight . . . !' " [64]

As he often did, Roosevelt decided to adopt a middle course. He would not try immediately to push the bill through again, but if conditions appeared favorable, he would make an attempt later in the session. On April 21st, Ickes commented on this decision: "The President has not given up the reorganization bill. He is going to wait to see what strength he develops on legislation now pending and then if things look favorable, he will try to get the reorganization bill through this session. I am pessimistic enough to doubt whether this will be done. Pressure from the leaders on the Hill to go home for their campaigns will be too great, I fear, for the President to stand up against." [65]

In the end, Ickes' fears were realized, for on June 26th, he reported: "The President had to abandon the reorganization bill. . . . in the closing days of the session the Vice President bluntly told the President that he would have to choose between a filibuster in the Senate against the reorganization bill or having his spending bill passed. In the circumstances the President did the only thing that he could do. He abandoned the reorganization bill. I regret this very much indeed because this was something that was closer to my heart than anything else." [66]

Thus two regular sessions and one special session of Congress had come and gone without Roosevelt being able to secure the necessary authority to put through the comprehensive reorganization of the administrative organization which he desired.

In 1939, however, after the tumult and the shouting of "dictatorship" had somewhat subsided, Roosevelt was finally successful in getting some of the most basic of his reorganization proposals put into effect when the Seventy-sixth Congress approved a Reorganization Act on April 3rd.[67] This measure was very similar to the bill defeated in 1938, and it enabled the President to achieve many of his fundamental goals. In spite of the fact that several of the recommendations of the President's Committee on Administrative Management did not find their way into the final Reorganization Act of 1939, the approved bill was still a measure of the first magnitude in enabling the President to effect executive reorganization. "The substance of the bill," as Herbert Emmerich has said, ". . . conformed to the principle enunciated by the President's Committee two years earlier." [68]

At long last, Roosevelt had finally received from Congress the authority to overhaul the administrative organization. As shall be seen, his authority was not without serious limitations, but it was sufficient to allow him to make numerous organizational changes of major significance.

CHAPTER VII

OVERHAULING THE ADMINISTRATIVE ORGANIZATION

DURING THE SECOND TERM

Under the provisions of the Reorganization Act of 1939, the President was authorized, until January 20, 1941, to submit to Congress specific plans for the reorganization of the administrative organization.[1] Such plans were to become effective sixty days after transmittal, unless within that time they were disapproved by a concurrent resolution passed by both houses of Congress. The Reorganization Act called upon the President to investigate the organization of the departments and agencies of the government, and to determine what changes should be made to accomplish any of five general purposes:

" (1) To reduce expenditures
" (2) To increase efficiency
" (3) To consolidate agencies according to major purposes
" (4) To reduce the number of agencies by consolidating those having similar functions and by abolishing such as may not be necessary
" (5) To eliminate overlapping and duplication of effort." [2]

The President's authority was limited, however, in that the Act provided that he could make no changes in the names or number of the ten existing departments. In addition, Congress specifically exempted the following twenty-one agencies from the President's reorganization authority: Civil Service Commission, Coast Guard, Engineer Corps of the United States Army, Mississippi River Commission, Federal Communications Commission, Federal Power Commission, Federal Trade Commission, General Accounting Office, Interstate Commerce Commission, National Labor Relations Board, Securities and Exchange Commission, Board of Tax Appeals, United States Employees' Compensation Commission, United States Maritime Commission, United States Tariff Commission, Veterans Administration, National Mediation Board, National Railroad Adjustment Board, Railroad Retirement Board, Federal Deposit Insurance Corporation, and the Board of Governors of the Federal Reserve System.

During the time the Reorganization Act was in effect, Roosevelt submitted a total of five reorganization plans, none of which was disapproved by Congress. His Plan No. I was transmitted on April 25, 1939, just twenty-two days after Congress had approved the Act. Once the Act was passed, Roosevelt had lost no time in making use of its provisions. He called Louis Brownlow at once by telephone and asked him to arrange for the members of the President's Committee on Administrative Management to come to Washington as soon as possible to draft the reorganization plans the President wished to submit to Congress. Brownlow, Merriam, and Gulick set to work immediately, assisted by Roosevelt's newly appointed Director of the Budget, Harold D. Smith, and within a week had prepared Reorganization Plans I and II. Following a three hour session with Brownlow and Smith at which all aspects of Plan I were discussed, Roosevelt submitted it to Congress.[3] In his message accompanying the plan, Roosevelt reemphasized the purposes which motivated his reorganization efforts by stating:

"My whole purpose in submitting this Plan is to improve the administrative management of the Republic, and I feel confident that our Nation is united in this central purpose, regardless of differences upon details.

"This Plan is concerned with the practical necessity of reducing the number of agencies which report directly to the President and also of giving the President assistance in dealing with the entire Executive Branch by modern means of administrative management."[4]

In this message, Roosevelt announced that it was his intention to carry out his comprehensive reorganization program in a series of three steps, which he described as follows:

"The first step is to improve over-all management, that is to do those things which will accomplish the purposes set out in the law, and which, at the same time, will reduce the difficulties of the President in dealing with the multifarious agencies of the Executive Branch and assist him in distributing his responsibilities as the chief administrator of the Government by providing him with the necessary organization and machinery for better administrative management.

"The second step is to improve the allocation of departmental activities, that is, to do those things which will accomplish the purposes set out in the law and at the same time help that part of the work of the Executive Branch which is carried on through executive departments and agencies. In all this the responsibility to the people is through the President.

"The third step is to improve intradepartmental management, that is, to do those things which will enable the heads of departments and agencies the better to carry out their own duties and distribute their own work among their several assistants and subordinates."[5]

Reorganization Plan No. I was designed to accomplish two major changes: (1) it established the Executive Office of the President and transferred to it the Bureau of the Budget from the Treasury Department and the functions of the National Resources Committee, which had been operating independently; and (2) it created three large department-like agencies, a Federal Security Agency, a Federal Works Agency, and a Federal Loan Agency, and placed under them most of the agencies of the government which had been set up outside the regular departments, except those which had been specifically exempted by the Reorganization Act.

Plan No. I was divided into four main parts. In discussing Part One, which deals entirely with the Executive Office of the President, Roosevelt set forth his reasons for transferring the Bureau of the Budget from the Treasury Department:

"It is apparent from the legislative history of the Budget and Accounting Act that it was the purpose in 1921 to set up an executive budget for which the President would be primarily responsible to the Congress and to the people, and that the Director of the Budget was to act under the immediate direction and supervision of the President. While no serious difficulties have been encountered because of the fact that the Bureau of the Budget was placed in the Treasury Department so far as making budgetary estimates has been concerned, it is apparent that its coordinating activities and its research and investigational activities . . . will be facilitated if the Bureau is not a part of one of the ten executive departments."[6]

Part One also provided that "the functions of the National Resources Committee . . . and all of the functions of the Federal Employment Stabilization Office in the Department of Commerce . . . are hereby transferred to the Executive Office of the President. The functions transferred by this section are hereby consolidated, and they shall be administered under the direction and supervision of the President by the National Resources Planning Board . . . which shall be composed of five members to be appointed by the President."[7] These transfers were made, according to Roosevelt, so that "the President will be given more direct access to and immediate direction over that agency which is concerned with planning for the utilization and conservation of the national resources, an indispensable part of the equipment of the Chief Executive." [8]

In his message, Roosevelt expressed his displeasure at the failure of Congress to allow the President to transfer "the administration of the third managerial function of the Government, that of personnel," [9] to the Executive Office. Since the Reorganization Act, however, had authorized the President to appoint six administrative assistants to aid him in the performance of his duties, Roosevelt informed Congress that it was his intention to use one of these administrative assistants as his liaison agent on all matters involving personnel management. In this way, he hoped to accomplish at least some of the objectives set forth by the President's Committee on Administrative Management in its recommendation of a single civil service administrator directly responsible to the President.

Although the President's Committee had recommended the creation of two new executive departments, one for Social Welfare and one for Public Works, Congress, in writing the Reorganization Act, had turned a deaf ear to this suggestion and had specifically prohibited the President from increasing the number of departments. Nevertheless, Roosevelt was able to accomplish much the same result by creating the Federal Security Agency and the Federal Works Agency, which were to function as departments in every respect but name. In addition, he also decided to establish a Federal Loan Agency to bring together most of the independent lending agencies of the government. He emphasized the semi-departmental status of the three new agencies by inviting their heads to meet regularly with the Cabinet.

Part Two of Reorganization Plan No. I was devoted to the Federal Security Agency in which Roosevelt grouped "those agencies of the Government, the major purposes of which are to promote social and economic security, education opportunity and the health of the citizens of the Nation." [10] The President's Committee on Administrative Management and Roosevelt had originally proposed the creation of a Department of Social Welfare. According to Brownlow's account the new Federal Security Agency was given the name "security" instead of "welfare" because Vice President John Nance Garner told Roosevelt that there was a great objection to the terms "welfare," "social welfare," and "public welfare," etc., in Congress, but that "there was no objection to the word 'security' because it looked as if the Social Security Board might be a pretty good thing." [11]

The new agency, headed by a Federal Security Administrator,

brought together the U. S. Employment Service (from the Depart-
ment of Labor), the Office of Education (from the Department of
Interior), the Public Health Service (from the Department of the
Treasury), the National Youth Administration (from the Works
Progress Administration), and the Social Security Board and the
Civilian Conservation Corps, both of which were independent
agencies.[12]

Part Three created the Federal Works Agency, which was to consolidate "those agencies of the Federal Government dealing with
public works not incidental to the normal work of other departments,
and which administer Federal grants or loans to State and Local
Governments or other agencies for the purposes of construction."[13]
The Federal Works Agency, under the direction of a Federal Works
Administrator, was to be composed of the Bureau of Public Roads
(from the Department of Agriculture), the Public Buildings Branch
of the Procurement Division of the Treasury Department, the Branch
of Buildings Management of the National Park Service (from the
Department of Interior), the United States Housing Authority (from
the Department of Interior), and the two major public works agencies
set up during the depression, the Federal Emergency Administration
of Public Works (PWA), and the Works Progress Administration
(WPA), except for its subsidiary, the National Youth Administration.[14]

Part Four dealt with the Federal Loan Agency which was created
to bring together "those independent lending agencies of the Government which have been established from time to time for the purpose
of stimulating and stabilizing the financial, commercial and industrial
enterprises of the Nation."[15] The agencies placed under the jurisdiction of the Federal Loan Administrator, as head of the Federal Loan
Agency, were: the Reconstruction Finance Corporation, Electric
Home and Farm Authority, RFC Mortgage Association, Federal
Home Loan Bank Board, Home Owners' Loan Corporation, Federal
Savings and Loan Insurance Corporation, Federal Housing Administration, and Export-Import Bank.[16]

Neither the President's Committee nor the President had originally
recommended the creation of a Federal Loan Agency. The Committee
had discussed with Roosevelt the possibilities of consolidating all of
the government's loan agencies in either the Department of Commerce
or the Department of the Treasury. Roosevelt quickly vetoed the
suggestion of the Treasury, saying to the Committee, as Brownlow

recalls, "That won't work. If they put them in the Treasury, not one
of them will ever make a loan to anybody for any purpose. There
are too darned many glass-eyed bankers in the Treasury." [17] Accordingly, Roosevelt was prepared to recommend that all of the loan
activities should be placed in the Commerce Department. However,
the powerful head of the Reconstruction Finance Corporation, Jesse
Jones, was strongly opposed to being transferred into the Department
of Commerce. "So it happened," according to Brownlow, "that Mr.
Jones, together with Vice President Garner and Speaker Rayburn,
all three Texans, all three party leaders, told the President where to
get off. The result was the Federal Loan Agency." [18]

In addition to creating the Federal Loan Agency, Part Four of
Plan I also stipulated that several independent agencies which had
been set up for the purpose of providing loans for the stimulation and
stabilization of agriculture should be placed with all other agricultural
activities of the government in the Department of Agriculture. The
agencies so affected were the Farm Credit Administration, the Federal
Farm Mortgage Corporation, and the Commodity Credit Corporation. [19]

After a two hour discussion of Reorganization Plan II with Brownlow and Smith on May 3, 1939, Roosevelt submitted it to Congress on
May 9. He regarded it as a partial fulfillment of the second step in
his comprehensive reorganization program. Whereas Plan No. I had
been concerned entirely with improving the overall organization and
management of the administrative organization, Plan No. II was
devoted entirely to the transfer and redistribution of already existing
agencies and functions among various departments and agencies.
Consequently, no new administrative machinery was created by Plan
No. II, but numerous agencies were shifted from one location in the
administrative organization to another. According to Roosevelt, Plan
No. II was "concerned with the sole purpose of improving the administrative management of the Executive Branch by a more logical grouping of existing units and functions and by a further reduction in the
number of independent agencies." [20]

In a message which he sent to Congress along with Plan No. II,
Roosevelt stated that he did not intend to submit any more reorganization plans at that session, because of the lateness of the date and
because the reorganizations of an intradepartmental character — the
third step in his reorganization program — "require a great deal of
research and careful painstaking detailed work." [21] In addition, he

informed Congress that despite the large number of changes made by Plans I and II, "Not all of the interdepartmental transfers and consolidations that are necessary and desirable have been accomplished," and he added that he was "directing the Bureau of the Budget to study these problems . . . with the view of sending other reorganization plans involving both interdepartmental and intradepartmental reorganizations to the Congress at its next session." [22]

In order that the the effective date of the changes made in Plans I and II could coincide with the beginning of the government's fiscal year, Congress set aside the normal sixty day waiting period prescribed in the Reorganization Act of 1939 and provided that both plans should go into effect on July 1, 1939. [23]

On September 8, 1939, Roosevelt issued his Executive Order 8248 to implement the provisions of Plans I and II pertaining to the Executive Office of the President. In describing the preparation of this Executive Order, Louis Brownlow has written that on September 1, the day World War II started with Hitler's invasion of Poland, he received a call to come to the White House. His account continues:

". . . The President was very busy that day. I had perhaps three or four minutes with him. He said he already had talked with Harold Smith, the director of the budget, and had told Smith that he would like to have me draw up an Executive Order activating the Executive Office of the President and its several divisions.

"The next two or three days, along with Harold Smith, Donald C. Stone, head of the administrative management division of the budget, and Judge Townsend of the Department of Justice, I was very busy. I myself wrote the final draft of the Executive Order. Mr. Smith took it to the White House, and it was given to the President just before he was leaving by train to go to Hyde Park for the week end.

"In it I set up the several divisions of the Executive Office of the President according to the general plan that the Bureau of the Budget had worked out, which had been approved generally by the President and had been talked over by him with me." [24]

Executive Order 8248 set forth in detail the organization of the component parts of the Executive Office. The functions and duties of the five principal divisions of the Executive Office were defined as follows:

"1. *The White House Office*

"In general, to serve the President in an intimate capacity in the performance of the many detailed activities incident to his immediate office. To that end, the White House Office shall be composed of the following principal subdivisions, with particular functions and duties as indicated:

" (a) *The Secretaries to the President.* — To facilitate and maintain quick and easy communication with the Congress, the individual members of the Congress, the heads of executive departments and agencies, the press, the radio, and the general public.

" (b) *The Executive Clerk.* — To provide for the orderly handling of documents and correspondence within the White House Office, and to organize and supervise all clerical services and procedures relating thereto.

" (c) *The Administrative Assistants to the President.* — To assist the President in such matters as he may direct, and at the specified request of the President, to get information and to condense and summarize it for his use. These Administrative Assistants shall be personal aides to the President and shall have no authority over anyone in any department or agency, including the Executive Office of the President, other than the personnel assigned to their immediate office. In no event shall the Administrative Assistants be interposed between the President and the head of any department or agency, or between the President and any one of the divisions in the Executive Office of the President.

"2. *The Bureau of the Budget*

" (a) To assist the President in the preparation of the Budget and the formulation of the fiscal program of the Government.

" (b) To supervise and control the administration of the Budget.

" (c) To conduct research in the development of improved plans of administrative management, and to advise the executive departments and agencies of the Government with respect to improved administrative organization and practice.

" (d) To aid the President to bring about more efficient and economical conduct of Government service.

" (e) To assist the President by clearing and coordinating departmental advice on proposed legislation and by making recommendations as to Presidential action on legislative enactments in accordance with the past practice.

" (f) To assist in the consideration and clearance and, where necessary, in the preparation of proposed Executive orders and proclamations, in accordance with the provisions of Executive Order No. 7298 of February 18, 1936.

"(g) To plan and promote the improvement, development, and coordination of Federal and other statistical services.

"(h) To keep the President informed of the progress of activities by agencies of the Government with respect to work proposed, work actually initiated, and work completed, together with the relative timing of work among the several agencies of the Government; all to the end that the work programs of the several agencies of the Executive Branch of the Government may be coordinated and that the monies appropriated by the Congress may be expended in the most economical manner possible with the least possible overlapping and duplication of effort.

"3. *The National Resources Planning Board*

"(a) To survey, collect data on, and analyze problems pertaining to national resources, both natural and human, and to recommend to the President and the Congress long time plans and programs for the wise use and fullest development of such resources.

"(b) To consult with Federal, regional, state, local and private agencies in developing orderly programs of public works and to list for the President and Congress all proposed public works in the order of their relative importance with respect to (1) the greatest good to the greatest number of people, (2) the emergency necessities of the Nation, and (3) the social, economic, and cultural advancement of the people of the United States.

"(c) To inform the President of the general trend of economic conditions and to recommend measures leading to their improvement of stabilization.

"(d) To act as a clearing house and means of coordination for planning activities, linking together various levels and fields of planning.

"4. *The Liaison Office for Personnel Management*

"In accordance with the statement of purpose made in the message to Congress of April 25, 1939, accompanying Reorganization Plan No. I, one of the Administrative Assistants to the President, authorized in the Reorganization Act of 1939, shall be designated by the President as Liaison Officer for Personnel Management and shall be in charge of the Liaison Office for Personnel Management. The functions of this office shall be:

"(a) To assist the President in the better execution of the duties imposed upon him by the provisions of the Constitution and the laws with respect to personnel management especially the Civil Service

Act of 1883, as amended, and the rules promulgated by the President under authority of that Act.

"b) To assist the President in maintaining closer contact with all agencies dealing with personnel matters insofar as they affect or tend to determine the personnel management policies of the Executive Branch of the Government.

"5. *The Office of Government Reports*

" (a) To provide a central clearing house through which individual citizens, organizations of citizens, State or local governmental bodies, and, where appropriate, agencies of the Federal Government may transmit inquiries and complaints and receive advice and information.

" (b) To assist the President in dealing with special problems requiring the clearance of information between the Federal Government and State and local Governments and private institutions.

" (c) To collect and distribute information concerning the purposes and activities of executive departments and agencies for the use of the Congress, administrative officials, and the public.

" (d) To keep the President currently informed of the opinions, desires, and complaints of citizens and groups of citizens and of State and local Governments with respect to the work of Federal agencies.

" (e) To report to the President on the basis of the information it has obtained possible ways and means for reducing the cost of the operation of the Government." [25]

In addition to these five main divisions, Roosevelt and Brownlow also provided in Executive Order 8248 that the Executive Office should contain "in the event of a national emergency, or threat of a national emergency, such office for emergency management as the President shall determine." [26] Except for this one vague reference, the potential sixth division of the Executive Office, which Clinton Rossiter has aptly called "an office in embryo," [27] was not mentioned in Executive Order 8248.

In a Presidential statement, drafted by Brownlow and issued by Roosevelt along with the Executive Order, it was pointed out that in periods of emergency it has "always been found necessary to establish administrative machinery in addition to that required by the normal work of the government. Set up in a time of stress these special facilities sometimes had worked at cross purposes both within themselves and with the regular departments and agencies. In order that the Nation may not be again caught unaware, adequate resources for management should be provided in advance of such periods of emergency." [28] Inclusion of this provision in the Executive Order was later to provide Roosevelt with a legal basis for creating the Office for Emergency Management which he was to use as the official foundation upon which he established most of the special wartime organizations set up during World War II.[29] This was a novel and unprecedented development in American administration in that it permitted the President to act immediately in time of emergency to establish new administrative agencies to deal with the emergency conditions without having to wait to secure prior Congressional authorization by regular legislation.

On the same day that he created the Executive Office of the President, Roosevelt also issued Proclamation No. 2352 in which he proclaimed a "Limited National Emergency," because of the European War which had just started.[30] In discussing the juxtaposition of these two Presidential actions, Robert E. Sherwood has written:

"On September 8, 1939, the day when Roosevelt issued his Limited National Emergency Proclamation after the outbreak of war in Europe, he also issued an Executive Order which received scant attention in the press and the vital importance of which has never been even remotely apparent to the American people. It provided for reorganization of the Executive Office of the President and involved the transfer of the Bureau of the Budget to that office from the Treasury Department. I have heard this action compared to the invention of the radio as an asset to Roosevelt in his exercise of authority, and that is not so much of an exaggeration as one might think. [31]

There has been widespread agreement among students of public administration that Roosevelt's establishment of the Executive Office of the President was one of the most significant events in the history of national administration. By creating a central staff office for the Presidency, in which he placed those agencies concerned with the problems of over-all administrative management, particularly budgeting, planning, and personnel, Roosevelt equipped the President for the first time with some of the tools needed to enable him to cope effectively with his job as the chief administrator of the whole administrative organization. It was fortunate that Roosevelt was able to bring about the establishment of the Executive Office of the President when he did, for it seems certain that he could not have met the tremendous administrative demands during the years of World War II nearly as well without the assistance received from the staff of the Executive Office. Wayne Coy, one of Roosevelt's administrative assistants during the war years and a former Assistant Director of the Budget, has emphasized the importance of the Executive Office:

"It is . . . clear to me . . . that the largest step toward enabling the President to 'take care' of the effective operation of the administrative system occurred in 1939, with the establishment of the Executive Office of the President. . . . In a professional field rich in differences of opinion, it is extraordinary indeed to notice how widespread is the agreement on this particular point. . . . It is difficult to imagine how wartime government in the executive realm could have functioned in a generally effective manner without the services the President obtained from his Executive Office." [32]

The establishment of the Executive Office of the President provided definite evidence of Roosevelt's desire to place major reliance upon top-level coordination of the administrative organization from his own office rather than placing major reliance upon the Cabinet departments for general administrative coordination. It was a clear reflection of his underlying attitude that the Cabinet should always remain subordinate to the over-all administrative leadership and coordination of the White House. And it was indicative of Roosevelt's strong personal wish to centralize the direction and coordination of the administrative organization in his own hands as much as possible.

In 1940 Roosevelt submitted three more reorganization plans to Congress. Reorganization Plan No. III, transmitted on April 2, was designed to carry out the third step of his reorganization program by providing for several organizational improvements which were intradepartmental in character.[33] In Reorganization Plan No. IV, submitted on April 11, 1940, Roosevelt took further action toward completing the second step of his program by proposing a number of additional interdepartmental transfers of agencies and functions.[34]

One of the most significant of the changes made by Plan No. IV, which should be singled out for further comment, was that which placed the independent Civil Aeronautics Authority in the Department of Commerce. The plan further provided that the three-member Air Safety Board, which had been set up in the Civil Aeronautics Authority to investigate aircraft accidents, was abolished and its investigatory functions were transferred to the five-member board of the Civil Aeronautics Authority, which was officially re-named the Civil Aeronautics Board. It was also provided that the Civil Aeronautics Board and the Administrator of Civil Aeronautics would together constitute the Civil Aeronautics Authority, which would be administratively responsible to the Secretary of Commerce. The Civil Aeronautics Board, however, was to continue to exercise its quasi-legislative and quasi-judicial functions of rule-making, adjudication, and investigations independently of the Secretary of Commerce.

In dealing thus with the Civil Aeronautics Authority, Roosevelt followed closely the recommendation of the President's Committee on Administrative Management, which had urged that all of the independent regulatory commissions should be placed under various departments for administrative purposes, but that their quasi-judicial and quasi-legislative functions should be separated from their administrative functions and performed independently of departmental control. The large number of agencies which were exempted from the provisions of the Reorganization Act of 1939 made it impossible for Roosevelt to apply this method to the other independent regulatory commissions.

Roosevelt originally thought that Reorganization Plan No. IV would be the last which he would submit under the Reorganization Act of 1939. Consequently, in his message to Congress with Plan IV, he concluded by stating that the task of reorganization was still by no means completed and he urged Congress to reenact the Reorganization Act so that future reorganization needs could be met:

"The reorganization plans thus far submitted do not exhaust the transfers, consolidations, and abolitions that may be necessary and desirable. Some changes that now appear to have merit require further study. It is the responsibility of the President as Chief Executive to see that needed adjustments and improvements in administrative organization are made. But this he cannot adequately accomplish without proper statutory authority. The present Reorganization Act entirely exempts some twenty-one administrative agencies from consideration. Furthermore, this Act expires on January 20, 1941.

"I strongly recommend the reenactment of the Reorganization Act, without exemptions. The structure and management of our Government, like the activities and services it performs, must be kept abreast of social and economic change." [35]

On May 22, 1940, however, Roosevelt was prompted by new developments to submit to Congress a fifth reorganization plan in order to transfer the Immigration and Naturalization Service from the Department of Labor to the Department of Justice. [36] This was the only change included in Plan No. V. It was designed to afford more effective control over aliens in this country in view of what Roosevelt called "the startling sequence of international events which has occurred," [37] i.e., the fall of France and Hitler's domination of almost all of Europe. Roosevelt had seriously considered making this transfer earlier; he had mentioned it as a future possibility which needed additional study in the message he sent to Congress in 1939 with Plan No. II.[38] He had not included it in his previous plans, however, because "much can be said for the retention of these functions in the Department of Labor during normal times." [39] Nevertheless, the paramount needs of national defense and possible threats to the internal security of the country finally convinced him that under the prevailing circumstances immigration and naturalization activities could best be carried on if integrated with the Department of Justice. In this way, the government would be able "to deal quickly with those aliens who conduct themselves in a manner that conflicts with the public interest." [40]

Thus Roosevelt concluded his reorganization efforts under the authority which Congress had granted him in the Reorganization Act of 1939. The serious limitations which Congress imposed upon his authority had prevented him from carrying through a truly comprehensive reorganization of the whole executive branch, as he had wished to do. Within those limitations, however, he had been able to accomplish much during his second term toward overhauling the administrative organization. By structural integration, he had substantially reduced the number of independent agencies reporting directly to the President. By transfers and consolidations of agencies and functions he had eliminated much of the overlapping and duplication of jurisdiction and of work. Most important of all, he had organized the Executive Office of the President in such a way that the President was provided for the first time with the kind of regular staff assistance which he needed to carry out his Constitutional responsibilities of managing and coordinating the entire administrative organization.

Chapter VIII

MEETING THE EXPANDING NEEDS OF NATIONAL
DEFENSE: THE PLANNING STAGE

During the latter half of his second term, President Roosevelt found it necessary to devote greatly increased amounts of time and attention to the expanding needs of national defense. The ominously deteriorating international situation which had been worsening progressively during the late 1930's, finally culminated in the outbreak of World War II on September 1, 1939, when German armed forces invaded Poland. In view of these developments, Roosevelt became more and more concerned with the problems involved in adjusting the administrative organization to the task of providing adequate defense production to meet the possible needs of the country if involvement in a major war should actually materialize.

Fortunately the reorganization plans which Roosevelt initiated under the provisions of the Reorganization Act of 1939 had made a substantial number of administrative improvements which helped to free him somewhat from some of his earlier Administrative burdens so that he had more time available in which to deal with the defense problems and armaments expansion. Considerable progress had been made under the reorganization plans toward simplifying and integrating the administrative organization. Many of the agencies which had been created during the depression were integrated into the regular departments or into the three large new special agencies, the Federal Security Agency, The Federal Works Agency, or the Federal Loan Agency. The number of agencies and administrators reporting directly to the President was substantially reduced. Many of the regular peacetime activities of the government were consolidated and as a result a substantial amount of duplication was eliminated.

In addition to the integration and consolidations under the Reorganization Act, the establishment of the Executive Office of the President improved the over-all control and coordination of the administrative organization from the White House. The authorization of six administrative assistants to the President, the strengthening of the Bureau of the Budget by Roosevelt, and the revitalization of the Bureau under its new Director, Harold D. Smith,—all of these made it somewhat easier for Roosevelt to function as the administrative chief of the government. These changes in 1939 released him to at least a greater degree than would have been true previously to work on the increasing problems of defense and to give a larger share of his time to the management and coordination of the military preparedness program.

Among the major administrative decisions Roosevelt had to make in 1939 concerning the defense program was whether to follow the ready-made Industrial Mobilizaiton Plan which had been prepared under the auspices of the Army and Navy Munitions Board. Following America's experience with industrial mobilization in World War I, Congress enacted the National Defense Act of 1920 which recognized the desirability of having plans immediately available if the country should ever have to enter any other such conflict. Under the terms of this Act, primary responsibility for industrial preparedness had been placed upon the Assistant Secretary of War. Two years later, on July 22, 1922, the Army and Navy Munitions Board had been established by administrative action to coordinate the mobilization requirements of both the Army and the Navy. In 1931 the Board published its first Industrial Mobilization Plan which contained provisions concerning proposed emergency legislation, war-time administrative organization, and procedures for military production, distribution and procurement. Later revisions of the original plan were issued by the Board in 1933, 1936, and 1939. All of the revisions held in common the basic assumption that the conduct of mobilization in the event of any future war should be placed largely in the hands of American industry.

On August 9, 1939, the Assistant Secretary of War, Louis Johnson, with the President's approval, appointed a civilian advisory committee to the Army and Navy Munitions Board to consider possible future revisions to the Industrial Mobilization Plan. This committee, named the War Resources Board, was composed of four prominent figures in industry, a banker, a president of a major university who was also a distinguished scientist, and an economist who headed a leading national research organization. These seven members were Edward H. Stettinius, Jr., Chairman of the Board of the United States Steel Corporation; Walter S. Gifford, President of American Telephone and Telegraph Company; John Lee Pratt, a director of General Motors Corporation; General Robert E. Wood, Chairman of Sears, Roebuck and Company; John Hancock, a Lehman Brothers partner; Karl T. Compton, President of Massachusetts Institute of Technology; and Harold G. Moulton, President of the Brookings Institution.[1]

The War Resources Board was attacked almost immediately as being chiefly representative of so-called "Big Business," with no representation of the interests of labor, of agriculture, of consumers, or of other groups in the society. Secretary of the Interior Harold L. Ickes recorded in his diary on September 16, 1939, the great concern which John L. Lewis, then President of the Congress of Industrial Organizations, expressed to him about the Board because it contained no labor representative. A short time later Ickes wrote of a meeting in his office attended by "Frank Murphy, Bob Jackson, Tom Corcoran, Ben Cohen, Jerome Frank, Isador Lubin, and Lauchlin Currie . . . . All of us are opposed to the efforts being made by Assistant Secretary Johnson . . . to bring into the Administration as advisers such men as the War Department and Henry Morgenthau have been gathering together lately." Ickes added, however, "I did not believe it was the intention of the President to allow the fat cats of Wall Street to run the war activities if war should come." [2]

The Industrial Mobilization Plan of 1939 [3] was designed to be put into effect immediately at the outset of a war to insure sufficient munitions for the military, essentials for the civilian population, and to provide for general economic stability. It was to depend upon the quick enactment by Congress of a whole range of emergency legislation to allow the creation of a War Resources Administration which would control and coordinate everything necessary for industrial mobilization, including prices, profits, wages, labor allocation, a selective service system, imports and exports. The Army and Navy Munitions Board had intended that its advisory War Resources Board would eventually be established as the new War Resources Administration called for in the Industrial Mobilization Plan, with dominant administrative leadership assigned to an Administrator to be appointed by the President. The Administrator was to be assisted by an Advisory Council composed of the heads of the various divisions of the War Resources Administration plus delegates from the State, War, and Navy Departments.

The War Resources Board was never destined to fulfill this expectation. After reviewing the Industrial Mobilization Plan, the Board submitted a report containing its recommendations. Even before the submission of its report, there were widespread rumors in Washington that the Board was soon to be disbanded. Commenting on the Board in his diary on September 16, 1939, Ickes wrote that "it was not the purpose of the President to recognize it officially or deal with it directly in the event of war." [4] After receiving its report, Roosevelt did officially dissolve the Board on November 24, 1939, with a warm public letter of thanks and appreciation upon the completion of the Board's work.[5] The report submitted by the Board was immediately classified "Top Secret" and it was not publicly released until 1946, in spite of the fact that great pressure was brought to bear to make it public in the early days of the war.

When the report was finally released following the war, it indicated that after the President had told the Board that he was not favorable to any plan which would delegate full and centralized authority over the civilian economy, the group had agreed to work out an "organization plan that would be more in line with the ideas of the President" than that originally contained in the Industrial Mobilization Plan. Consequently, the Board's report set forth two alternative proposals. One suggested a super-agency along the lines of the War Resources Administration contemplated in the Industrial Mobilization Plan, with "almost complete control of the economic life of the Nation." The other proposal called for the establishment of seven separate war agencies, each exercising a specific delegated war power, each reporting directly to the President, and each operating directly under his supervision and control. According to this proposal the heads of the seven agencies were to coordinate their activities among themselves and through the President.[6]

Although the approach advanced in the Industrial Mobilization Plan had wide support, both in Congress and out, Roosevelt decided against its adoption. The reasons which led him to this decision were probably both numerous and complex. The Industrial Mobilization Plan assumed the existence of a state of war with an "M-Day" when full war mobilization and organization could be undertaken at one time, and almost any power could be obtained from Congress for the asking in order to meet the needs of fighting the war. These conditions, of course, did not obtain in 1939 and 1940 and it was both politically unrealistic to think that such an all-encompassing plan could have been put into effect without serious modification even if Roosevelt had wished to do so.

Undoubtedly another factor of fundamental importance in Roosevelt's rejection of the Industrial Mobilization Plan was its provision for the creation of a single administrator, the Administrator of the War Resources Administration, with vast powers over both the administrative organization and policies of the government. Delegation of such extensive powers as provided in the Industrial Mobilization Plan would have made it much more difficult for the President to exercise personal control over the general strategy of defense preparations during a critical period. Roosevelt was completely unwilling to delegate such broad authority to another person at that time and wished to retain in his own hands the direction and coordination of the preparedness program. Still another reason was Roosevelt's fear that the Industrial Mobilization Plan would give too much power to the military in war production and procurement, functions which he wished to keep essentially under the final control of civilian authorities. He believed that the plan might well allow greater military influence in the administration of governmental affairs than he thought wise or politically desirable at the time.

Since 1940 was to be an election year, and since prevailing public opinion in the United States was still strongly opposed to any direct participation in the war, Roosevelt was undoubtedly sensitive about supporting a plan originated by the Army and Navy Munitions Board and calling for immediate full-scale war mobilization of unprecedented scope. Such action might easily be construed by the people of the country as a big step toward America's entry into the war, which in turn might well have unfortunate repercussions upon the fortunes of the Democratic Party in the forthcoming election.[7]

In his memoirs, Louis Brownlow has written a revealing account of some of Roosevelt's thoughts concerning the Industrial Mobilization Plan and the recommendations of the War Resources Board as expressed in conversations between the two men in August 1939. Brownlow wrote:

"One day I was invited to lunch at the White House with the President. He asked me if I had read the published industrial mobilization plans. I had not. He asked me to read them, to let him know what I thought about the administrative aspects of the recommendations, what I thought could be done about obtaining from Congress special legislation for special organizational plans for preparedness, and what I thought could be found in the statute books that would enable him to proceed without new legislation.

"During this conversation a good deal was said about President Wilson's difficulties with administrative organization. More especially

we talked about how Wilson had found it necessary not only to go
to the Congress for every new agency that the situation required but
to return to the Congress to get that agency abolished or changed.

"A few days later I saw the President, again at his request . . . .
I was invited to come to the White House to lunch on Tuesday,
August 29, 1939.

" 'What is your report?' he asked after a rather longish dis-
cursive talk over the luncheon at his desk.

" 'Well, it seems to me that any President who accepts the recommendations of these mobilization plans would do a little better to
resign.'

" 'In other words, you think resignation is more dignified than
abdication.'

"I said, 'Certainly.'

"He went on:

" 'Yes indeed. If I were to set up a scheme such as recommended
by this reoprt, turning over the sole administration of the economy
of the country, even the public relations of the White House, to a
single war administrator—even though he were appointed by me—I
would simply be abdicating the presidency to some other person. I
might choose that person, but I would be expected to select him from
a small group of big businessmen whose names were submitted to me
by a committee, most of the members of which would desire above
everything else in the world that some person other than F.D.R. were
President of the United States."

" 'Next question,' said the President. 'How will I go about it?'

" 'Mr. President,' I said, 'I believe that the only way to proceed
is to use the act of August 29, 1916, setting up the National Defense
Council. Re-create it . . . and then set it up in the Executive Office of
the President. The power to do this has been granted to you in
the Reorganization Act of April 3, this year.'

" 'Several people have told me that the act of August 29, 1916,
was probably my only recourse, but I had not thought before of
utilizing the Executive Office.'

" 'That, I think, Mr. President, will give you the necessary power
to control the operation of the council and enable you to grant or to
withhold power, to create or dissolve subsidiary agencies and committees, and to retain control over them all.'

" 'That's an idea. The council, of course, is composed of six members
of the Cabinet, but the law authorized an advisory committee. I could

reconstitute the council, tell the Cabinet officers to get lost, and run the thing through the advisory committee as part of my own office.'

" 'That, I think, is your way out.'

" 'But,' he said, 'tomorrow I am going to talk to the Stettinius board. It will have a recommendation for me. I don't know just how I will handle it. I don't know whether I will handle it at all at this time. I am going to sleep on it tonight, but on the whole I am inclined to think that you are right and that the thing to do is to revive the old Council of National Defense and pull it right straight into my own office. If we are really headed for trouble, I will at least be my own boss and will not be compelled to turn over the presidency of the United States to some other man, a man who, I am sure, would never be nominated by a Democratic convention and never be elected by the people.' " [8]

Consequently, in early September 1939, when Brownlow was requested by Roosevelt to draft an executive order to create the Executive Office of the President, he provided, in rather brief, vague guage, for the possible establishment therein of an Office for Emergency Management. This "agency in embryo" provided the means whereby Roosevelt was able to retain control, direction, and coordination of the administrative organization for national defense securely in the White House under his own direct supervision.

Another question of fundamental importance which Roosevelt faced in developing the administrative organization for national defense was whether to place most of the new defense work under the already-existing permanent departments and agencies or to set up new, specialized, and presumably temporary agencies not responsible to the regular departments but responsible directly to the President and created for the purpose of performing only the specific tasks assiged to them. This was essentially the same problem he had faced in 1933 in working out the administrative arrangements to fight the economic crisis. At that time his decision had been to create the whole host of new "alphabet agencies" to administer the respective programs of the New Deal. This method had resulted in a lot of administrative duplication, conflict, and confusion.

Roosevelt had hoped to straighten out the situation, at least to considerable degree, through his reorganization proposals stemming from the work of the President's Committee on Administrative Management. Although the restrictive terms of the Reorganization Act of 1939 had rather limited the consolidations and integration which could be obtained, Roosevelt had acted to reduce the duplication substantially through his reorganization plans of 1939 which he submitted at a time when he was already giving serious thought to the defense preparation program. Roosevelt had been distressed by the administrative difficulties and confusion resulting from his approach during the early New Deal years, and he desired to achieve the administrative improvements which he hoped would result from the reorganization plans. Consequently, in the early days of the expanding defense program he apparently intended originally to handle the new activities as much as possible through the existing departments, or at least he expressed the desire to do this to some of those who were closely associated with him at the time.

According to a statement by former Secretary of Labor Frances Perkins, Roosevelt had "originally intended before the war to place the wartime agencies and functions under the responsible heads of the existing departments, with the additional liaison and coordination which would be necessary to be provided for by the White House. Rather elaborate plans," Perkins added, "were worked out in advance by all of the regular agencies to accomplish this purpose. Roosevelt thought Wilson had created too many separate wartime agencies and he wanted to avoid this." [9]

Another Cabinet member, Secretary of the Interior Harold L. Ickes, wrote in his diary on June 2, 1940, that "the idea of the President all along has been that he didn't want to set up any separate authority aside from the regular establishments of the Government, through which he expected to work, except for certain advisory and coordinating jobs that would be subordinated to the regular establishments." [10] Ickes followed this up on June 12, 1940, by writing that Roosevelt had "started out with the firm announcement that he was not going to have a supergovernment, that the people whom he would bring to Washington would have to work through the regular establishments." [11]

In a White House press conference on May 23, 1940, Roosevelt's Press Secretary, Stephen Early, stated that the "president had no intention of creating an involved administrative machinery for defense purposes. Some business executives would be invited by the President into the government; but places would not be found for them by the establishment of new agencies." [12]

Despite these statements as to his original intent, several factors led Roosevelt to decide to pursue a different course of action on this important question. For he soon proceeded to meet the defense emergency by the establishment of a large number of new and separate independent agencies, just as he had done to meet the economic emergency seven years earlier. Robert Sherwood has written that Harold Smith, Roosevelt's Budget Director from 1939 to 1945, "expressed the belief that if Roosevelt had had ample time to prepare for war—and the authority to do so—he might have reorganized the Departments to meet the emergency, which would certainly have involved some drastic changes in personnel. But," Sherwood continues, "there was not ample time and Roosevelt had to improvise as best he could.'[13] This pressure of time and events apparently combined with some of Roosevelt's basic attitudes towards administration and the nature of the Presidency to impel him to follow this procedure. Among the possible reasons, those discussed below seem to have been especially important in his thinking.

Frances Perkins has expressed the opinion that the "main reason Roosevelt weakened" in his intent to have the defense program administered through the regular departments "was because several important men the President wanted in the government for certain jobs were reluctant to come to Washington unless they were given sufficiently high rank and position out from under the regular Cabinet departments. Because of this," according to Perkins, "Roosevelt created several new agencies for these people to head and bestowed Cabinet rank upon them."[14]

Wayne Coy, another of those closely associated with Roosevelt as one of the President's Administrative Assistants and later as Assistant Director of the Bureau of the Budget, has summarized what he believed to be the main reasons underlying Roosevelt's decision in the following passage:

"As our defense effort got underway, the question soon presented itself whether the emerging civilian control functions should be vested in the permanent departments or in agencies set up for this specific purpose. There were technical pros and cons for either alternative. The weightiest consideration, it seemed to me, was essentially political. Establishment of special war agencies promised not only a welcome influx of fresh blood and outside talent, but also a desirable opportunity for drawing into the government both representatives of important interests and exponents of the political opposition. The organizational solution then adopted was dictated in the main not by administrative arguments in the narrow sense, but by the quest of national unity—a paramount factor in the hour of peril." [15]

Unquestionably another factor in Roosevelt's thinking was his belief that the regular departments were not geared to meet the extraordinary and urgent demands of defense preparations and possible eventual wartime administration. The departments, Roosevelt feared, were too bound by custom, tradition, red-tape, and bureaucratic fear of undue haste and irregularity to be able to adjust to the faster pace and new procedures which the developing emergency would inevitably make necessary. In addition, some of the established personnel in a regular department might disagree with the objectives or methods of a new program. Their active hostility in the internal competition within a department would make it far more likely that the new program would suffer serious impairment than if it were set up in a separate agency directly under the President.

Another important consideration stems from the fact that Congress is usually inclined to look with suspicion upon any substantial increases in the powers, staff, and funds of the permanent departments, as it is axiomatic in Congressional thinking that once a new function is established in a regular department it is extremely hard to get it ended. On the other hand, temporary agencies created only to perform emergency functions can be abolished, and expect to be, when the emergency is over. Consequently, Roosevelt may have thought that Congress would probably not object so strongly to granting extensive authority over a specific program to a newly-created temporary agency as it would to giving such authority to one of the permanent departments. Finally, the success of many of the new defense programs was so closely related to the need for Presidential leadership, support, and control that Roosevelt wanted to maintain close personal contact with those responsible for administering them rather than having to deal only indirectly with the program through the head of a regular department with whom he already had to deal about a host of other programs.

This approach undoubtedly increased Roosevelt's administrative work-load very substantially as he had to see and keep in touch with a rapidly expanding number of defense agency administrators. He was helped in this regard, of course, by the creation of the Executive Office of the President and the expansion of his White House staff in accordance with the terms of the Reorganization Act of 1939. Despite this, however, his approach made it very likely that there would be some duplication, conflict, confusion, and uncertainty in the administration of the defense program because of Roosevelt's sheer inability to deal as expeditiously as needed with the many problems arising from all of the agencies to which he had to give his personal attention. But at least it meant that Roosevelt would be in direct personal charge of the various aspects of the defense preparation program. This he regarded as a necessary and proper exercise of his Presidential authority commensurate with the full responsibility for the program which the Constitution placed squarely upon him.

As set forth in the above statement by Wayne Coy, Roosevelt was concerned from the beginning of the expanded preparedness program about bringing some leaders of the opposition Republican party into his defense administrative organization. Samuel Rosenman has reported that, "The President had said frequently that he was not going to repeat what he thought was Wilson's mistake—leaving the Republicans out of the handling of the emergency." [16] In early September 1939, shortly after the outbreak of the war in Europe, Ickes wrote in his diary that Roosevelt had discussed with him the possibility of appointing the Republican Presidential and Vice Presidential candidates of 1936, Alfred E. Landon and Frank Knox, to positions in his Cabinet. [17] And Louis Brownlow has written in his autobiography that Roosevelt had discussed this subject with him as early as the spring of 1939 following the surrender of Czechoslovakia to Germany. [18]

On September 20, 1939, Roosevelt invited Landon and Knox and a small group of other leading citizens of both political parties to the White House to discuss the war policies of the country. In connection with this meeting, Landon made three public statements, one in Topeka before starting to Washington, one in Chicago on his way, and one on the White House steps immediately following the conference. In all of these, he uttered remarks critical of the Roosevelt Administration. In a subsequent interview in New York two days after the meeting he demanded that Roosevelt announce that he would not be a candidate for a third term. According to Brownlow's account, "Not only did Governor Landon make these public statements, but in the conference in the President's office he was markedly uncooperative. The President told me not long afterward that during the meeting Landon 'acted like a bad little boy.' At a still later time, Colonel Knox, in talking to me about the meeting, characterized Landon's behavior on that occasion in much saltier and more forceful words." [19]

Apparently Landon's conduct dampened whatever enthusiasm Roosevelt may have had for his appointment. In any case, in the following December, Roosevelt proceeded to invite Frank Knox alone to come into his cabinet as Secretary of the Navy without tendering any similar offer to Landon. Although Knox was both interested and complimented, he declined on the basis, as he told Ickes, that "he would be regarded by his Republican friends as having sold out," unless at least one other Republican was brought into the Cabinet at the same time to establish something in the nature of a coalition Cabinet. Ickes replied that "if this offer had come at the time of the convening of the special session of Congress, with an offer also to Landon to go into the Cabinet, both could have accepted then, and there would have been no criticism." According to Ickes, "Knox agreed with this, as he did with my statement that Landon had talked so much on that occasion that he had made it impossible for the President to carry out what was in his mind." [20]

During the following few months Roosevelt continued intermittently to give consideration to the possibility of appointing Knox and an additional Republican to the Cabinet. One prominent Republican considered for such a position was the well-known New York lawyer, William J. Donovan, who was later appointed by Roosevelt as Coordinator of Information in the defense program and still later as head of the wartime Office of Strategic Services. At one stage, Roosevelt also gave very serious thought to appointing Mayor Fiorello LaGuardia of New York as Secretary of War.[21] By June 1940, however, he had finally settled on offering the position of Secretary of War to Henry L. Stimson who had served in that capacity in the Taft Administration and as Secretary of State under Hoover, despite the fact that Stimson was almost 73 years of age. On that same date, he once again offered the position as Secretary of the Navy to Knox who readily accepted this time.[22]

The appointments of Stimson and Knox were announced on June 20, 1940, at a time when Germany's complete conquest of France was fast becoming an established fact and just four days before the Republican National Convention was to convene. Roosevelt's action aroused both violent denunciation and hearty approval. The chairman of the Republican National Committee, John Hamilton, tried to read both Stimson and Knox out of the Republican party, and Roosevelt was denounced by many Republican leaders for trying to disrupt their party on the eve of its national convention. On the other hand, the President was widely praised throughout the country for having brought two of the outstanding Republican leaders into his Cabinet at a time of great national peril in an effort to insure that the administration of the defense program would be non-partisan and non-political. After rather lengthy, intensive, and often hostile questioning before the Senate Armed Services Committee, led by Senators Robert A. Taft and Arthur Vandenberg, who were not members of the Committee but were invited to question the appointees, the Senate finally approved both men by comfortable margins, Stimson by 56 to 28 and Knox by 66 to 16.

Throughout the period of defense preparation and certainty after America's direct entry into the war following Pearl Harbor, Roosevelt appointed many individuals to the new emergency agencies who were Democrats, many who were Republicans, and many who were not strongly identified with either of the two major parties. The basically non-partisan character of most of the new agencies was established so early and so clearly that often even the newspapers failed to set forth the party affiliation of many of the men brought in as heads of important new programs.[23]

It was on May 25, 1940, that Roosevelt formally established the first, and in some ways also the most important, of his new national defense agencies. This was the Office for Emergency Management which he activated in the Executive Office of the President by a brief administrative order which reads as follows:

"1. There is established in the Executive Office of the President an office to be known as the Office for Emergency Management, which shall be under the direction of one of the Administrative Assistants to the President, to be designated by the President.

"2. The Office for Emergency Management shall:

"(a) Assist the President in the clearance of information with respect to measures necessitated by the threatened emergency;

"(b) Maintain liaison between the President and the Council of National Defense and its Advisory Commission and with such other agencies, public or private, as the President may direct, for the purpose of securing maximum utilization and coordination of agencies and facilities in meeting the threatened emergency;

"(c) Perform such additional duties as the President may direct."[24]

The activation of the Office for Emergency Management was to serve three important purposes. First of all, as Roosevelt himself stated it, "The paramount purpose of the Office for Emergency

Management is to enable me to plan and direct all phases of the defense program." [25] Through the Office for Emergency Management the President could coordinate, supervise and, when he wished or found it necessary, personally direct the work of the agencies engaged in emergency defense activities. Secondly, it provided the President with some additional staff assistance in the coordination and direction of the defense program, especially in dealing with the numerous specialized agencies which Roosevelt brought into existence.

The third purpose, however, was to prove to be of even considerably greater importance than the second. For the Office for Emergency Management provided Roosevelt with the legal authority necessary for the establishment of such new agencies as he saw fit to create. It served him very well "as a great legal convenience," to use Herman Somers' phase.[26] With very few exceptions, most of the new administrative organizations necessary for defense, and later, for war originated as parts, or divisions, of the Office for Emergency Management. It gave Roosevelt a handy, easy to use "holding company" device to utilize when setting up the emergency agencies without having to try to get the express authorization of Congress each time through specific legislation.[27] Thus the President was able to act much more quickly than before without the possible delay of having his requests for the creation of new agencies bogged down in lengthy and acrimonious Congressional debate, with of course the risk always present that Congress might refuse the requests altogether.

Roosevelt had been greatly concerned about the problem of having to get Congressional approval and authorization for settling up any new agencies. He had discussed this subject at length with Louis Brownlow in August 1939 when he expressed concern "about how Wilson found it necessary . . . to go to the Congress for every new agency that the situation required." [28] He was looking for a way to avoid this difficulty and Brownlow's suggestion for the establishment of the Office for Emergency Management in the Executive Office of the President provided him with the answer.

Roosevelt made very extensive use of the Office for Emergency Management as the main framework within which he set up almost all of the civilian defense and wartime agencies. As Wayne Coy has written, "The Office for Emergency Management, originally merely an institutional peg on which to hang temporary agencies in case of an emergency, passed through a period of tropical growth during the war." [29] Among the more important of the "constituent agencies" or "divisions" which were to be established in the Office for Emergency Management were the Foreign Economic Administration, The National War Labor Board, the Office of Production Management, the Office of Alien Property Custodian, the Office of Civilian Defense, the Office of the Coordinator of Inter-American Affairs, the Supply Priorities and Allocations Board, the Office of Defense Health and Welfare Services, the Office of Defense Transportation, the Office of Economic Stabilization, the Office of Scientific Research and Development, the Office of War Information, the War Manpower Commission, the War Production Board, the War Relocation Authority, the War Shipping Administration, and the Office of War Mobilization. [30]

To head the Office for Emergency Management, Roosevelt designated one of his original Administrative Assistants, William H. McReynolds, under the title of Liaison Officer for Emergency Management. [31] A veteran government official with 34 years of service at the time of his appointment, McReynolds had first entered Federal employment in the Post Office Department in 1906 and had served successively in the Bureau of Efficiency, the Bureau of the Budget, and as assistant to the Secretary of the Treasury prior to his appointment to the White House in 1939. There he was named as the Administrative Assistant to serve as Liaison Officer for Personnel Management, a position he continued to hold until 1945.

McReynolds served as the Liaison Officer for Emergency Management until April 1941 when he was succeeded by Wayne Coy, a former Indiana newspaper editor who had entered government service as a protege of Indiana Governor Paul V. McNutt, and who was serving as Assistant Administrator to McNutt in the Federal Security Agency when appointed as the Liaison Office for Emergency Management. Subsequently, in 1942, Coy was appointed as the Assistant Director of the Bureau of the Budget, and he held both positions simultaneously until he relinquished the Liaison Officer job in June 1943 following the establishment of the Office of War Mobilization.

The Director of the Office of War Mobilization, former Senator and Supreme Court Justice James F. Byrnes, also assumed the position of Liaison Officer of the Office for Emergency Management and held that title until November 3, 1943, when he resigned from the post. It was then decided by Roosevelt that no successor should be appointed as the duties previously performed by the Liaison Officer had been assimilated into the Office of War Mobilization. Thus the liaison activities of the Office for Emergency Management were terminated, though the Office itself continued in existence throughout the duration of the war as the convenient legal base for nearly all of the important war agencies.[32]

On May 28, 1940, just three days after the establishment of the Office for Emergency Management, Roosevelt moved to complete his long-planned administrative organization for defense by reviving the Advisory Commission to the Council of National Defense as his second important step toward the coordination and control of the economy for defense purposes. As already indicated above, statutory authority still remained on the books in an act passed on August 29, 1916, during the First World War for the appointment of a Council of National Defense composed of six Cabinet officers—the Secretaries of War, Navy, Interior, Agriculture, Commerce, and Labor. In addition, the statute required the Council to nominate for Presidential appointment an advisory commission "of not more than seven persons, each of whom shall have some special knowledge of some industry, public utility, or the development of some natural resource, or be otherwise specially qualified." [33]

As appointed by Roosevelt, the Advisory Commission consisted of the following: Edward R. Stettinius, Jr., Chairman of the Board of Directors of the United States Steel Corporation, as Adviser on Industrial Materials; William S. Knudsen, President of General Motors, as Advisor on Industrial Production; Sidney Hillman, President of the Amalgamated Clothing Workers, as Adviser on Employment; Chester C. Davis, member of the Federal Reserve Board and former Administrator of the Agricultural Adjustment Administration, as Adviser on Farm Products; Leon Henderson, member of the Securities and Exchange Commission, as Adviser on Price Stabilization; Ralph Budd, Chairman of the Board of the Chicago, Burlington, and Quincy Railroad, as Adviser on Transportation; and Harriet Elliott, a political scientist and Dean of Women at the University of North Carolina, as Adviser on Consumer Protection.[34]

The newly-appointed Liaison Officer for Emergency Management, William H. McReynolds, was designated as the secretary of the Commission. On June 27, 1940, Donald M. Nelson, Executive Vice President of Sears, Roebuck and Company, who was already in Washington working as an adviser to the Treasury Department, was appointed as Coordinator of National Defense Purchases and functioned from then on in fact as a member of the Advisory Commission though he was not an official member because of the statutory limitation of seven members.

As set forth in the statute, the general functions assigned to the Conncil of National Defense were "to coordinate industries and re- sources for the national security and welfare and to create relations that would make possible the immediate concentration and utiliza- tion of the resources of the Nation in time of need. Specifically, it was the duty of the Council to direct investigations and make recommendations to the President and the heads of executive depart- ments regarding such defense activities as the utilization of railroads and waterways, the mobilization of military and naval resources, the production of materials essential to the Nation during any interrup- tion of foreign commerce, the development of seagoing transporta- tion, and the production of military supplies." [35]

The functions of the Council were very quickly transferred to the Advisory Commission by Roosevelt. Although the Commission in form was intended to be advisory to the Council, in fact it was made advisory to the President with the Council remaining almost dormant. In his press conference announcing the establishment of the Council and the Advisory Commission on May 28, 1940, Roosevelt said, "The Council consists merely of six Cabinet Officers, who will meet every Friday anyway and who work and who are expected to work on the coordination of the whole picture, through this Commission . . . ." [36]

At a White House meeting with the President on May 30, 1940, attended by the members of the Council of National Defense, some of the other Cabinet members, the members of the Advisory Com- mission, and a few Congressional leaders, Roosevelt made it clear that the Council would meet and act only at meetings of the Cabinet, and that the Advisory Commission would deal with the Council only through the President or his Liaison Officer for Emergency Manage- ment, William H. McReynolds. In commenting on this meeting in his diary, Harold Ickes wrote:

"Barkley raised a question about the relationship of this commis- sion to the Council of National Defense created during the world war, which consists of the Secretaries of War, Navy, Interior, Agri- culture, Commerce, and Labor. The President's reply was that there would be no connection, that the Council of National Defense would operate only through the Cabinet, since it consisted entirely of Cabinet members, and it would probably not hold a meeting as a separate body." [37]

Thus, in effect, the revived Council itself actually served only as an instrument which the President used to create the Advisory Commission and divisional agencies set up under it which he wished to have established for the defense program.

Certainly one of Roosevelt's major reasons for relying on the old 1916 statute to set up his national defense administrative organization was his desire to avoid seeking action directly from Congress. He was reluctant to open the matter with the politicians on Capitol Hill for fear of the lengthy and highly controversial debate which would probably ensue before anything would be done, and because he was afraid that Congressoinal action might result in a straightjacket of administrative inflexibility at a time when he believed the greatest possible flexibility was needed. In addition, Congress was in the midst of its consideration of his proposals for the establishment of selective service and Roosevelt did not want to do anything to jeopardize this legislation by the introduction of additional urgent Presidential requests. As Robert Sherwood has put it, ". . . he used antiquated and generally inadequate legislation as his authority for action because he did not want to risk possible conflict with the Congress on any issue other than what he considered the main one—which was Selective Service. As Commander in Chief in a time when the national security was imperiled, he had to put first things first . . . ." [38]

Roosevelt's desire to direct the defense program himself, his unwillingness to delegate broad powers to any other individual, and his reluctance to propose an all-out, super defense agency at a time when he thought that limited powers and action were probably about all that public opinion was ready to support—all of these reasons undoubtedly also affected his decision. [39] Preparation for defense was a matter of very questionable popularity with many people in the country who were bound and determined to stay out of war. Isolationist sentiment was still quite strong throughout the land and Roosevelt was already being accused of leading the country into war in a surreptitious manner without revealing his true intentions. In addition, the political situation of the country (and, of course, of Roosevelt personally) was highly complex and delicate. The national party conventions and the Presidential campaign were rapidly approaching and political speculation was in a state of even greater than normal confusion because of uncertainty as to the effects of the war emergency and as to whether Roosevelt would run for a third term as President. Regarding Roosevelt's own position at that time, Robert Sherwood has written:

"His personal position was far weaker than at any other time in the New Deal or war years. Whatever unity and harmony and even loyalty there had been in his Administration was to a serious degree disrupted by the third term issue and the selection of the Vice-Presidential nominee. During the most critical weeks of May and June, it was not known whether Roosevelt would run again, or, if he did whether he would be able to overcome the obstacles of isolationist sentiment and of popular respect for the tradition established by George Washington and solidified by Thomas Jefferson."[40]

Consequently, in view of all these complications, Roosevelt had moved very cautiously and carefully in creating his defense organization. The decision to establish the National Defense Advisory Commission when he did was based upon a careful evaluation of all the relevant factors discussed above, as well as upon the growing urgency of the international situation as Hitler's armies advanced through France. Fundamentally, he made an important administrative decision primarily upon the basis of his judgment as to what it was best to do under the political conditions existing at the time. At his press conference on May 28, 1940, he explained his decision as follows:

"This is not complete, immediate national mobilization. We are not talking at the present time about a draft system either to draft men or women or money or all three. We are trying to expend about a billion and a quarter dollars more than the normal process. And in order to do that, it has seemed wise to put into effect what has been ready and planned for, for a long, long time, under an existing statute, without having to go and propose something entirely new in the way of legislation that would take weeks and months and a great deal of pro and con discussion, partisan and otherwise, and would probably end up in practically the same thing that we have on the statute books now." [41]

As was true also of the appointment of Henry L. Stimson and Frank Knox to his Cabinet three weeks later, Roosevelt's establishment of the National Defense Advisory Commission was, at least to some degree, "a move to have all major groups united in the common defense. It was an attempt to build a National Government." [42] Roosevelt developed this theme in his press conference on May 28, 1940, in the following passage: "These seven people who are set up here on this Commission cover, for the present, the various fields of activity that have to be coordinated . . . . Through these seven people, we have taken in practically all of the necessary activities of civilized life in the United States at the present time . . . ." [43]

In some extemporaneous remarks to a group of representatives of national civic organizations on August 2, 1940, he emphasized this same approach. Referring to the National Defense Advisory Commission, he said: "When we came down to establishing it, we tried to cover all the elements of American life, because that is another way of saying total defense. Instead of putting just one industrialist or financier at the head of this organization we tried to gather all the component parts of American life that were essential to defense. And if you will go down the list, you will see what I did." [44]

As a group the Commission was far more representative of the varied interests of the country than the earlier War Resources Board, or than the organization similar to it envisioned in the Industrial Mobilization Plan would have been. Among the members of the Commission most of the significant political and economic viewpoints of the time were reflected. This was undoubtedly of considerable help in securing wider popular support for the President's defense program. Also, the deliberations of the Commission were to prove of substantial value in working out compromises in the positions of major interest groups and in developing reconciliations of conflicting opinions in order that the defense effort might get to moving along. Most of the members of the Commission were to continue to work in leading positions of responsibility throughout the remainder of the defense and war emergency. Their period of service on the Commission was one of great educational benefit in that it exposed them to deeply held and forcefully expressed views which often differed sharply from their own, and which had to be given serious consideration in carrying on the defense program.

Each of the advisers found himself faced by two major tasks. First of all, he had to assume administrative responsibilities for getting a current job done of coordinating the civilian affairs of the country in the respective field of activity in which he was designated. In addition, and perhaps of greater importance, he had to supervise the making of thorough studies and detailed plans as to the defense needs of the country, especially as to what would have to be done if the country should actually get into war. Thus, each member was responsible for conducting investigations and making recommendations, as well as for organizing defense activities and facilitating the progress of the preparedness program in his specific field of assignment. As Roosevelt himself was to write in May 1941, "The Commission was designed to aid in ascertaining precisely what America needed in the way of defense materials, where she could get them, and what was the best way to obtain them." [45] In meeting the problem of preparing plans for whatever might come, each of the advisers proceeded to assemble small staffs which later were to provide the nucleus around which most of the larger, more elaborate war agencies were developed.

Although the official title of Advisory Commission to the Council of National Defense seemed to indicate otherwise, the statute under which the members were appointed did not provide for them to constitute a collegial body or to engage in group functions. Actually, however, any expectation that each adviser would function independently within only his own particular field was soon dispelled. The members very quickly started having Commission meetings and assumed collective responsibilities and activities with all of them interesting themselves in almost all phases of defense policy. This was apparently Roosevelt's intention for in the initial meeting with the Commission and the Council members on May 30, 1940, he said that the Commission "ought to meet perhaps once a week in conference," and "should come in to see him about once a week." [46] And in the Advisory Commission's handbook which it drew up to explain its own operations, it was provided that, "The Commission meets regularly twice a week to consider activities by the Commission as a body." [47] The members tended to think of themselves as a Commission, not just as individual advisers to the President, and somewhat later they came to be called by the title "Commissioner" rather than "Adviser." The Commission acted as a body on matters of general defense policy and at times on such details as whether the construction of a particular plant should be authorized and where defense plants should be located. Reflecting in its own ranks the divergent views of several of the major interest groups of the country, the Commission had several serious and troublesome internal controversies on such basic questions as the degree of expansion of industrial capacity, curtailment of non-essential civilian production, and ways of dealing wtih organized labor. [48]

Although administratively it certainly was not a perfect mechanism for the conduct of defense mobilization, the Advisory Commission type of organization had several distinct advantages for the situation of 1940 which enabled it to make some substantial contributions. In

terms of accomplishments, the Commissoin expedited the execution
of the production and procurement program authorized at the time,
brought many new and badly needed personnel into the government
service, carried through numerous studies and surveys, prepared many
plans for future developments, and directed attention to the types
and seriousness of problems and controversies which would almost
inevitably continue to arise. This period of the Advisory Commission
also gave Roosevelt a good opportunity to study and evaluate the
performances of a sizable number of new people he was bringing into
leading positions in the government so that he could decide which
ones he would advance into positions of heavier responsibility if the
developing circumstances should demand it. As far as Roosevelt personally was concerned, the Advisory Commission arrangement had
the great virtue of enabling him to retain full control and direction
over the defense program. According to both Ickes and Brownlow,
near the end of the Advisory Commission's first meeting with the
President on May 30, William Knudsen asked who was to be boss of
the Commission. Roosevelt replied simply, "I am."[40] And he left
little doubt in his dealings with the Commission but that he regarded
himself as the Constitutionally responsible person for supervising all
defense activities.

Although Roosevelt's insistence upon occupying the predominant
role in the defense program may have been necessary in his estimation in view of the uneasy and highly complex political situation of
1940, and although it may have been desirable in enabling him to
build the administrative organization in a highly flexible manner so
that it could be adjusted and modified easily to meet changing circumstances, it also unfortuantely resulted in the two major weaknesses of
the Advisory Commission arrangement.

The first of these weaknesses was that the Commission had no
chairman or other operating head, other than the President. Consequently, as the Commission moved along more and more out of the
planning stage and became involved increasingly in operations, the
more it suffered from lack of sufficient internal coordination, and the
more its liaison relationships with other agencies became difficult since
no one person could speak as the Commission's representative. The
second significant weakness was that the Commission lacked clear-
cut, specific authority and direction and operated with considerable
ambiguity and disagreement as to exactly what it was supposed to

do. In discussing this point, Donald M. Nelson was later to write of the Advisory Commission:

"It operated in a climate of uncertainty; its powers were blurred around the edges; its job was ill defined or not defined at all . . . . The NDAC was not a war production board, nor was it an office to 'manage production.' It was an 'advisory commission,' and I believe it went, patriotically, beyond the advisory function without any real authority to do so, and that the nation is lucky the commissioners had the fortitude to exceed—at least in a measure—their vaguely stipulated powers." [50]

Partly, this vagueness and uncertainty was undoubtedly due to the inadequacy of the old statute under which the Commission was created and partly it was due to the uncertainty prevalent throughout the body politic of the country as to what the purposes and aims of the United States were in view of the political confusion accompanying a Presidential election year. Partly, also, it should be attributed to the fact that Roosevelt himself may not have been absolutely clear in his own mind just exactly what he wished the Commission to do and how he wished it to operate. The report which Harold Ickes wrote in his diary after attending the first meeting of the Advisory Commission and the Council of National Defense bears this out. Some allowance should perhaps be made for the fact that Ickes was opposed to the entire idea of the Advisory Commission, as he wanted the defense program to be managed through the established departments. Nevertheless his account provides a revealing commentary upon the vague way in which Roosevelt launched the Commission on its way:

"I became depressed as I sat at this meeting and listened to the President. He must have talked for about an hour straight, and I was reminded of other occasions when he was developing a new idea. He was conciliatory and persuasive and plausible, and yet, it seemed to me, ineffective. He didn't give such an impression of strength as I think this situation calls for, and the plans that he outlined for the members of the commission were nebulous and inchoate. Probably it took him a long time to explain his scheme because it was somewhat intangible even in his own mind.

"In sum, what he said got down to this: The commission was not to be executive so much as co-ordinating, and yet it appeared to be given certain executive powers; he had appointed no chairman, but the members might select their own chairman if they wanted one;

however, they might feel that they would prefer to get along without a chairman; with this in mind he had designated McReynolds, who 'was wise and experienced in Government business,' to work with them; McReynolds might even call them together and preside at their meetings if they wished him to; they ought to meet perhaps once a week in conference, but, after all, each was to be assigned independent duties . . . ." [51]

The failure to appoint a chairman was regarded by Donald Nelson as the Advisory Commisison's great weakness. In an illuminating statement about both the Commission and Roosevelt, he wrote:

"It was an unusually sturdy and well balanced array of talent. But note that no one was designated to act as chairman. I believe that this was a serious mistake, and that the Board's most critical weakness stemmed from this omission. This weakness I was able to spot later when I sat in with the Commission and saw how aimless an organization without a directing and integrating force can become. Every member of the Commission was, in his own orbit, energetic and conscientious, and had definite notions about how to do his job, but there was no one to synchronize and guide the combined efforts of this group of strong individuals. There was no one to settle the arguments and quarrels which were inevitable when determined, able and well intentioned persons have different ideas as to how to reach the same goal. I admire the President as much as anyone who ever knew him, but I believe he made a serious mistake at this point.

"I believe that the President overestimated his own capacity. He undertook to direct the Commission, and frequent meetings were held with him in the chair, meetings at which basic policies and plans were investigated and talked over. When President Roosevelt could sit in with the commissioners, he was always able, thanks to that clear, incisive mind of his, to set courses and directions, to analyze the methods suggested for moving ahead. With ever surprising frankness, he kept them informed on up-to-the-minute developments in the war, and implied what part this country would ultimately have to play in it. Unquestionably, he saw earlier than almost anyone else I knew—certainly earlier than our military men, certainly earlier than Congress—that the United States would soon bear the major burden of defending the entire planet against the depredations of the Axis." [52]

Roosevelt, of course, was not able to meet with the Commission at all of its meetings and was not able to give it the kind of regular day-to-day direction and guidance which was needed. As the President did not see fit to designate a chairman, the Commission members themselves did not name one. Instead, they followed Roosevelt's suggestion of allowing their secretary, McReynolds, to preside at all of the meetings not presided over by the President. At his press conference announcing the appointment of the Commission, Roosevelt discussed the selection of McReynolds as secretary as follows:

"The man who will act as secretary to this Commission . . . is going to be our old friend McReynolds, for the very good reason that he knows every statute on the statute books and knows what each Government department or agency does, which very few outsiders when they first come down to Washington do know about. It generally takes them two or three months before they learn their way around the Capitol, or even the Department of Commerce Building." [53]

A little later in the conference, when questioned by the newsmen about the appointment of a chairman, Roosevelt engaged in this dialogue:

Reporter: "Did you say this Commission had no chairman? Did you say there is no chairman of this Commission?"

The President: "May [Miss Craig], I do not know. Why bring up the subject? I don't know."

Reporter: "It is hard to function without a chairman."

The President: "Let Mac [Mr. McReynolds] be the chairman; he is the secretary. In other words, let the secretary call the meeting together. I do not know what the procedure will be. I do not think it will be formal. I think it will get on." [54]

McReynolds, as Liaison Officer, possessed no real authority over the Commission and he was not empowered by Roosevelt to direct activities of the members, either in his own name or in that of the President. Instead, Roosevelt seemed to think of McReynolds' role as primarily that of a "clearing house" of information, as he phrased it in the press conference. [55] As pointed out by Herman Somers, "Top officials will not bring their troubles to a man without authority; nor do they want an intermediary to deal with the decision-maker; they want to present their own case." [56] Ickes clearly put his finger on this difficulty in discussing the appointment of McReynolds, of which he was highly critical:

"The selection of McReynolds to work with the commission seemed to be particularly unhappy. He is a career man of probably some thirty years' service who, during the last two or three years, has

become very garrulous. I never thought that his selection by the
President as an Administrative Assistant was a good one. He is by
no means strong enough to be a dominating figure on the commission
and it is hard for me to imagine that men like Knudsen and Stettinius
would view with patience an attempt on the part of an old-time
Government employee, who has always worked under someone else,
to give them orders or directions." [57]

Despite these manifest shortcomings, the accomplishments and administrative significance of the Advisory Commission were substantial. In terms of administrative organization, it should be kept in
mind that the defense program prior to the 1940 election was limited
mainly to planning and trying to get established only partial administrative machinery for only partial industrial mobilization. The Commission and Roosevelt's administrative conduct in establishing and
dealing with it must be looked at in the light of what it was politically
feasible and desirable to do at a time when the people of the country
were trying to make up their collective mind about what should be
done in regard to the European war, and when the country was
badly split politically by the internal turmoil of a national Presidential election campaign. The political and special interest group divisions of the country were reflected clearly in the type and rate of
development of the administrative organization for defense which
Roosevelt devised, as well as in the top-level personnel which he appointed to major positions.

Inevitably the uncertainty and lack of clear-cut agreement as to
what the nation should do in international affairs made its way into
the uncertainty and lack of clear-cut agreement as to the nature of
the administrative organization. If there had been more widespread
agreement that the United States would probably eventually be
attacked and drawn into the war, a more rapid rate of military
preparedness and industrial mobilization would undoubtedly have
been attempted, and Roosevelt's decision as to the kind of governmental administrative machinery needed might well have been different.

In spite of its loose-knit and uncohesive form, the Advisory Commission did much to determine the future nature and development of
the defense and wartime agencies which followed it. The Commission,
which has been aptly referred to as "a practical administrative stop-
gap," [58] contained in embryonic form almost all of the important
agencies which were to be set up and developed more fully later.

Within the Commission as it existed prior to the 1940 election were the seeds from which germinated the Office of Production Management, the Office of Price Administration and Civilian Supply, the Office of Defense Transportation, the War Manpower Commission, the Economic Defense Board, the National Housing Agency, the Coordinator of Commercial and Cultural Relations between the American Republics, and the Council of National Defense. In addition, the major coordinating agencies established later can be said to have grown to considerable degree indirectly from the Advisory Commission experience, namely the Supply Priorities and Allocations Board, the War Production Board, the Office of Economic Stabilization, and the Office of War Mobilization and the Office of War Mobilization and Reconversion.

Prior to the 1940 election, the plans had been made and the operations started for a truly gigantic program to construct new plants and expand old ones for the manufacture of arms and munitions, though it is true that by the date of the election only a relatively small amount of war material was actually coming from the factories. Nevertheless, an administrative framework had been developed and a foundation provided for greatly expanded preparedness activities. Before the election, Roosevelt had moved quite cautiously and slowly, subordinating his administrative determinations to the complicated and delicate political situation which faced him. He did not wish to "rock the boat" too violently in the troubled and uncharted waters across which the country and his own political future were sailing. With the successful conclusion of the election, his position was greatly strengthened and he began to consider possibilities for further steps in the development of the administrative organization for defense. After lengthy study of possible courses of action, he finally put into effect an organizational change of major proportions just a few days before his inaugural on January 20, 1941, as the only third term President in the country's history. In effect, he had decided that it was time to move from what had been essentially a planning stage to what would be essentially an operating stage.[50]

CHAPTER IX

MEETING THE EXPANDING NEEDS OF NATIONAL

DEFENSE: THE OPERATING STAGE

As both the year 1940 and his second term as President came to an end, Roosevelt was deeply involved in the formulation of new proposals for the revision of the adminisrative organization for national defense. The National Defense Advisory Commission, functioning since the end of May 1940, had provided a significant first step in developing the administrative machinery to meet the needs of the defense program. The individual members of the Commission had been active in preparing plans for what might be required to meet the possible needs of the future, and had taken initial steps in carrying some of their plans into operation.

Due to the continuing deterioration of the international situation as seen both in the success of Germany in the European war and in the expansionist activities and threats of Japan in the Far East, there was need for the United States to develop and accelerate its military production program still further. Many people were urging that a more highly centralized and elaborate governmental machinery should be provided for the defense effort. Some of the questions which had not been regarded as too urgent and which were only in the planning stage when the Advisory Commission was established, such as price stabilization, labor supply, agricultural production and distribution, and transportation needs, were gradually becoming problems of sufficient concern to warrant moving them from the planning stage into the stage of operational action. In addition, the major demonstrated weaknesses of the Advisory Commission—its loose structure and lack of a chairman or any co-ordinating head other than the President, and its lack of clear-cut, precise authority and direction as to what it was supposed to do—were subjecting it and Roosevelt increasingly to sharp criticisms from many sources, among the most outspoken of which were the press, members of Congress, and leaders of business and industry. There was widespread demand for the designation of a single top administrator to head the entire defense program.

Underlying much of the controversy as to what the structure of the administrative organization for defense should be was actually the fundamental question of who was going to dominate and run the industrial mobilization program. Because of the strong position and outspoken views of some of the special interest groups in American society, the question of the possible appointment of a single individual as defense czar took on very great significance. Business and industry groups naturally thought that some outstanding leader from their ranks should be placed in command. Organized labor, on the other hand, feared the loss of some of the gains and strengthened position it had obtained during the New Deal years if industrial and financial interests were allowed to dominate the defense program.

Roosevelt knew that something had to be done to correct the deficiencies of the Advisory Commission arrangement and to move the program ahead into speeded up operations. In November, soon after the election, he asked the Director of the Bureau of the Budget, Harold Smith, to review the administrative aspects of the defense organization and to submit some alternative reorganization proposals for his consideration. He also requested proposals from others serving in the government, including William S. Knudsen, the Adviser on Industrial Production of the Advisory Commission. Knudsen's plan, submitted to the President in late November, illustrates well the point of view of those supporting a much more centralized system. In essence, Knudsen's proposal was very similar to the Army-Navy Munitions Board's Industrial Mobilization Plan which Roosevelt had rejected previously. It would have transformed the Adviser on Industrial Production into a Director of Industrial Mobilization with power to direct almost the entire defense preparedness program. Under the plan, the Director would have been put over subordinate administrative offices in charge of production, planning, materials, procurement, transportation, labor, price control, export and import control, and domestic requirements.[1]

By the end of the year, after intensive consideration of the matter, Roosevelt decided that it was still inadvisable to designate a single individual to head all defense activities as the Knudsen plan advocated. Instead he worked out an ingenious solution which was not a victory for any particular group, but which tried still to keep the leaders of various interests united in support of the program with no single group in a dominant position or enjoying special advantages. To do this, he decided to take out of the National Defense Advisory Commission the parts of its work headed by William Knudsen (Production), Edward Stettinius, Jr. (Materials), Sidney Hillman (Employment), and Donald M. Nelson (Purchases) and to place them in a new agency, the Office of Production Management, which he would establish in the Office for Emergency Management. The new agency would concentrate its attention on the problems of production, priorities, and procurement while the problems of price control, consumer protection, agriculture, and transportation would be continued under the jurisdiction of the respective offices of the Advisory Commission.

The President discussed the general administrative structure of the new organization in a press conference on December 20, 1940, while announcing that an executive order setting forth the details would be forthcoming sometime soon after the first of the year. A sizable extract from Roosevelt's statement to the newsmen is presented here because it sets forth his thinking on what he called the "cardinal principles" which guided him in setting up the new agency.

"About a month ago it became apparent that we were coming to the end of the study period, and had learned thereby of certain needs. During the past month the various methods of organization to meet those needs have been studied, and all manner of suggestions have been received. There were two or three cardinal principles; and one of them is the fact that you cannot, under the Constituiton, set up a second President of the United States.

"In other words, the Constitution states one man is responsible. Now that man can delegate, surely, but in the delegation he does not delegate away any part of the responsibility from the ultimate responsibility that rests on him.

"The second principle is that this is a Government of laws as well as of men; and the administrative procedure has to follow as closely as possible the laws of the United States, or there must be changes in the laws—one or the other. If it is possible to accomplish better organization through existing laws without asking for changes, that's the method of procedure.

"The third criterion is the thing that is so often forgotten by amateurs, and that is in every process of production there are three elements, which in practically no case are present in any one individual's experience.

"Let's take, as an illustration, any article: a gun, an airplane, an office desk, or a lamp. The three elements are, first the combined element of the buyer and the user. . . . In the case of the national defense program the buyer and the user, because it is military and naval, are the two defense departments, the War Department and the Navy Department. That is one element.

"The other two elements are things we have talked about and written about—they are nothing new. They are management and labor. . . . Into the production of every article there go those two elements. . . . it is impossible to find any one 'Czar' or 'Poobah' or 'Akhoond of Swats,' who combines all three of those elements in his own person. Therefore, the amateurs who talk about sole responsibility in one man, prove their ignorance. Nobody ever found that paragon yet, and as I explained the other day, nobody did in the World War either." [2]

After a fairly lengthy review of the organization of the Executive Office of the President and the Office for Emergency Management, the President continued:

"I am setting up in that authorized Office for Emergency Management a new organization. . . . It will be called the 'Office of Production Management.'

"We then come down to the problem of how to simplify and concentrate responsibility. And coming back to the parable of the desk and the gun, or whatever it is that is made for defense, we still have those three elements. And therefore the Office of Production Management will consist of those three elements, divided among four people—the Director, Mr. Knudsen, and the Associate Director, Mr. Hillman. That gives you the two elements of management and labor; and the third element, which is what I call the buyer and the user, will be the Secretary of War and the Secretary of the Navy, because the two of them put together are the buyer and the user of all these things that are turned out." [3]

Some of the newspapermen were especially interested in the question of Roosevelt's relationship to the new agency, which prompted the following exchange:

Reporter: "Mr. President, as this now stacks up, will you be the top?"

The President: "No, I am not the top, except constitutionally. You cannot divest yourself of the responsibility of that. It rests in this office of which Knudsen is Director and Hillman Associate Director, and the Secretaries of War and Navy, who are orderers and users, are the other two people."

Reporter: "Mr. President, just to what extent can you divest yourself of responsibility?"

The President: "I can't, under the Constitution."

Reporter: "Mr. President, will this Board have power to make decisions and all that, without referring them to you?"

The President: "Yes, sir."

Reporter: "Mr. President, you don't have to give the final approval?"

The President: "No, no, but believe me, if they make some kind of a decision which goes wrong, and I say that it is contrary to the national interest, I shall probably call them in and say, 'Here, here, what is this?' "[4]

Despite Roosevelt's disclaimers, it seemed reasonably certain that he was going to continue to exercise substantial control over the new organization. In this connection Donald M. Nelson has written of the new arrangement as follows: "The President's announcement of December 20, 1940, had informed us that he was going to run the new show just as he had run the headless NDAC. He was not going to cede or delegate any powers to any 'economic czar.' The new machine was to operate with co-pilots, a Director General and an Associate Director General—which apparently meant that the Boss would be the Super-Director General, just as he had been with NADC."[5]

To the Bureau of the Budget fell the chore of drafting an executive order for Roosevelt to issue which would embody the administrative set-up upon which he had decided. This proved to be an extremely difficult and tedious piece of work. More than a dozen proposed drafts were prepared for the President's consideration and for discussion and possible revision by the interested parties in the government. The most difficult part of the job was to set forth in clear and unequivocal terms the relationship which would exist between the Director General and the Associate Director General in regard to the administrative management of the new organization. The Budget Bureau was never able to work this out to Roosevelt's satisfaction in drafting the order and finally the President himself took a pencil and wrote into the final draft the following provision:

"The Director General, in association with the Associate Director General, and serving under the direction and supervision of the President, shall discharge and perform the administrative responsibilities and duties required to carry out the functions specified . . . subject to and in conformity with the policies and regulations (not inconsistent with such regulations as may be issued by the President) prescribed by the Office of Production Management."[6]

When Roosevelt issued the executive order[7] on January 7, 1941, he held a lengthy press conference at which he went over the order section by section to explain it to the news writers. As might have been expected, most of the questioning centered around the question of the relationship and relative authority of Knudsen and Hillman. To the dubious newspapermen, Roosevelt explained that the two men would exercise joint authority in directing the defense program. He said:

The President: "I suppose the easiest way to put it is that these four people—the Office of Production Management, Knudsen, Hillman, and the two Secretaries—fix the policy, and then Knudsen and Hillman carry it out, just like a law firm that has a case; say there are two partners, and they carry it out as a law firm. Anybody that knows anything about management will realize that that is the practical way to handle that kind of a matter, just like a law firm with two main partners."

Reporter: "Are they equals?"

The President: "That's not the point; they're a firm. Is a firm equals? I don't know. See what I mean? Roosevelt & O'Connor was a law firm in New York; there were just two partners. I don't know whether we were equal or not. Probably we might have disagreed in regard to a catch question of that kind; but we never had a dispute or an argument. . . ."

Reporter: "Why is it you don't want a single, responsible head?"

The President: "I have a single, responsible head; his name is Knudsen & Hillman."

Reporter: "Two heads."

The President: "No, that's one head. In other words, aren't you looking for trouble? Would you rather come to one law firm, or two?"

Reporter: "I don't think that's comparable."

The President: "Just the same thing, exactly. Wait until you run into trouble."

Reporter: "I would rather avoid trouble."

The President: "I think they will. They think they will—that's an interesting thing." [8]

Surprisingly enough Knudsen and Hillman did get along together much better in managing the program than most of the critics had anticipated. They apparently avoided any fundamental clashes over jurisdiction or irreconcilable conflicts regarding the direction the program was to go, and their joint positions at the head of the defense effort had a very substantial significance for the country in that it symbolized a national political coalition in a time of emergency.

The new organization was by no means received with great enthusiasm by all member of the Roosevelt Administration. On December 20, 1940—the day Roosevelt first publicly announced he was setting up the Office of Production Management, Harold Ickes wrote at length in his diary concerning his misgivings:

"I talked to the President about his defense setup. . . . He had made up his mind and was ready to announce a new group including Knudsen as director, Sidney Hillman as associate director, and Stimson and Knox as members. . . . When I suggested that Knox would be a better man in the key position than Knudsen, the President replied: 'But he is not a businessman.' My answer was that a man had to have some politics in him to run a government job successfully; that the President himself was able to conduct the biggest business in the world because he was a politician. I predicted that Knudsen would not be able to do the job successfully and then the President said, in effect, although I cannot quote his exact words, that this might be the way to solve the Knudsen and 'businessman' problem. My reply to this was that the price was altogether too high. However, since the President's mind was already made up in the matter, I did not labor the question.

"Considering the state of public opinion, and the demand for a businessman such as Knudsen for chairman of the defense activities, I suspect that the President adopted the only course that was open to him. Knudsen has been functioning on defense, he has had a tremendous newspaper buildup, and if the President had gone over his head and put someone else in charge, there would have been a tremendous uproar in all parts of the country. So the President really had no other option, nor could have done otherwise than he did originally when he brought Stettinius and Knudsen to Washington. Originally his hand was forced by the event of the coming campaign and, more recently, it was forced by the high estimation that Knudsen enjoys in the minds of the public—an estimation that in my judgment is grossly exaggerated. I do not believe that Knudsen can make the grade, but I hope that he can.'"

Shortly after, Ickes also reported in his diary about a conversation with Secretary of the Treasury Henry Morgenthau in which the

latter had told Ickes "that when the President recently set up his
Defense Commission, consisting of Knudsen, Hillman, Stimson, and
Knox, he wanted Henry and the Director of the Budget to be ex-
officio members. Henry refused because he did not want to be a
member of this commission when the blowup came. . . . and that,
sooner or later, there will be a blowup there." [10]

The powers vested in the Office of Production Management were
spelled out in the executive order as follows:

"a. Formulate and execute in the public interest all measures
needful and appropriate in order (1) to increase, accelerate, and
regulate the production and supply of materials, articles and equipment and the provision of emergency plant facilities and services
required for the national defense, and (2) to insure effective coordination of those activities of the several departments, corporations,
and other agencies of the Government which are directly concerned
therewith.

"b. Survey, analyze, and summarize for purposes of coordination
the stated requirements of the War and Navy and other departments
and agencies of the Government, and of foreign governments for
materials, articles, and equipment needed for defense.

"c. Advise with respect to the plans and schedules of the various
departments and agencies for the purchase of materials, articles, and
equipment required for defense, to coordinate the placement of major
defense orders and contracts and to keep informed of the progress
of the various programs of production and supply.

"d. Plan and take all lawful steps necessary to assure the provision
of an adequate supply of raw materials essential to the production
of finished products needed for defense.

"e. Formulate plans for the mobilization for defense of the production facilities of the Nation, and to take all lawful action necessary
to carry out such plans.

"f. Determine the adequacy of existing production facilities and to
assure their maximum use; and, when necessary, to stimulate and
plan the creation of such additional facilities and sources of production and supply as may be essential to increase and expedite defense
production.

"g. Determine when, to what extent, and in what manner priorities
shall be accorded to deliveries of material as provided in Section 2 (a)
of the Act entitled "An Act to Expedite National Defense and for
other Purposes," approved June 28, 1940. Deliveries of material shall

take priority, as provided in said Act, in accordance with determinations and the orders issued in pursuance thereof by the Office of Production Management.

"h. Perform the functions and exercise the authorities vested in the President by Section 9 of the Selective Training and Service Act of 1940." [11]

The last provision above referred to the power to place compulsory orders, which had been given to the President under the Selective Service Act of 1940, and which the President was now delegating to the Office of Production Management.

As further evidence that the President would probably continue to exercise considerable control over the new agency, despite his press conference remarks, was the fact that he prescribed in detail the internal organization of the Office of Production Management in his executive order. It was provided that the organization should function through three main divisions—a Division of Production, a Division of Purchases, and a Division of Priorities—with the director of each division to be appointed by the Office of Production Management with the approval of the President. [12] John D. Biggers of Libbey-Owens-Ford, who had served with Knudsen in the National Defense Advisory Commission, became head of Production, Donald M. Nelson headed Purchases, and Edward Stettinius, Jr. headed Priorities. Very shortly after, these three operating divisions were supplemented by the establishment of a Labor Division, headed by Sidney Hillman, and a Bureau of Research and Statistics, headed by Stacy May who had performed the same job for the National Defense Advisory Commission.

Although the authority and functions of the Office of Production Management were much more definitely stated and went considerably beyond those of the National Defense Advisory Commission in regard to production for defense purposes, the new agency was by no means unlimited and in fact there were sizable gaps in its powers which kept it from exercising full jurisdiction over the mobilization program. First of all, the Office of Production Management was charged only with the responsibility of production for defense; responsibility for civilian production was a significant omission in the administrative organization which had to be dealt with later. Secondly, responsibility for the determination of the amount of military production required remained in the hands of the War and Navy Departments and the Office of Production Management could only "survey, analyze, and summarize for purposes of coordination the stated requirements" of the military services. Roosevelt was questioned about this in his January 7, 1941, press conference and made it clear that this function was still in the jurisdiction of the military authorities:

Reporter: "Mr. President, as I understood the reading of your order, you said this agency—these two men—would fix policy; does that mean that in fixing policy they will decide what the Army and Navy, under the defense program, need?"

The President: "Oh, no; the Army and Navy are military things; the Army and Navy naturally would decide."[13]

A third gap was that the legal power to award contracts for military facilities and materials also was left vested in the Army and Navy Departments, although the Office of Production Management was empowered to advise concerning defense purchasing and to coordinate the placement of major defense orders and contracts. Nevertheless, in spite of these weaknesses, the Office of Production Management was in a position to stimulate and plan the construction and use of many additional "war-plants" and other productive facilities and the conversion of many non-essential factories to the production of defense materials.

On the same day that he established the Office of Production Management, Roosevelt also issued an administrative order "further defining the status and functions of the Office for Emergency Management." Originally when the Office for Emergency Management was activated on May 25, 1940, its functions and role were left very vague and general with only the duties specifically assigned to it of serving as a liaison between the President and the defense agencies and of assisting the President in the clearance of information with respect to the emergency."[14] Consequently, the new administrative order was designed to broaden, clarify, and make more specific the functions of the Office for Emergency Management, which were set forth as follows:

"(a) To advise and assist the President in the discharge of extraordinary responsibilities imposed upon him by any emergency arising out of war, the threat of war, imminence of war, flood, drought, or other condition threatening the public peace or safety.

"(b) To serve as a division of the Executive Office of the President, with such subdivisions as may be required, through which the President, during any emergency, may coordinate and supervise and, in appropriate cases, direct the activities of agencies, public or private, in relation thereto.

"(c) To serve as a channel of communication between such agencies and the President concerning emergency activities, to keep the President currently advised of their progress, to assemble and analyze information concerning additional measures that should be taken, and to assist in the preparation of recommendations for any necessary legislation.

"(d) To provide and maintain liaison during any such emergency with other divisions of the Executive Office of the President and with other agencies, public or private, for the purpose of bringing about maximum utilization and coordination of their services and facilities.

"(e) To advise and assist the President upon or before termination of any such emergency with respect to any measures that may be needful to facilitate a restoration of normal administrative relations and to ameliorate the consequences of the emergency.

"(f) To perform such other duties and functions with respect to any such emergency as the President may from time to time direct."[15]

The administrative order further provided for the coordination in the Office for Emergency Management of the work and activities of the Office of Production Management and the National Defense Advisory Commission which was still left with jurisdiction over the defense programs in the fields of agriculture, transportation, price control, and consumer protection following the creation of the Office of Production Management.

This, then, was the situation pertaining to the administrative organization as it had been developed to meet the expanding needs of national defense on January 20, 1941, as Roosevelt completed his second term as President and took the oath of office to start his third term. The Office of Production Management had been established to carry the industrial production program for defense forward into a stage of expanding operations from the previous stage which had been primarily one of planning and laying the foundations for future activities. By the creation of the National Defense Advisory Commission and the Office of Production Management the groundwork had been provided for the general type of administrative organization which was to be continued throughout the entire war.

However, there was still much unfinished business remaining to be taken care of in building an adequate defense program. One of the main difficulties which continued to plague the entire preparedness effort was the widespread disagreement as to what actually constituted an "adequate" defense program. Eight months after the launching of a substantial rearmament drive with the creation of the National Defense Advisory Commission, this fundamental question of *what* should be done remained almost as bothersome and controversial as the question of *how* the program could best be carried out. The need to organize for defense at a time when the country was at peace probably made it almost unavoidable that debates and controversies would rage as to the formulation of the government's policies, and would delay and influence the government's administrative activities.

Many administrative problems arose from the pulling and hauling which took place both in the government and in the country in connection with the establishment of the National Defense Advisory Commission and the Office of Production Management. Fundamentally these administrative problems of how to devise a proper organization for national defense were surface manifestations of the underlying political problems involved in maintaining the cooperation of all the many groups needed to support a national defense effort. Industry and labor were suspicious and jealous of each other, and each was afraid the other would get the upper hand in the defense program. The relationship between the armed services and those in charge of civilian non-military activities was always potentially a source of almost unlimited trouble. Consequently, Roosevelt's decisions and the administrative organization which he developed resulted from his attempts to maintain a balanced working alliance among the major special interest groups represented in the defense program. He had not allowed himself to be pushed prematurely against his will into centralizing the administrative authority over the entire defense program into the hands of one group, one agency, or certainly not into the hands of any one man other than himself. As a result, in the entire administrative organization for defense there was in January 1940 no single individual other than the President who had enough authority to make a major administrative decision with the equivalent authority to enforce its execution.[16]

The end of the second term, of course, did not bring an end to Roosevelt's adjustments of the administrative organization to meet the expanding needs of national defense. As circumstances developed and new factors entered into the defense picture, Roosevelt devised new administrative machinery to supplement that already in existence in dealing with the changing conditions. Or, on occasion, he terminated some agencies and transferred their functions, and usually their personnel, to some other place in the administrative organization. Such adjustments and changes went on frequently throughout both the defense period prior to the war and the period of the war itself, and certainly one of the major hallmarks of Roosevelt's administrative management of the defense program was its flexibility. Old agencies were sometimes merged and gradually transformed into new agencies while some new agencies were created outright for the purpose of performing specific tasks and meeting pressing needs.

A brief outline of just the major top-level administrative agencies which Roosevelt established after his second term—and through which he continued to try to provide the over-all direction and coordination needed for the defense program—will indicate the evolutionary and pragmatic nature of the program, as well as its flexibility. To provide a detailed account of all the multitudinous developments in the administrative organization during the period of World War II goes beyond the limited scope of this present study and would merit and probably require another study of greater length than this one, if dealt with thoroughly. Suffice it to say here that Roosevelt established a long series of major agencies after January 1941 to help him handle the various aspects of the defense program. In the way in which he created these agencies he demonstrated for the most part his strong reluctance to delegate extensive authority and his desire to maintain the general direction of affairs in his own hands as much as possible.

Little by little, however, Roosevelt was pushed by the pressure of circumstances and the sheer weight of administrative necessity to yield some of his authority in gradually increasing amounts to the individuals he appointed to head some of the wartime agencies. The constant adjustment of these agencies and the men who headed them to each other and to Roosevelt on a sort of survival of the fittest basis eventually did culminate in late May 1943 in Roosevelt's creation of a true super-coordinating agency, the Office of War Mobilization. To this agency, under the direction of former Supreme Court Justice James F. Byrnes, who had earlier been for many years one of the leading members of the United States Senate, Roosevelt did delegate very extensive powers of coordination over most of the civilian aspects of the war effort.

In the somewhat over two years of his third term which elapsed before he reached the decision to establish the Office of War Mobilization, Roosevelt had utilized four other top-level agencies in addition to the Office of Production Management in trying to exercise over-all administrative direction and control of the emergency programs. The first of these was the Office of Price Administration and Civilian Supply, established on April 11, 1941, and designed to fill the gap left by the Office of Production Management, which concentrated entirely on industrial production for defense purposes, by providing for the regulation of production and allocation of supplies for civilian uses. Under the leadership of Price Administrator Leon Henderson, this new agency was an amalgamation resulting from the merger of the functions of the National Defense Advisory Commission's Adviser on Price Stabilization (Henderson) and Adviser on Consumer Protection (Harriet Elliott).

It was not long before serious conflicts broke out between the Office of Production Management and the Office of Price Administration and Civilian Supply over the jurisdictional lines separating the two agencies and over fundamental policy differences as to how much the production of civilian supplies would have to be slashed in order to guarantee the necessary level of production of defense items. The Office of Price Administration and Civilian Supply under Henderson took an urgent approach that civilian production should be cut stringently while the Office of Production Management under the influence of Knudsen and other business leaders took the position that the cuts in civilian production recommended by the Office of Price Administration and Civilian Supply were too severe and beyond what was necessary. This conflict between those who favored an "all-out" defense effort and those who didn't became quite intense by the summer of 1941 as described in the following passage by Donald M. Nelson:

"There were those who were convinced that total war was ahead for the United States, and that we were arming not only to help the nations with which we sympathized but to preserve our own country by strong, aggressive action. They were sometimes called 'expansionists' or 'all-outers.' They were for the quick conversion of industry, a longer-range policy for the accumulation of raw-material stockpiles, a firmer and deeper organization of the economy for war. On this side, Leon Henderson and I and our teams lined up. It also included some of the so-called New Dealers, the economists and statisticians and 'planners' and perhaps a few of the long-suffering 'professors.'

"Opposed to this group were men of equal sincerity who, in almost all cases, were heartily pro-Ally, but who thought that we could avoid a shooting war and that there was no need to shake our economy apart in anticipation of an emergency which would probably not occur. This frame of mind, which pervaded most government agencies, prevented the accumulation from foreign sources of commodity reserves which were still obtainable in quantities sufficient to meet our needs in whole or in part. The majority opinion in RFC advocated bargaining and going slow in the expenditure of the kind of money which would have been necessary. In OPM itself this school of thought not only retarded the importation of certain materials which were necessary in the processing of vital products such as steel and aluminum, but it also pursued a cautious course in the expansion of our manufacturing facilities."[17]

In addition, other strong pressures bearing upon the question of the priorities to be assigned for the allocation of American defense production were greatly intensified by the enactment of legislation for the Lend-Lease program on March 11, 1941,[18] and by the fact that Russia was brought under the program following the German invasion into Russian territory on June 22, 1941. All of these factors raised the fundamental question of what kind of additional administrative machinery could be devised to take into account the conflicting requirements for American military needs, for Lend-Lease, and for civilian supplies. It was clear that some new approach was necessary to establish methods of determining priorities among these various needs and to integrate and correlate the methods of allocating a limited amount of supplies among an almost unlimited number of demands.

As a result of these diverse ingredients, and following strong recommendations of the Director of the Bureau of the Budget, Harold Smith, and of Bernard Baruch, Chairman of the War Industries Board of World War I, that the control over production and priorities for both military and civilian needs should be further centralized, Roosevelt decided to create a new policy agency superimposed over both the Office of Production Management and the Office of Price Administration and Civilian Supply. This was the seven-member Supply Priorities and Allocations Board, established on August 28, 1941.[19] This Board was composed of the Director General and Associate Director General of the Office of Production Management, William S. Knudsen and Sidney Hillman respectively, Secretary of War

Henry L. Stimson, Secretary of the Navy Frank Knox, Price Administrator Leon Henderson, the Special Assistant to the President supervising the Lend-Lease Program, Harry Hopkins, and Vice President Henry Wallace as Chairman. Donald M. Nelson was named as the Executive Director. A little later in the year, Secretary of Commerce Jesse Jones was added to the Board as the supervisor of the Reconstruction Finance Corporation which administered much of the funds for constructing new defense plants, importing essential materials, etc.

In establishing the Supply Priorities and Allocations Board, Roosevelt was once again motivated strongly by a desire not to make the new organization a clear-cut victory for either of the contending factions, or for any particular individual or point of view. And he still was not ready to appoint any one person as the over-all director or coordinator of the defense effort, even though Baruch had strongly urged him to centralize authority in one man.[20]

Under terms of the executive order creating it, the Supply Priorities and Allocation Board was given power to make policy decisions on dividing the available supply of materials among military needs, Lend-Lease needs, and civilian needs. It was also enabled to determine the policies relating to the allocation of supplies among the various civilian industries and users within the United States. However the final authority to determine the distribution of all finished military production, such as planes, ships, tanks, and guns, remained in the President's hands. A White House press release issued along with the executive order creating the Supply Priorities and Allocations Board made it apparent that Roosevelt intended to retain a sizable amount of authority in his own grip as it stressed that the Board would follow the general policies enunciated by the President and would have no power to decide upon the division of finished materials.[21]

Despite its limitations of authority and its cumbersome organizational structure, the Supply Priorities and Allocations Board was able to accomplish some quite significant achievements. It has been characterized by Donald Nelson as follows: "SPAB was certainly an administrative anomaly, even for Washington, yet it worked surprisingly well, and during its brief life it took, in a number of vitally important, far-reaching cases, action which made possible the amazingly successful war production program that came into being after Pearl Harbor."[22] The fact that it was constituted as a top-level policy and coordinating agency without any direct operating responsibilities itself undoubtedly contributed to its success. For the first time during the defense effort, a centralized planning approach was adopted. The Supply Priorities and Allocations Board was able to act as a central agency for making decisions to be carried out by the various operating agencies such as the Office of Production Management and the Office of Price Administration which were subordinate to it. Although from a strictly administrative standpoint, the Supply Priorities and Allocations Board left much to be desired, it was nevertheless a most important step in bringing together in one agency diverse elements of the defense program which had differing ideas as to how the program should be managed. Gradually they were learning to work together cooperatively if not always harmoniously.

This administrative arrangement was the one which remained in effect on December 7, 1941, when the United States was plunged actively into the war by the Japanese attack on Pearl Harbor. Although it had worked surprisingly well, to the dismay of some of the President's critics, the Supply Priorities and Allocation Board's lack of sufficient authority and its cumbersome administrative structure centered attention on its weaknesses and inadequacies once the country was at war. There were renewed demands and urgings in Congress and out for the appointment of a "czar" over all defense activities and a substantial amount of dissatisfaction was expressed in Congress and in the press about the slowness and delay in building the war production program. It was obvious, of course, that with the country's actual participation in the war the production effort would have to be accelerated substantially and that the system of controls would have to be expanded and the administrative organization more centralized and better coordinated than previously.

Even before Pearl Harbor, Roosevelt had been thinking seriously about appointing a single top-level administrator over the entire defense effort. Prior to setting up the Supply Priorities and Allocations Board, he had given lengthy consideration to the possibility of appointing Associate Justice William O. Douglas of the Supreme Court to such a job.[23] And according to a memorandum written by Harry Hopkins on January 14, 1942, the President had continued to think of this possibility during the intervening months:

"For the past three months the President has been considering the appointment of a single person to direct war production but he never could find the right person. He discussed every conceivable possibility and played seriously with the idea of getting Bill Douglas off the Supreme Court and, in fact, talked to Douglas about it but Douglas never had much enthusiasm for it."[24]

Five weeks after Pearl Harbor, on January 16, 1942, Roosevelt issued an executive order establishing th War Production Board, with supervision over the entire war production program and with all of the President's authority to make final decisions on matters of production, materials, procurement, priorities, and allocation vested in the chairman, Donald M. Nelson. The Office of Production Management and the Supply Priorities and Allocations Board were abolished, and their duties and personnel transferred to the new agency, while the Army and Navy Munitions Board was ordered to report to the President thereafter through the chairman of the War Production Board.[25]

The authority delegated to Nelson constituted Roosevelt's greatest delcagtion of authority since he became President in 1933. All of the powers given the new agency were centered in Nelson's hands as the Board established in the executive order was purely advisory to the chairman in nature and served primarily to continue to bring together for a meeting each week to exchange information the heads of the Departments of War, Navy, and Commerce, the Vice President, the Price Administrator, and Harry Hopkins as the representative of the White House—the same men who had previously constituted the Supply Priorities and Allocations Board.

The executive order creating the War Production Board gave Nelson powers which were extensive enough to encompass practically all aspects of the country's domestic war activities. In most ways the power conferred on Nelson was not much less than that eventually delegated by Roosevelt in May 1943 to James F. Byrnes as director of the Office of War Mobilization. As of January 1942, it appears that Roosevelt finally had overcome sufficiently his reluctance to appoint one man over the entire war production program that he was willing to delegate into Nelson's hands adequate and relatively unreserved authority to direct, control, and coordinate most of the home-front war activities. Unfortunately, this power and authority given to the War Production Board and Nelson was dissipated, diffused, and diluted before too long so that before the end of the year the War Production Board was no longer regarded as the definite superior to all of the other war agencies and Nelson was no longer the supreme head of all civilian war work.

These developments were due to a variety of factors, but probably the most important were Nelson's own limited conception of his job and the role of the War Production Board which led him to surrender many of his powers to other agencies and individuals, and Roosevelt's tendency as time went on—possibly as a consequence of Nelson's attitude and failure to exercise full authority—to cease regarding the War Production Board as the one supreme super-agency over all of the war production program. Increasingly, the President came to look upon the War Production Board as just one more war agency on a relatively equal plane with several other war agencies. Instead of Nelson and the War Production Board settling top-level jurisdictional conflicts and providing over-all coordinative authority for the other agencies, Roosevelt found himself still having to do this with great frequency, with many of the disputes involving the War Production Board as one of the contesting parties among which he had to act as umpire. Rather than urging Nelson to fulfill the extensive authority which had been delegated to him, it appears that Roosevelt went along with Nelson's limited approach to his job. This meant, of course, that more decisions and more settlements of disputes would inevitably have to be made by the President.

Despite the intelligence, ability, and vigor which Nelson had convincingly demonstrated in his previous defense jobs in the National Defense Advisory Commission, the Office of Production Management, and the Supply Priorities and Allocations Board, which led Roosevelt to select him from among numerous other potential candidates for the job,[28] he was by temperament and viewpoint perhaps not so well suited as he might have been for the responsibilities of serving as the supreme head of the entire war production program. This can be seen from the way he described his conception of the chairmanship of the War Production Board:

"As interpreted and executed by me, it was not the one-man job conceived by the President when the Board was created. The economic power vested in me at that time was potentially greater than that ever held by any other civilian, except a wartime President. The records will show that of my own initiative I shed controls and authorities not directly germane to my principal function (which was war production) as rapidly as I could be sure that they had been placed in competent hands. This was done not to escape responsibility, but to allocate responsibility in such a way that the administrative capacity of no one person—including myself—would be spread so thin that it would lose its tensile strength. . . . I know I was criticized for whittling down my own job, but that is the kind of criticism I like."[27]

There is no doubt, of course, but that Nelson faced an exceedingly difficult task and one that inevitably would subject him to lots of criticism. The competing demands for the limited production and increasingly scarce resources of the country made it certain that a substantial amount of conflict was bound to occur and that the head of the War Production Board would be caught in the middle by pressure from all sides. However, Nelson's divesting himself of many of the powers delegated to him and placing them in the hands of others tended to create numerous situations of overlapping authority and conflicts of interest. His control of rationing, which he transferred to the Office of Price Administration in January soon after the creation of the War Production Board was one of the first powers which he gave away. This was to remain a major source of friction throughout the rest of the war. In April, Roosevelt offered Nelson the chance to have a new manpower control agency placed under his direction in the War Production Board but Nelson refused and allowed the War Manpower Commission, under the direction of Paul V. McNutt, to be established as a completely separate and independent organization. Some time after, in the late summer of 1942, Roosevelt established an Office of the Rubber Director, headed by William M. Jeffers, and placed it in the War Production Board. Nelson, however, announced that Jeffers would exercise all of the authority given to the War Production Board over the rubber program and would issue final orders to all government agencies concerned with rubber.

Shortly after the establishment of the War Production Board, Nelson had also begun to yield some of his powers to the military services. In agreements between the War Production Board and the Army and Navy Departments in March 1942, Nelson conceded to the armed services the right to continue to exercise their procurement authority, with the War Production Board exercising only general policy and planning functions. These agreements did not eliminate serious jurisdictional conflicts as the armed services duplicated many of the War Production Board's activities to such a degree that disputes were certain to occur. As time went on such disputes became more frequent and bitter.[28]

The disputes between the armed services and the War Production Board were by no means the only ones raging between the leaders of the various war agencies. In fact the public airing of such controversies became so bad that Roosevelt was moved on August 21, 1942, to issue a public letter to all of his agency heads stating that he would no longer countenance such behavior. He wrote, in part, as follows:

"In dealing with the many complex war problems which we face today, it is unavoidable that there be wide differences of opinion between agencies of the Federal Government—opinions sincerely and honestly held. However, too often in recent months, responsible officials of the Government have made public criticism of other agencies of the Government; and have made public statements based either on inadequate information or on failure to appreciate all the aspects of a complex subject which is only partially within their jurisdiction.

"This is inadvisable at any time. But in times of war it is particularly contrary to public policy. It contributes only to the confusion of the public, which naturally does not know what to believe on an involved issue when it gets different stories on successive days from officials of equal standing, though not necessarily of equal understanding.

"Such divergencies, especially when coupled, as they often are, with express or implied criticisms of other officials, are a direct and serious handicap to the prosecution of the war. Officials divert to quarrels with each other the time and energy they ought to be devoting to fighting the enemy. The people, confused by these contradictory voices, are apt to obtain the false impression that the Government as a whole is uncertain as to its objectives and general method and that it does not know its job.

"This feeling is of course pounced upon, exploited, and intensified by opponents of our war effort. Our enemies use this raw material of discord provided for them by men who ought to be making trouble for the enemy and not for one another.

"These differences between agencies often deal with matters of fact which can be harmonized by fuller investigation, or questions of policy which should be adjusted by conference between the agencies or by reference to me as the responsible head of the Government. Disagreements either as to fact or policy should not be publicly aired, but are to be submitted to me by the appropriate heads of the conflicting agencies. The policy of the Government should be announced by me, as the responsible head thereof. Disagreement as to facts can be resolved, if necessary, by investigations and surveys directed by me.

"Will you please see to it that your particular department and its various bureaus and divisions comply with these instructions."[29]

Roosevelt's admonition resulted in only a temporary respite in the fussing, feuding, and fighting. Nelson either did not try to exercise sufficient authority over such disputes, or he was not able to do so, which pointed up the fact that short of the President himself, who was seriously over-burdened with problems of military strategy and international affairs connected with the war, there was no one available in the government with sufficient power and stature to settle these arguments.

Roosevelt took steps to alleviate this situation partially on October 3, 1942, when he set up the Office of Economic Stabilization. The executive order creating the new agency set forth its powers as follows:

"The Director, with the approval of the President, shall formulate and develop a comprehensive national economic policy relating to the control of civilian purchasing power, prices, rents, wages, salaries, profits, rationing, subsidies, and all related matters—all for the purpose of preventing avoidable increases in the cost of living, cooperating in minimizing the unnecessary migration of labor from one business, industry, or region to another, and facilitating the prosecution of the war. To give effect to this comprehensive national economic policy the Director shall have power to issue directives on policy to the Federal departments and agencies concerned."[30]

The President appointed as director of the Office of Economic Stabilization Justice James F. Byrnes, who resigned from the Supreme Court to accept the new position, and announced that Byrnes' office would be located in the White House. Although officially Byrnes' jurisdiction extended only to questions involved in economic stabilization, or the fight against inflation, Roosevelt rather quickly let it be known that he was going to rely on Byrnes to handle personally some of the tasks of top-level coordination and settling of disputes which fell beyond the official compass of Byrnes' office. According to Byrnes' later account, Roosevelt told him at the time of his appointment:

"Jimmy, most of my time is devoted to the consideration of problems intimately and directly connected with the conduct of the war. It just isn't possible for me to devote sufficient time to the domestic problems. All these new agencies we have had to create mean an increasing number of jurisdictional conflicts which come to me for decision. I want you to settle these conflicts for me; I'll issue an executive order giving you power to settle them, and I'll let it be known that your decision is my decision."[31]

As a result of the nature of Byrnes' appointment, his location in the White House, and Roosevelt's public exhibition of confidence and support for Byrnes on numerous occasions, it became obvious that Byrnes had replaced Nelson as the top official in the home-front war program. Whenever Byrnes dealt with matters in the areas of War Production Board responsibility, as frequently happened, it became known that the final judgment of the Director of Economic Stabilization would prevail rather than that of the Chairman of the War Production Board.

The Office of Economic Stabilization had extensive powers, great prestige, and strong Presidential support so that it was able to do a very significant job of coordination in the President's behalf. However, its effectiveness was limited by the fact that officially it was charged with responsibility only for those parts of the war program having to do with economic stabilization. Although Byrnes, with Roosevelt's approval, sometimes ranged beyond his formal area of responsibility, he was given only a part of the total coordination job to handle so that he was by no means in charge of coordination of the whole civilian war effort. As a result, although Byrnes helped substantially in reducing the internal conflicts and jurisdictional disputes bothering the President, such conflicts were by no means ended by his presence but continued to break out virulently with considerable frequency in late 1942 and early 1943.

Undoubtedly the most publicized and bitter of the disputes during this period was a running feud which seemed to flare up intermittently between Vice President Henry A. Wallace, in his capacity as Chairman of the Board of Economic Warfare, and Secretary of Commerce Jesse Jones, in his role as head of the Reconstruction Finance Corporation. Roosevelt had created the Board of Economic Warfare (originally under the name of Economic Defense Board) on July 30, 1941, to control all exports from the United States (other than Lend-Lease) and to purchase essential materials in foreign countries to meet our own needs or to keep such materials from falling into the hands of the enemy.[32] The financial aspects of these activities, however, were to be carried out through subsidiaries of the Reconstruction Finance Corporation which were in charge of the disbursement of funds, fiscal accounting, and the acceptance and delivery of the materials. Such a separation of financial control from the determination of what was to be purchased seemed likely to provoke differences, and this likelihood was certainly in no way diminished by the radically differing personalities and viewpoints of the two powerful and ambitious men heading the agencies, Wallace and Jones.

In December 1942, the Senate Banking and Currency Committee released to the press the testimony which the two men had presented before an executive session of the Committee. The account was replete with violent charges and counter-charges.[33] Jones complained that Wallace was exercising undue interference in RFC matters and that the RFC was no longer allowed to prevent unwise loans for foreign purchases which the Board of Economic Warfare certified as strategically necessary. Wallace, in turn, charged that the RFC had excessively delayed approving the funds for many of the projects which the Board of Economic Warfare had authorized, and that the RFC tended to judge such matters primarily from the point of view of normal, peacetime business practices and sound fiscal responsibility rather than as necessary emergency measures in a program of economic warfare. This difference in views was reflected clearly by a statement made by Jones that "The Reconstruction Finance Corporation does not pay $2 for something it can buy for $1."[34] In the eyes of Wallace, this may have been excellent business practice but it was not the way to engage successfully in economic warfare.[35]

In May and June 1943, the dispute erupted publicly again with first Wallace and then Jones releasing to the press a series of charges which revealed the depth and seriousness of the differences between them. Shortly thereafter the exasperated President eventually removed from both Wallace and Jones their respective responsibilities as Chairman of the Board of Economic Warfare and head of the Reconstruction Finance Corporation, and created a new Office of Economic Warfare to consolidate all of the functions of the two agencies in regard to arranging and financing foreign purchases and imports. Final authority for the coordination of these activities with the other departments and agencies of the government was vested in the hands of Justice Byrnes.[36]

Although the Wallace-Jones fight was the most flamboyant and serious, it was by no means unique. During late 1942 and the first few months of 1943 there was a spate of jurisdictional battles involving several of the leading personages of the administration. Among those who figured most prominently in one or more of these

fights were Under Secretary of War Robert Patterson, Under Sec-
retary of the Navy James Forrestal, Secretary of the Interior Harold
Ickes, Rubber Director William M. Jeffers, War Information Director
Elmer Davis, the Office of Price Administrator Prentis Brown, War
Manpower Director Paul V. McNutt, Selective Service Director Gen-
eral Lewis Hershey, War Production Board Vice Chairman Ferdinand
Eberstadt, and Chairman Donald Nelson.[37]

Many of these disputes grew out of duplication and overlapping
functions of various agencies and intensive competition for resources
which were in short supply. In addition, they frequently reflected
personality conflicts of busy men who were both able and aggressive
in trying to meet the responsibilities of their positions, and who often
could not do so without infringing upon the jurisdictions of others.

Because of these conflicts and disputes, an increasing amount of
Congressional criticism of the war organization was expressed. Much
of it was aimed at the failure of the War Production Board to exercise
the authority originally bestowed upon it and the corresponding
tendency to disperse its authority among numerous other subordinate
agencies. Many of the Congressional criticisms called for the establishment of a strong centralized authority over the entire war production, procurement, and allocations program. For example, the
Committee headed by Senator Harry S. Truman, the Special Committee Investigating the Defense Program, issued a report early in
May 1943 in which it was stated that the principal difficulty in the
war program was caused by the continued dilution of the original
broad powers given to Nelson. The report concluded, "Today discussion of the over-all legal authority of the WPB is mere pedantry.
Although the authority may exist, it has not been exercised."[38] Shortly
thereafter, the Senate Military Affairs Committee's Subcommittee on
War Mobilization reported as follows:

"The Executive Order establishing the War Production Board
clearly intended to set up a central agency fully empowered to
mobilize the Nation's resources for war. . . . It would appear, however,
that most of these powers were delegated to the various agencies
which now compete with one another in such a way as to engender
conflicts inimical to maximum production." [39]

In view of these Congressional criticisms and the sentiment which
was gradually developing in Congress in favor of establishing a new
supreme war agency by legislation, and in view of the generally good
results which had been obtained on a limited scale by the Office of

Economic Stabilization under the leadership of Byrnes, Roosevelt decided in late May 1943 to proceed to set up the Office of War Mobilization with Byrnes as its director, as mentioned earlier. The Office of War Mobilization was based to considerable extent upon the Office of Economic Stabilization model in its organization and methods of operation with Byrnes proceeding to act in much the same way as before except that now he had jurisdiction over the entire civilian war mobilization program.

In his new position, Byrnes was quickly labeled by the press as the "Assistant President," and he certainly did merit that title more than anyone else who ever served with Roosevelt. However, his role was never that of a general "Chief of Staff" to the President or an all-around "Presidential Deputy," as Sherman Adams later became for President Dwight Eisenhower, for Byrnes's authority extended only to the home front, or the civilian parts of the government's activities, and he had little to do with the administration of military or foreign affairs matters, which Roosevelt continued to reserve to himself.

The creation of the Office of War Mobilization was a recognition by Roosevelt that he could no longer give sufficient personal direction to all of the emergency agencies. Circumstances had eventually forced him to realize that he had to turn over to someone else in large measure the coordinating role which he had been carrying on with diminishing success as the developments of the war confronted him with increasing military and international problems which pre-empted his time. The Office of War Mobilization marked the first time that Roosevelt actually deviated from his practice of providing the top-level coordination of the administrative organization himself, through his own office, and instead relied for such coordination upon a sub-Presidential but supra-departmental coordinator who would act in the President's name. The pressures of the war had become so demanding that Roosevelt finally had to admit that he could no longer supervise adequately both the foreign and the domestic affairs of the country.[40]

Roosevelt continued to operate with Byrnes as his top-level co-ordinating assistant over the whole administrative organization until only ten days before the President's death on April 12, 1945.[41] On October 3, 1944, however, Congress saw fit to expand the title of the Office of War Mobilization to Office of War Mobilization and Reconversion when the agency was given statutory recognition and was assigned new responsibilities of planning for the problems involved

in reconversion and demobilization.⁴² Byrnes stayed on in the White
House as the Director of the Office of War Mobilization and Reconversion and there was no disturbance in the continuity of operations
between the Office of War Mobilization and the Office of War Mobilization and Reconversion. The transition was an easy and undramatic
one because of the carry-over of all of the top personnel who kept on
doing the same things that they had been doing all along. In fact,
the Office of War Mobilization and Reconversion was really a new
agency in name only, except for the addition of the reconversion
responsibilities, and it continued to serve Roosevelt just as before in
coordinating the activities of all the civilian agencies of the government.

In retrospect, as one reviews the developments Roosevelt brought
about in the administrative organization to meet the expanding needs
of national defense, the period from May 1940 until almost the end
of the second term in January 1941 can properly be thought of as
mainly a planning stage in war preparations in which plans were
developed and launched in the basic fields of industrial production,
labor and manpower, prices, agriculture, materials, transportation,
and consumer problems. Throughout this period, the new administrative organization for defense remained loosely knit and flexible with
Roosevelt retaining securely in his own hands the reins of control
to such an extent that he was subjected to a considerable amount of
criticism from many who would have favored a more centralized
organization with much of the power over defense matters delegated
by Roosevelt to others.

Despite these criticisms and despite the loose and amorphous
administrative structure during this period, the administrative foundations were nevertheless effectively laid for all of the later developments in the defense and war production programs. The National
Defense Advisory Commission was the embryonic agency from which
practically all of the later defense agencies evolved. The component
parts of the entire defense program were included in the Advisory
Commission and the descent of almost all of the later organizations
could be traced back to its seven original divisions. The Advisory
Commission also clearly forecast the general outlines of the type of
flexible and easily adjustable administrative organization which
Roosevelt would use throughout the war, modifying and adapting it
to changing circumstances as they developed.

By the end of his second term Roosevelt had probably moved ahead about as far and as fast as sharply divided public opinion, an often hostile Congress, and several major political considerations of importance in the year 1940 would allow him to go in preparing for national defense and developing an administrative organization for that purpose. He was following an evolutionary and pragmatic procedure in keeping with the march of events on the domestic political scene and with the intensifying pressures of world affairs. As the second term ended, extensive planning had been done for very substantial increases in the industrial military preparedness of the country, even including the possible eventuality of active American participation in World War II. To a considerable degree, a basic groundwork for later developments in the defense program had been provided, but some rather glaring shortcomings and weaknesses had become apparent which would need to be dealt with before the defense program could successfully move ahead into an all-out operational stage. The administrative structure was too cumbersome and divided, with too much overlapping and duplication of functions and responsibilities. There was need for a considerably more centralized and integrated structure which could proceed to operate in a relatively unified way without a large number of internal conflicts and jurisdictional disputes.

In the first part of 1941, Roosevelt tried to lessen some of the shortcomings by the establishment of the Office of Production Management, the Office of Price Administration and Civilian Supply, and the Supply Priorities and Allocations Board. Although the military production of the country expanded greatly as the defense program moved into the operating stage with rapid strides during 1941, the above administrative agencies created by Roosevelt were only partially successful in providing satisfactory administrative mechanisms for the direction and control of the defense activities. The evolution of the administrative structure had been inextricably intertwined with Roosevelt's problem of providing effective political leadership in a time of crisis, and the closely related problem of trying to maintain proper balance and support among the different elements of the country and among the different interests represented in the defense program. Because of these factors Roosevelt had not thought it advisable to move any faster than he had done in centralizing the administrative system along more hierarchical lines. As the program expanded, however, this lack of a unified administrative system pointed up very clearly the pressing need for constant top-level coordination of all the diverse parts of the system if they were to work together effectively.

True to his nature and his conception of the Presidency, Roosevelt did not wish to centralize authority too much in the hands of others, but wished to retain the main control over top-level coordination as much as possible in his own hands. He did this as long as he could, until changing circumstances, the sheer pressure of events, and the magnitude of the demands made upon his time and attention by the war forced him to do otherwise. He wanted to continue to be his own chief coordinator, as he had been through the crisis of the depression and during the remainder of his Presidency prior to the defense emergency. As he made clear in his press conference of December 20, 1940, when he announced the establishment of the Office of Production Management, he was reluctant to delegate his authority because he could not, under the Constitution, delegate any of his responsibility. As long as he was to be responsible personally for the conduct of the Presidency, he preferred to exercise the authority of the Presidency personally as well.

As we know, Roosevelt did eventually delegate very broad authority to coordinate the entire civilian war program, first to Donald M. Nelson as Chairman of the War Production Board, and later to James F. Byrnes as Director of the Office of War Mobilization. In the first instance, the authority was so dispersed and dissipated by Nelson that in practice Roosevelt continued to serve as his own coordinator much as before. With Byrnes, of course, this was not the case. He served most effectively from October 1943 until April 1945 to relieve Roosevelt from having to take care personally of a great many conflicts and disputes arising from the war program which otherwise would have ended up squarely at the President's desk. This also served unquestionably to improve the administration of the war program by providing both quicker decisions and decisions based upon fuller consideration of the issues and interests involved than if everything had been forced to wait for the consideration and decision of Roosevelt himself in the very limited time at his disposal.

Chapter X

ROOSEVELT'S ENDURING INFLUENCE

We come now to the task of attempting to answer the last of the nine questions which were set forth in the first chapter: What were some of the enduring effects which Roosevelt had upon the role of the President as the chief administrator of the executive branch? Recognizing that it still may be too early to make definitive and final judgments as to the full effects of Roosevelt's years as President upon the administrative organization, it nevertheless seems possible to advance at least a few conclusions as to several effects which may be regarded as significant.

Perhaps the most obvious effect of Roosevelt's Presidency was the tremendous expansion which took place in the size of the administrative organization. This, of course, was the inevitable accompaniment of an equally tremendous expansion in the range of activities of the national government. Although this growth took place to some degree throughout his years as President, it was most marked during two particular periods: First, during his first two years in the White House when he sharply increased both the functions and the number of administrative agencies in his efforts to combat the severe economic depression, and again after 1940 when he did the same thing in developing the national defense system of the country following the outbreak of war in Europe. Between his first inauguration in 1933 and his untimely death in 1945, Roosevelt literally doubled the size of the administrative organization through the creation of many new agencies, commissions, boards, bureaus, and other miscellaneous forms of organization.[1]

As we have seen, Roosevelt followed the policy of setting up a host of new, specialized agencies separate from the regular departments to deal with both the emergency conditions of the depression and of the national defense and war programs. He seems to have regarded such independent agencies as almost an essential mechanism in dealing with emergencies. He was well aware that the creation of so many such agencies would complicate his job as the administrative head of the government because of the increased difficulty of coordinating the activities of the new agencies with those of the regular departments, and because of the added number of administrative subordinates who would have to report directly to the President. He felt, however, that a number of advantages, which have been discussed earlier, more than outweighed such disadvantages. As a result, the number of independent agencies and the over-all size of the administrative organization grew by very sizable proportions.

This expansion in the number of agencies was also accompanied by a correspondingly large increase in the number of personnel working for the government. When Roosevelt became President in 1933, the national government employed slightly less than 600,000 persons. By 1939 the number had grown to 920,310 as a result of the additions during the New Deal years, and in 1940, as the expansion of the national defense program was getting underway, the number of employees advanced to slightly over one million for the first time in the history of the country. By the time Pearl Harbor plunged the country into war, the number had increased to over a million and a half, and by 1943 it had soared to over three million. An all-time peak was reached in January 1945 when a total of 3,375,000 civilians were employed by the Federal Government.[3]

This great increase in the size of the government, as reflected in the expansion in the number of administrative agencies and the number of governmental personnel, has had a permanent influence upon the Presidency, of course, and upon the administrative conduct of all of Roosevelt's successors in the White House. It was impossible to return to anything resembling pre-New Deal and pre-World War II standards. Although government employment was curtailed sharply after World War II, it has never fallen to less than two million persons under any of the Presidents following Roosevelt, in contrast to the less than 600,000 of March 1933 when he took office. Following Roosevelt, "Big Government" was here to stay, with all of its implications for the problems of administrative organization and coordination. All of the subsequent Presidents have inevitably found it necessary to conduct the administrative work of the Presidency on something of a Rooseveltian "model" because of the government's sheer size and complexity and its degree of involvement in all aspects of American life.

Even President Dwight D. Eisenhower, as unlike Roosevelt in outlook, manner, training, and Presidential "style" as any man could be, found that he had to operate the executive branch with much the same scope of activities and on much the same scale as had Roosevelt and President Harry S. Truman, despite the fact that he had come into office strongly committed to effecting substantial reductions in the Federal Government's functions, size, and costs. Although he was subjected to continuing Congressional demands from members of his own party for reducing the number of people on the government payroll, Eisenhower found it necessary to retain over two million employees in the Federal service throughout his Presidency, and as he left office the number had grown to almost two and a third million. In addition, it had seemed essential for him to present the biggest budget and accumulate the biggest budget-deficit of any peace time administration up to that time. Subsequently the more activist-oriented and problem-plagued administrations of Presidents John F. Kennedy and Lyndon B. Johnson, which seemed more directly reminiscent of Roosevelt's years in office, have not witnessed any diminution in the size of the administrative organization or the number of government personnel employed, with the latter gradually ranging upward from two and a third million to approximately two and a half million persons.

A second significant effect which Roosevelt had upon the administrative organization, but one which is not so readily obvious as the one previously discussed, was the substantial amount of structural integration which he accomplished. In trying to improve the President's administrative management of the executive branch, it is possible to proceed in two ways. Either the organizational structure can be better integrated by combining all of the administrative agencies and functions together under relatively few line departments, with the President then dealing directly with the department heads and relying primarily on them to aid him in coordinating all the activities of their subordinate divisions and branches. Or specific functions can be placed in specialized, individual agencies out from under the regular departments and responsible directly to the President, with improvements being made in the staff facilities and services available to the President to assist him in coordinating the activities of the departments and agencies through his own office. In other words, structural integration and functional coordination may be thought of as alternative possibilities to use in attempting to provide better management of the administrative organization.

Perhaps Roosevelt devoted considerably more attention to trying to improve the coordination of the various parts of the executive branch than he did to accomplishing its structural integration. The important fact should not be overlooked, however, that at different times he tried to do both. In the years 1933 to 1936 he created many new agencies to administer the New Deal programs and he made some attempts through use of the Executive Council and the National Emergency Council to provide administrative mechanisms for improved coordination. At the same time, he also made some efforts to improve the government's structural integration by consolidating, transferring, and eliminating a considerable number of agencies and functions under the broad reorganization authority which he had been granted by Congress from 1933 to 1935.

It was during the years from 1936 to 1940, however, that Roosevelt made his main effort to achieve improved structural integration. It should be remembered that one of the major recommendations of the President's Committee on Administrative Management was that all of the more than 100 governmental agencies then in existence should be integrated into a total of twelve departments. Roosevelt supported this proposal wholeheartedly in his recommendations to Congress and in his two-year battle to secure Congressional approval for his comprehensive reorganization program.

When Congress finally did enact the Reorganization Act of 1939, it seriously limited what the President could do in the way of integration by excluding twenty-one of the more important agencies from his reorganization authority. Roosevelt did, nevertheless, try to accomplish something along this line by creating three new "superagencies" with almost all the attributes of regular departments except the name and statutory authorization—the Federal Security Agency, the Federal Works Agency, and the Federal Loan Agency. He went ahead to place most of the previously independent agencies into either one of the three new agencies or into one of the regular departments, and by his five reorganization plans which went into effect in 1939 and 1940 he achieved a considerable degree of integration through a large number of consolidations and transfers which reduced substantially the number of agencies reporting directly to the President.[3] It soon proved to be of great benefit that he had managed to get the normal, peacetime agencies of the government set up in this way, on a permanent, integrated basis, before the administrative organization was subjected to the strains of the tremendous expansion which took place as a result of the national defense and wartime programs.

A third significant effect of Roosevelt's years as President was the positive assertion by both word and deed and the increased gen-

eral acceptance of the concept of the President as the "chief administrator" or "general manager" of the entire administrative organization. From the day he became President, Roosevelt acted upon the
assumption that the Constitution made him the responsible head
of all the administrative work of the executive branch. It was his
view that the President had no more fundamental responsibilities
than the direction and operation of the government's administrative
machinery and, in the words of Arthur Schlesinger, Jr., "Little fasci-
nated Franklin Roosevelt more than the tasks of presidential administration."[4] Certainly he devoted a very great amount of his
time and energy to the superintendence and coordination of the
activities of his administrative subordinates, and he tried to keep
closely in touch with the details of as many things as possible which
were going on throughout the departments and agencies. No other
President in the twentieth century has matched Roosevelt in the
amount of attention which he gave to the administrative work of the
departments and agencies and in the personal knowledge which he
possessed about the detailed activities of the entire administrative
organization. Perhaps President Lyndon Johnson has come the closest
to doing so as there is a considerable degree of similarity in both their
extensive knowledge and in their intense concern about governmental
operations and procedures.

In addition to Roosevelt's personal example in actually trying his
best to serve as the over-all "chief administrator" of the government,
the concept of the President as the head of the entire administrative
organization was greatly clarified and strengthened by the work of
the President's Committee on Administrative Management, and by
Roosevelt's strong support of the Committee's recommendations.
Among all of the things which the Committee did, it is probably true
that "its most important effect," as Wayne Coy has written, "was
a much clearer conception of the role of the President as the responsible head of the whole administrative establishment."[5]

At the core of the Committee's proposals was the basic idea that
the President urgently needed help to enable him to fulfill the responsibilities imposed upon him by the Constitution, and that without
such increased assistance the President could not exercise adequate
direction and control over the functions performed in his name and
under his authority throughout the executive branch. To this end,
the Committee proposed that the President's immediate office should
be augmented by the addition of six administrative assistants, that

the three top-level governmental functions of budgeting, planning, and personnel management should be supervised by persons serving directly as administrative arms of the President, and that the entire branch should be integrated and streamlined in such a way that the chain of command from the White House down would be tightened up and made more responsive to the President's direction.

The President's Committee strongly urged that the President should be given badly needed help in doing his job instead of trying to devise ways of reducing the size and scope of the job. There was no recommendation at all for the increased delegation of the President's administrative functions. He was to be provided with substantially increased staff assistance to help him in performing his many duties, but there was no provision for the duties to be diminished. The Committee accepted the premise as strongly as did Roosevelt that the President should properly serve as the chief administrator of the government in fact as well as in name. Although this premise has certainly not lacked influential and vocal critics among political scientists and students of public administration, it has nevertheless remained at the heart of all later studies of the administrative aspects of the Presidency. Friend and foe alike have to recognize the validity of George Graham's statement that "The Report of the President's Committee on Administrative Management is a landmark from which all subsequent discussions of the Presidency must take their bearings."[6]

One important example of the pervasiveness of the Committee's view of the President as the chief administrator is to be found in the work done by the Commission on Organization of the Executive Branch of the Government—the Hoover Commission, as it is more familiarly known. In its report dealing with the Presidency, the Hoover Commission expressed almost exactly the same viewpoint as the President's Committee.[7] The major emphasis was placed upon providing the President with more and better staff assistance in order to make it possible for him to perform his duties more effectively. The general concept of the Presidency expressed by the Hoover Commission in 1949 was no different in any important way from that expressed by the President's Committee in 1936-1937. And except for the Hoover Commission's proposal that a new position of Staff Secretary should be established in the White House Office, nothing additional was proposed over and above what the President's Committee had previously recommended.

Certainly all of Roosevelt's successors have acted in general conformity with this view of the President as the administrative manager of the executive branch as enunciated by Roosevelt and the President's Committee. Although President Dwight Eisenhower seemed to hold the opinion that the President should be politically and administratively above and beyond intimate involvement in the day-to-day details of administrative affairs in the way that Roosevelt had always been, under his Administration the White House Office nevertheless remained the central focal point in the supervision of government operations with administrative direction and control centralized to a considerable degree in Sherman Adams in his capacity as The Assistant to the President from 1953 to 1958. For all practical purposes, Adams served as Eisenhower's "Chief of Staff" and acted in the President's name and with his authority in managing the administrative affairs of the government. After Adams' decline and fall from power, his role as "Chief of Staff" passed to General Wilton B. Persons for the remainder of Eisenhower's time in office, although Persons was not able to operate with the same degree of authority and independence as Adams.

Among Roosevelt's other successors, Presidents Truman, Kennedy, and Johnson, there has certainly been no move away from an acceptance of the view that the President should be the general manager of the administrative organization. All three have exerted strong leadership in administrative affairs personally, as well as through the use of such important White House assistants as Clark Clifford and John R. Steelman under Truman, Theodore Sorenson, Kenneth O'-Donnell and McGeorge Bundy under Kennedy, and Walter Jenkins, Bill Moyers, and Joseph Califano under Johnson. None of these occupied anything like the predominant position of Sherman Adams under Eisenhower because each of the Presidents whom they served preferred to be his own "Chief of Staff" as Roosevelt had been. Nevertheless, the importance attached to all of these individuals and the fact that each was regarded around Washington as being at least as significant in the administrative conduct of the government's business as any Cabinet member illustrates the continuity of the concept advanced by Roosevelt and the President's Committee that the President and those associated most closely with him in the White House Office are responsible for the over-all direction of the government's administrative activities.

A fourth significant effect which Roosevelt had upon the admin-

istrative organization was his creation in 1939 of the Executive Office
of the President. It is probably true that no other single administrative action by Roosevelt has received such widespread approbation
from informed observers of the Presidency as has this one. For example, Executive Order 8248, by which Roosevelt established the
Executive Office, has prompted Clinton Rossiter to write, "For some
years now it has been popular, even among his friends, to write off
Mr. Roosevelt as a 'second-rate administrator.' In the light of Executive Order 8248, an accomplishment in public administration superior to that of any other President, this familiar judgment seems a
trifle musty and platitudinous."[8] Among other examples which might
be cited are statements by Herman Somers: "Establishment of the
Executive Office of the President is a grand landmark in the administrative history of our government;" George Graham: "The creation
of the Executive Office of the President was a milestone in the history of the Presidency . . . ;" and Fritz Morstein Marx: "There is
widespread agreement . . . that the formation of the Executive Office
under the Reorganization Act of 1939 has been a most constructive
move."[9]

Shortly after the Executive Office was set up, the unprecedented
burden of national defense and wartime problems placed an exceedingly heavy administrative load upon Roosevelt and the new organiaztion. For the most part, the components of the Executive Office
met this severe test quite well, though not always with uniform
success, and there can be little doubt but that Roosevelt would not
have been able to meet nearly so well the extraordinary demands
which the war made upon him without the assistance of the Executive Office, especially of his expanded White House Staff, of the
Bureau of the Budget, and of the Office for Emergency Management.
In the years since, despite the numerous changes in the composition
of the Executive Office as some of the old components have been
eliminated and several new ones added, the general acceptance of
the Executive Office has become so complete that it is now virtually
impossible to conceive of the Presidency being able to operate without some sort of institutionalized system of a similar nature. In fact,
it is undoubtedly true to say that whereas the Executive Office
exists only to help the President to do his job, the Presidency itself
could no longer exist as we have thought of it in recent years without
the Executive Office. Today, many of the services of the Executive
Office are absolutely essential to the President if he is to perform

his duties in a way which even approximates an effective manner.

Only two of the original five component parts of the Executive Office of the President as established in 1939—the White House Office and the Bureau of the Budget—now remain, performing essentially the same basic functions as at the beginning, though both of them have been expanded greatly in terms of personnel employed and range of services rendered to aid the President in the execution of his tasks. In spite of the numerous organizational changes which have occurred in the composition of the Executive Office, the fundamental concept which motivated the President's Committee and Roosevelt in creating it has not undergone any significant change. The structural changes which have taken place have conformed to the general outline which was described in the report of the President's Committee.

Of the original agencies other than the White House Office and the Bureau of the Budget, the National Resources Planning Board fell afoul of increasing Congressional antagonism and a probable feeling of the need to reassert Congressional authority after much of it had been virtually abdicated to the President in the early part of World War II. The activities of the Planning Board had been viewed with a considerable amount of suspicion by Congress from the outset and it is probable that the agency would have been killed in either 1941 or 1942 if Roosevelt had not made strenuous efforts to secure its continuance. His appeals in its behalf proved not to be sufficient in 1943 and the Board was abolished in the summer of that year when Congress voted to withhold any appropriations from the agency, to forbid the President from using money from his emergency fund to continue the Board, and to prevent the transfer of the Board's functions to any other agency.

Approximately three years later, Congress proceeded to fill a substantial part of the vacancy caused by the demise of the Planning Board when it established the three-member Council of Economic Advisers, which was placed in the Executive Office of the President under the terms of the Employment Act of 1946. The Council of Economic Advisers fulfills what had been one of the major areas of the Planning Board's responsibility, the study and reporting of economic trends, in assisting the President in the preparation of his annual economic report to the Congress, and in aiding him by analyzing economic developments, appraising the economic implications of governmental programs and activities, and formulating national economic policies.[10]

The Liaison Office for Personnel Management functioned throughout Roosevelt's last five years in the Presidency under the direction of William H. McReynolds, who provided staff assistance to Roosevelt in matters of personnel administration and served as the President's liaison with the Civil Service Commission and with the personnel officers of the departments and agencies. Donald S. Dawson served as the Liaison Officer for Personnel Management during the time President Harry S. Truman occupied the White House and continued the functions which McReynolds had inaugurated. In dealing with the Civil Service Commission and the departments and agencies, Truman delegated to Dawson the general authority to make final decisions in the President's name on most personnel matters. In addition, Dawson was Truman's right-hand man in all matters involving the dispensing of political patronage and represented the President in contacts with Senators, Democratic party officials, state and local political leaders, etc., in regard to filling appointive government jobs.

In 1953, President Dwight Eisenhower finally obtained approval for a reorganization move which brought the personnel management function in the Executive Office somewhat closer to what the President's Committee had proposed when he followed a recommendation of the Hoover Commission and designated Chairman Philip Young of the Civil Service Commission as his personal adviser on government personnel matters, and eliminated the post of Liaison Officer for Personnel Management. The Chairman was also given increased authority to direct the administrative work of the Commission. This arrangement has been continued under both the Kennedy and Johnson Administrations with John W. Macy, Jr. serving as both the chariman of the Civil Service Commission and the personnel adviser to the President.

The last of the original Executive Office agencies, the Office of Government Reports, which had been the last surviving remnant of the National Emergency Council, was made a part of the Office of War Information when that agency was created in June 1942. After the dissolution of the latter, President Truman issued an executive order in December 1946 to reestablish the Office of Government Reports in the Executive Office of the President on the same basis and with the same functions as it had performed prior to its assignment to the Office of War Information. Its renewed life as a separate agency was destined to be brief, however, for Congress in 1947, as part of a legislative onslaught on many of the information services provided by government agencies, failed to apropriate any funds for the Office of Government Reports so that its activities had to be terminated.

Since 1939 it has been the Bureau of the Budget which has always continued to be the backbone of the Executive Office of the President. In fact, Roosevelt's transfer of the Budget Bureau to the Executive Office of the President, his increased utilization and expansion of the Bureau's services, and the emphasis which he placed upon the Bureau as the most important single institutional instrument which he had available to help him manage the activities of his administrative subordinates—these combine to form a fifth significant effect which Roosevelt had upon the administrative organization of the executive branch.

As discussed in Chapter IV, Roosevelt had already made substantially greater use of the Bureau of the Budget before 1939 than had his predecessors, but a combination of factors tended to prevent him from relying upon it as much as he was to do after that date. One of these factors, though only one among several, was the location of the Bureau in the Department of the Treasury. In formulating its recommendations, the President's Committee had to consider the possibility of leaving the Bureau in the Treasury and proposing to rebuild the Treasury Department into an institution somewhat more like the British Treasury whereby it would be the agency which would unify the budgetary process with all the other major fiscal functions of the government. Although there undoubtedly might have been some beneficial results from this approach, the Committee decided that they were outweighed by other considerations and recommended that the Budget Bureau should be taken out of its somewhat anomalous position in the Treasury and placed immediately under the President to whom it had been directly responsible, in fact, since its establishment in 1921.

This decision reflected the view that the concept of a national executive budget requires an over-all perspective which has to encompass the entire government, and that under our Constitutional system the President is the only one who has to look at the whole administrative organization, above and beyond the particular interests of the individual departments and agencies. Because of this, it was thought preferable to strengthen and improve the Budget Bureau as a staff agency to assist the President in providing the over-all management of the executive branch rather than delegating a part of the President's managerial authority to the Secretary of the Treasury as a subordinate line officer who would have to supervise in some ways the activities of all his fellow line officers. Also, it was thought that the problems which would be involved in transforming a long-established operating agency like the Treasury into an agency with over-all management responsibilities would undoubtedly be very substantial. Roosevelt, in supporting the recommendation of the President's Committee, cited particularly that the expanded co-ordinating functions which he hoped to obtain from the Budget Bureau would be facilitated if the Bureau was not a part of one of the departments.[11] Consequently, the Bureau was placed in the Executive Office of the President and the concept of the executive budget, prepared and administered by the Bureau of the Budget under the direction of the President, has become firmly established in the United States. At least it was established firmly enough that when A. E. Buck, in his study for a Hoover Commission Task Force on Fiscal, Budgeting, and Accounting Activities, recommended that the Bureau be returned to the Treasury, the full Commission emphatically rejected his recommendation and said that it "would be a step backward."[12]

The sizable increase in the functions and importance of the Bureau of the Budget after Roosevelt transferred it to the Executive Office of the President in 1939 is attributable to several factors. First of all, the President was badly in need of the increased help which the Bureau could provide. As Roosevelt himself was to write later, "It seemed evident that I had to be provided with expanded staff facilities to assist in the job of administrative management. One obvious move was the strengthening of the Bureau of the Budget."[13] The field for assisting the President in managing and coordinating the executive branch was a relative void, except for what the Budget Bureau had already been called upon to do along these lines, for as we have seen, Roosevelt had not developed any effective or lasting institutional machinery for coordination in the years before 1939. The resulting near-vacuum was thus available to be filled by a staff agency whose leadership demonstrated ability, ambition, and imagination.

The second major factor was the new Director of the Bureau whom

Roosevelt apointed in 1939, Harold D. Smith. Smith had all three of the attributes mentioned above in quite generous amounts. He possessed a broad, dynamic view as to the functions of the Bureau and the services which a Presidential staff should perform. He wrote, "The main function of the Bureau is to serve as an agent of the President in coordinating operations and in improving the administrative management of the government." [14] This was a quite different conception from that of many of his predecessors who believed that the only important function of the Bureau was to try to insure a balanced budget. In addition, Smith very quickly established a good personal relationship with Roosevelt. This was very important as Roosevelt frequently tended to view administration in terms of personalities and relied most upon those for whom he felt a close personal affinity.

A third factor was the inevitable interrelationship and overlapping between the budget function and the other functions involved in administration and coordination. A comprehensive executive budget is in effect a master plan for the administrative activities of the entire government, and the budgeting process must unavoidably impinge to some degree upon how the administrative activities are to be carried out. So given this inevitably close relationship between budgeting and administrative management, given Roosevelt's increasing need for help in the years from 1939 to 1945, and given Harold Smith's eagerness and ability to provide such help, it is not surprising that Roosevelt looked more and more to the Budget Bureau so that it came to occupy an increasingly important place at the very heart of the President's administrative organization. To some degree this was reflected in the fact that the Bureau quadrupled both its funds and its personnel within the first two years after Smith became director. [15] With Roosevelt's encouragement and Smith's leadership, the Bureau developed some of the methods of managing the administrative organization in the President's behalf to a quite high level of accomplishment. Its position of vital importance in the national administrative system has been maintained and strengthened by the Bureau down to the present day. The current Director of the Budget, Charles L. Schultze, is virtually always involved by President Johnson in all major questions concerning administrative policies and procedures.

The sixth and last significant effect to be singled out here was Roosevelt's establishment and utilization of the Office for Emergency

Management in conjunction with the national defense and wartime emergency resulting from World War II. Placing a provision in Executive Order 8248 in September 1939 which authorized the later creation of the Office for Emergency Management in the Executive Office of the President can be characterized as almost a sheer stroke of both administrative and political genius on the part of Roosevelt and Louis Brownlow. It is difficult to overstress the importance of this action—which Brownlow has described as "putting a rabbit in the hat" to be pulled out by the President later [16]—as it was a novel and completely unprecedented administrative approach which allowed the President to move ahead in devising new emergency agencies for defense and war in a much easier, much faster, and much more flexible way than would undoubtedly have been the case if he would have had to secure approval for the organizational structure and powers of each of the new agencies by a statute obtained through the regular processes of Congressional action. The Office of Emergency Management served as an effective "holding company" for almost all of the new defense and war agencies. They were created with no statutory base or authorization other than the President's reorganization authority as set forth in the Reorganization Act of 1939, in Roosevelt's Reorganization Plan No. 1, and in Executive Order 8248. In this way Roosevelt was able to avoid having to go to Congress to secure approval for the great majority of his new defense agencies; through use of the Office for Emergency Management he managed to eliminate what had often plagued Wilson and earlier wartime Presidents—the difficulty of obtaining Congressional sanction for each new emergency organization.

Despite Roosevelt's important use of the Office for Emergency Management, it is also of interest to note what he did not do with the agency. At no time did he delegate to it the authority to act as a central coordinating agency in his behalf. In many ways this seems unfortunate, as the Office for Emergency Management's location in the Executive Office of the President as the parent body to which almost all of the emergency agencies belonged would have made it eminently suited to serve as a strong coordinative body acting for and with the approval of the President. Roosevelt, however, apparently never intended to use the Office for Emergency Management as a supreme coordinative device other than to provide him with a channel through which he could establish whatever new agencies he deemed necessary, and which he would coordinate himself.

The Office for Emergency Management did serve as an auxiliary agency with general housekeeping functions for its numerous component parts, and it provided central administrative services and a coordinated information service. However the Liaison Officers for Emergency Management, William H. McReynolds and his successor, Wayne Coy, were never given any power to direct or control the operations of the subordinate organizations. It is interesting to conjecture if the story in this regard would have been different if it had worked out for Roosevelt to appoint Louis Brownlow as his Liaison Officer, as he had offered to do in 1939. It seems probable that a person of Brownlow's character and leadership ability might have tried to invest the job with considerably more authority than was true under McReynolds, although Brownlow was later to write that the agency functioned along the lines he and Roosevelt had envisioned for it:

"I had originally conceived of the Office of Emergency Management in the Executive Office of the President as a holding company —an agency which was to do little or nothing on its own but which was to establish continuous lines of instantaneous communication between the President and any of the defense organizations to be set up and which was also to serve as a catalyzer so that the President on his own motion at any time, without having to seek legislation from the Congress, could create, modify, consolidate, or dissolve any particular agency set up for the emergency. In that respect, despite many difficulties, I believe the agency justified itself, and materially advantaged the operations during the years of preparedness. It made possible the greatest effort ever made by any nation through its governmental machinery to equip an army and navy—the army and navy that won World War II." [17]

Almost certainly there would have been a substantial difference in the way the Liaison Officer for Emergency Management operated if Roosevelt had followed through on his inclination to appoint Fiorello LaGuardia to the job as he seriously contemplated doing at the time he was planning to establish the Office of Production Management in December 1940. [18]

In retrospect, it appears to some degree strange that Roosevelt did not see fit to develop the Office for Emergency Management as his top-level coordinative agency. Since it was in the Executive Office of the President and was the legal "home" of all the specialized defense and war agencies, it could have been developed into some-

thing similar to what the Office of War Mobilization ultimately came
to be, with someone like Justice Byrnes or another respected and
capable political leader gifted in the art of compromise and concilia-
tion as its head. This would have served Roosevelt's purpose in
preventing the establishment of anything like the superagency provided for in the Industrial Mobilization Plan with a supreme director
from the ranks of business, which Roosevelt was determined to avoid.
At the same time, however, it would have allowed him to appoint
one important top-level figure in whom he had great confidence to
assist him in the White House, as Byrnes did later, by heading-up
the coordination of the activities of the defense agencies and in
settling the conflicts and jurisdictional disputes which were inevitably
going to occur.

Such a move might possibly have been made at the time of the
establishment of the Office of Production Management at the beginning of 1941, although the time may not have seemed suitable
politically that early. In any case it could undoubtedly have been
done by no later than the establishment of the War Production Board
in early 1942, shortly after Pearl Harbor. Again in retrospect, it would
seem that this might have been a better solution than delegating
extensive authority for coordination to Donald M. Nelson, the Chairman of the War Production Board, who concentrated his attention
primarily on developing the War Production Board as the chief
industrial and military production agency rather than as the top-level
coordinating agency which Roosevelt and the war program needed
by that time. Such a step could have substantially eased Roosevelt's
administrative and coordinative burdens well in advance of the date
when he finally established the Office of War Mobilization in May
1943. It also might have improved the general administration of the
war effort by providing faster, and, in some cases, better decisions
based on more information and fuller consideration of the facts.

Viewed from hindsight, Roosevelt's failure or unwillingness to use
the Office for Emergency Management in such a way and his slowness
in making important delegations of his coordinative authority must
be reckoned as a weakness in his administration of the Presidency
which may have hindered and delayed to some degree the accomplishment of the defense and war production programs.

In looking at Roosevelt's record as Chief Administrator, it must
be recognized that several other Presidents undoubtedly administered
the presidential office in a better and more orderly manner than he

did, if evaluated only in accordance with the more usual, routine administrative standards of efficiency and economy. Nevertheless, it seems equally true—and more important—to state that no other President has had a more significant total effect upon the scope, the structural arrangement, and the functioning of the administrative organization of the executive branch.

That Roosevelt did not get all of the administrative reforms made which needed to be made goes almost without saying. The extensive recommendations of the two Hoover Commissions made this abundantly clear, along with the extensive reorganization measures which have been put into effect by Presidents Truman, Eisenhower, Kennedy and Johnson. Partly his failure to accomplish additional worthwhile changes in the administrative system was due to deficiencies on his own part. Mostly, however, it was due to limitations and restrictions placed upon his reorganizational efforts by Congress and by numerous political considerations. Some of his earlier interest in improving the administrative organization of the government, as expressed over a period of many years before he became President, remained relatively obscured during his first term by his political and legislative activities in trying to put into effect the economic programs and social reforms which he thought necessary to get the country out of the depression. The same can also be said of the last year of his second term and his entire third term. He might well have undertaken more administrative reforms if the national defense emergency and World War II had not occurred to preoccupy almost all of his time and effort.

Although Roosevelt was always interested throughout his career in questions of administrative organization, it is accurate to say that his interest in administration was subordinate to his interest in politics. Perhaps it is really more accurate to say that Roosevelt as President never actually distinguished politics and administration from each other in any clear-cut way. In his thinking, everything which he did as President was inevitably political. It seemed almost second nature, or a sort of automatic reflex-action in his mental processes, for Roosevelt to consider the political consequences of every administrative action and to weigh constantly the implications of all that he did in terms of his political leadership of the Democratic party, of Congress, and of the country.

As President, it appears that Roosevelt was not particularly concerned about being a good administrator as such; he was probably not even particularly concerned with being a good politician as such. What he was concerned about, it seems clear, was being a good President. Rather than as "a great administrator" or "a great politician," he wished for history to call him "a great President." He knew from his close study of the lives of many of his predecessors that neither political achievements alone nor administrative achievements alone would be sufficient to secure the mantle of Presidential greatness. Instead, a combination of both, joined together in varying amounts with other essential ingredients in some sort of mysterious and elusive formula, was required. He well recognized the truth of what Herman Somers was later to write: "Long experience has demonstrated that a President is likely to succeed in most of his jobs or in none. They are mutually dependent. . . . The President is not politician *and* administrator; he is rather a *political administrator*." [19]

Consequently, in his administrative actions and in the changes which he brought in the administrative organization, Roosevelt was motivated not so much by a desire to be a better administrator but because he wanted to be a more effective President. Certainly he regarded one of his major administrative accomplishments, the creation of the Executive Office of the President, as considerably more than a device for enabling him to manage the administrative organization more efficiently and economically. He was interested in devising improved machinery to help him perform his administrative tasks, but he was even more interested in establishing the Executive Office as a means of reducing his administrative burdens to a sufficient degree that he would be helped in performing all of his other duties more effectively. In his administrative methods he was usually concerned most of all, not with whether they were neat and orderly, or whether they were especially efficient or in conformity with a logically designed, elaborate plan, but with the questions of whether they worked or not, and what effect they might have upon the over-all performance of his presidential obligations. Robert E. Sherwood has discussed this point in the following passage:

"Roosevelt's methods of administration . . . were to say the least, unorthodox. They filled some practical-minded observers with apprehension and dismay, and some with disgust; they filled others with awe and wonder . . . but there is one thing that can be said about these methods—whether they were good or bad, sensible or insane, they *worked*." [20]

In this connection, Sherwood went on to quote from a lengthy interview which he had with Harold Smith, the "modest, methodical, precise man, temperamentally far removed from Roosevelt," who served as Roosevelt's Budget Director from 1939 to 1945. He quotes Smith as follows:

"A few months ago . . . a magazine asked me to write an article on Roosevelt as an administrator. I thought it over and decided I was not ready to make such an appraisal. I've been thinking about it ever since. When I worked with Roosevelt—for six years—I thought as did many others that he was a very erratic administrator. But now, when I look back, I can really begin to see the size of his programs. They were by far the largest and most complex programs that any President ever put through. People like me who had the responsibility of watching the pennies could only see the five or six or seven per cent of the programs that went wrong, through inefficient organization or direction. But now I can see in perspective the ninety-three or -four or -five per cent that went right—including the winning of the biggest war in history—because of unbelievably skillful organization and direction. And if I were to write that article now, I think I'd say that Roosevelt must have been one of the greatest geniuses as an administrator that ever lived. What we couldn't appreciate at the time was the fact that he was a real *artist* in government." [21]

There seems to be little serious doubt on the part of most students of American government and politics but that history will eventually accord Franklin D. Roosevelt a secure place somewhere among the galaxy of great American Presidents, along with Washington and Lincoln, Jefferson and Jackson, Theodore Roosevelt and Wilson. It has long been held by many, however, that Roosevelt's administrative shortcomings constituted a major detraction from his over-all performance as President. "Even his stoutest friends admit that Roosevelt was not much of an administrator," Clinton Rossiter has observed; but then he adds, ". . . it is possible that his friends give away too much to his enemies on this particular count." [22]

Certainly Roosevelt's over-all effects upon the role of the President as the chief administrator of the executive branch were most significant. All of the Presidents since his day have operated administratively under the broad shadow which Roosevelt cast after him and have necessarily proceeded along lines which his administrative views and activities clearly foreordained. The work of his successors has been shaped and greatly facilitated by the administrative reorganization measures which Roosevelt initiated in his effort to enable the

President to manage a vastly expanded executive branch. And they have carried on their work through essentially the same institutionalized administrative framework in the White House Office and the Executive Office of the President which Roosevelt created to help the President discharge his responsibilities more effectively.

The view that Roosevelt's administrative record was mainly one of failure resulted from premature judgments based upon perspectives too limited in scope. It is the considered conclusion of this study that when one carefully weighs the pros and cons of Roosevelt's effects upon the role of the President as chief administrator, the balance clearly indicates that his administrative achievements should properly be recognized as significant contributions to his presidential reputation.

REFERENCES

CHAPTER I

1. Don K. Price, "The Presidency: Its Burdens and Its Promise," *The Strengthening of American Political Institutions* (Ithaca, New York: Cornell University Press, 1949), p. 97.

2. Wayne Coy, "Basic Problems," *The American Political Science Review* 40:1135, December, 1946.

3. Louis Brownlow, *The President and the Presidency* (Chicago: Public Administration Service, 1949), p. 90. Although Brownlow did not endeavor to write a complete analysis of the President as chief administrator, this little volume of miscellaneous reminiscences, illustrative anecdotes, and random observations does much to illuminate many phases of the President's administrative work.

4. Sidney Hyman, *The American President* (New York: Harper and Brothers, 1954), p. 9.

5. Edward H. Hobbs, *Behind the President* (Washington: Public Affairs Press, 1954), p. 3.

6. *The Presidency*, Vol. II, prepared in the Division of Administrative Management of the U. S. Bureau of the Budget (unpublished) under the direction of A. L. Dean, 1948, pp. 7-8. Quoted here from Hobbs, *op. cit.*, p. 3.

7. Brownlow, *op. cit.*, p. 62.

8. Harold J. Laski, *The American Presidency* (New York: Harper and Brothers, 1940), p. 89.

9. Charles Hyneman, *Bureaucracy in a Democracy* (New York: Harper and Brothers, 1950), p. 181. Clinton Rossiter has summarized the point succinctly as follows: "Whether it is his letters or his taxes that the ordinary citizen wants more efficiently collected, he looks first of all to the President as business manager of the administration." Clinton Rossiter, *The American Presidency* (New York: Harcourt, Brace and Co., 1956), p. 9. Rossiter's book, which this writer regards as the best yet written concerning the Presidency in all its aspects, devotes considerable attention to the President's administrative role, and contains an especially perceptive discussion of the major difficulties which confront a President in managing the administrative organization. See especially, pp. 40-43 and pp. 150-152.

10. *The Constitution of the United States*, Article I, Section 8 (the "necessary and proper" clause); and in two separate clauses in Article II, Section 2, dealing with the powers of the executive.

11. *Ibid.*, Article II, Section 2.

12. *Ibid.*, Article II, Section 3.

13. Edward S. Corwin, *The President: Office and Powers* (New York: New York University Press, 1948), p. 96 and p. 423.

14. Rossiter, *op. cit.*, p. 6.

15. Price, *op. cit.*, p. 92.

16. Paul H. Appleby, "The Significance of the Hoover Commission Report," *The Yale Review*, Autumn, 1949, p. 8.

17. Caleb Perry Patterson, "The President as Chief Administrator," *Journal of Politics*, 11:231, February, 1949.

18. A good definition of coordination as it is meant here was provided many years ago by the French student of administration, Henri Fayol: "To coordinate is to bring harmony and equilibrium into the whole. It is to give to things and to actions their proper proportion. It is to adapt the means to the end and to unify disconnected efforts and make them homogeneous." See Fayol, "The Administrative Theory in the State," in Luther Gulick and L. Urwick, editors, *Papers on the Science of Administration* (New York: Institute of Public Administration, 1937), p. 103.

19. Brownlow, *op. cit.*, p. 97.

20. Marshall E. Dimock, "Administrative Efficiency Within a Democratic Polity," *New Horizons in Public Administration* (University, Alabama: University of Alabama Press, 1945), pp. 37-38.

21. An excellent account of Roosevelt's record pertaining to the government's personnel program is given in Leonard D. White, "Franklin D. Roosevelt and the Public Service," *Public Personnel Review*, 6:139-146, July, 1945.

CHAPTER II

1. Anne O'Hare McCormick, "Roosevelt's View of the Big Job," *New York Times Magazine*, September 11, 1932, Section 6, p. 1.

2. Raymond Moley, *27 Masters of Politics* (New York: Funk and Wagnalls Company, 1949), pp. 81-82.

3. The most comprehensive account of Roosevelt's service as Assistant Secretary of the Navy is provided in the first two volumes of Frank Freidel's biography, *Franklin D. Roosevelt: The Apprenticeship* (Boston: Little, Brown and Company, 1952), pp. 135-372, and *Franklin D. Roosevelt: The Ordeal* (same publisher, 1954), pp. 3-50. (Hereafter cited respectively as Freidel I and Freidel II.) Another excellent account is found in Ernest K. Lindley, *Franklin D. Roosevelt* (New York: Blue Ribbon Books, Inc., 1931), pp. 115-185. Though less detailed, the following are also helpful for this period: James MacGregor Burns, *Roosevelt: The Lion and the Fox* (New York: Harcourt, Brace and Company, 1956), pp. 47-66; John Gunther, *Roosevelt in Retrospect* (New York: Harper and Brothers, 1950), pp. 207-215; Frances Perkins, *The Roosevelt I Knew* (New York: The Viking Press, 1947), pp. 15-22; and Arthur M. Schlesinger, Jr., *The Age of Roosevelt: The Crisis of the Old Order* (Boston: Houghton Mifflin Company, 1957), pp. 344-367.

4. Roosevelt was only thirty-one years of age when appointed to the position, the youngest Assistant Secretary in Navy Department history. Gunther, *op. cit.*, p. 209.

5. Freidel I, *op. cit.*, pp. 160-161.   6. Gunther, *op. cit.*, p. 210.

7. Freidel I, *op. cit.*, pp. 254-255; Burns, *op. cit.*, p. 61. The Statute creating the Council of National Defense is found in 39 *Stat.* 649.

8. See Chapter VIII.   9. See Chapters VII and VIII.

10. Lindley, *op. cit.*, p. 140; Perkins, *op. cit.*, p. 19.

11. George Fort Milton, *The Use of Presidential Power* (Boston: Little, Brown and Company, 1944), pp. 252-253.   12. Freidel I, *op. cit.*, p. 307.

13. Burns, *op. cit.*, p. 67.   14. Perkins, *op. cit.*, p. 21.

15. Louis Brownlow, *The President and the Presidency* (Chicago: Public Administration Service, 1949), p. 62.

16. Freidel I, *op. cit.*, p. 135.

17. 66th Congress, 1st Session, House of Representatives Select Committee on Budget, *Hearings* (Washington, 1919), pp. 649-677.

18. *Ibid.*, pp. 665-677. Also see Louis Brownlow, "A General View," *Public Administration Review*, 1:104, Winter, 1941. After discussing some of the views Roosevelt presented in 1919, Brownlow concludes with a remark that the ideas expressed in the report of the President's Committee on Administrative Management in 1937 were "nothing new to the President for whom it was drafted." Another close observer of Roosevelt, Rexford G. Tugwell, has written that in this testimony before Congress, Roosevelt provided "something of a preview of his sophistication, as he entered the Presidency, in such matters. . . . As many still living can testify, one of the most obsessive preoccupations of Roosevelt as President was to be the reorganization of government; and he had an intense interest in budget matters, which was part of his whole concern for detail and arrangement. This was a built-in characteristic." Rexford G. Tugwell, "The Sources of New Deal Reformism," *Ethics*, 64:272-273, July, 1954.

19. Freidel II, *op. cit.*, pp. 33-34.   20. Burns, *op. cit.*, p. 68.

21. Freidel II, *op. cit.*, pp. 77-78.   22. *Ibid.*, pp. 160-161; Burns, *op. cit.*, p. 89.

23. Freidel II, *op. cit.*, p. 161.

24. Good accounts of Roosevelt as Governor of New York are provided by Samuel I. Rosenman, *Working with Roosevelt* (New York: Harper and Brothers, 1952), pp. 13-66; Ernest K. Lindley, *op. cit.*, pp. 26-40 and pp. 200-379; Frances Perkins, *op. cit.*, pp. 41-110; John Gunther, *op. cit.*, pp. 250-261; James MacGregor Burns, *op. cit.*, pp. 105-122; Arthur M. Schlesinger, Jr., *op. cit.*, pp. 386-395; and by the entire third volume of the Freidel biography: *Franklin D. Roosevelt: The Triumph* (Boston: Little, Brown and Company, 1956), 414 pp. (Cited hereafter as Freidel III.) Many of Roosevelt's addresses and other public statements during his years as Governor are found in *The Public Papers and Addresses of Franklin D. Roosevelt*. Vol. I, Samuel I. Rosenman, editor (New York: Random House, 1938), 911 pp. (Cited hereafter as *Public Papers* I.) The volume also contains copious explanatory annotations which are very helpful. Considerable information about his work as Governor is also contained in *F.D.R., His Personal Letters, 1928-1945*, Vol. I, Elliott Roosevelt, editor (New York: Duell, Sloan and Pearce, 1950), pp. 3-316.

25. Woodrow Wilson, *Congressional Government* (Boston: Houghton Mifflin Company, 1885), p. 253.

26. Finla G. Crawford, "New York State Reorganization," *American Political Science Review*, 20:76-79, February, 1926.   27. Lindley, *op. cit.*, p. 27.

28. *Ibid.*, p. 317; Freidel III, *op. cit.*, pp. 122-123.

29. *Public Papers* I, p. 14.   30. *Ibid.*, pp. 16-19.

31. Freidel III, *op. cit.*, p. 361.   32. *Public Papers* I, p. 807.

33. *Ibid.*, pp. 808-810.

34. Raymond Moley, one of those associated most closely with Roosevelt at the time, has written: "The speech . . . at Pittsburgh . . . has been used to taunt him with increasing frequency as the years have passed. Suffice it to say that he was wholly aware of its implications when he made it. . . . So far as it is possible for anyone to be positive of anything, I am sure that the speech, as delivered, represented Roosevelt's wholehearted views. . . ." *After Seven Years* (New York: Harper and Brothers, 1939), p. 62.

35. Criticisms of this Pittsburgh speech continued to plague Roosevelt for many

years. In the note which he prepared in 1937 to accompany this speech in the first volume of his *Public Papers*, Roosevelt emphasized that the speech had also included the following passage: "The above . . . statements are aimed at a definite balancing of the budget. At the same time, let me repeat from now to election day so that every man, woman and child in the United States will know what I mean: If starvation and dire need on the part of any of our citizens make necessary the appropriation of additional funds which would keep the budget out of balance, I shall not hesitate to tell the American people the full truth and ask them to authorize the expenditure of that additional amount." He went on to stress in the note that, "Immediately upon assuming office I recommended and effected drastic economies in the regular expenditures of Government. . . . The great increase in the expenditures of Government came from the new extraordinary agencies . . . created to meet the emergency and from the necessities of meeting the widespread needs of the unemployed." *Public Papers* I, pp. 810-812.

36. Some of Roosevelt's letters between his election and his inauguration indicate that he discussed possible reorganization measures during that period with several people, including Owen D. Young, the industrialist; Swagar Sherley, a former Congressman from Kentucky to whom Roosevelt first offered the appointment as Director of the Bureau of the Budget; and Congressman Lewis W. Douglas of Arizona, who was appointed to that position after Sherley declined. See *F.D.R., His Personal Letters, op. cit.,* pp. 311-312 and pp. 321-322. Raymond Moley has also written that immediately after the election, "Roosevelt had . . . put Swagar Sherley and Lewis W. Douglas to work on the subject of governmental economy and reorganization." Moley, *After Seven Years, op. cit.,* p. 84.

CHAPTER III

1. 47 *Stat.* 413.

2. The party representation in the House of Representatives was Democrats 219, Republicans 207, and Farmer-Labor 1; the vote on the resolution disapproving the Hoover proposals was 198 yeas, 173 nays, and 53 not voting. *Congressional Record,* 72nd Congress, 2nd Session, Vol. 76, p. 2109, January 19, 1933.

3. 47 *Stat.* 1517.

4. Roosevelt's specific reorganization powers as he became President were set forth in Title IV of Part II of the Legislative Appropriations Act of 1933 as follows:

Sec. 401 . . . the President shall investigate the present organization of all executive and administrative agencies of the Government and shall determine what changes therein are necessary to accomplish the following purposes:

(a) To reduce expenditures to the fullest extent consistent with the efficient operation of the Government;

(b) To increase the efficiency of the operations of the Government to the fullest extent practicable within the revenues;

(c) To group, coordinate, and consolidate executive and administrative agencies of the Government as nearly as may be, according to major purposes;

(d) To reduce the number of such agencies by consolidating those having similar functions under a single head, and by abolishing such agencies and/or such functions thereof as may not be necessary for the efficient conduct of the Government;

(e) To eliminate overlapping and duplication of effort; and

(f) To segregate regulatory agencies and functions from those of an administrative and executive character.

Sec. 403. Whenever the President, after investigation, shall find and declare that any regrouping, consolidation, transfer, or abolition of any executive agency or agencies and/or the functions thereof is necessary to accomplish any of the purposes set forth in section 401 of this title, he may by Executive Order—

(a) Transfer the whole or any part of any executive agency and/or the functions thereof to the jurisdiction and control of any other executive agency;

(b) Consolidate the functions vested in any executive agency; or

(c) Abolish the whole or any part of any executive agency and/or the functions thereof; and

(d) Designate and fix the name and functions of any consolidated activity or executive agency and the title, powers, and duties of its executive head; except that the President shall not have authority under this title to abolish or transfer an executive department and/or all the functions thereof. 47 *Stat.* 1517.

5. 48 *Stat.* 16.   6. 40 *Stat.* 556.   7. 55 *Stat.* 838.

8. See Avery Leiserson, "Political Limitations on Executive Reorganization," *American Political Science Review*, 41:68-84, February, 1947.

9. The foregoing changes were made by Executive Order 6166, issued June 10, 1933. See *The Public Papers and Addresses of Franklin D. Roosevelt*, Samuel I. Rosenman, editor (New York: Random House, 1938), 1933 Vol., pp. 222-225. (The volumes of this set will be cited hereafter as *Public Papers*, with a notation of the particular yearly volume referred to.)

10. Executive Order 6084, issued March 27, 1933. *Ibid.*, pp. 84-90.

11. Executive Order 6694, issued May 1, 1934. *Ibid.*, p. 227.

12. Executive Order 6145, issued May 25, 1933. *Ibid.*, pp. 210-211.

13. Executive Order 6726, issued May 29, 1934. *Ibid.*, p. 227. In these early reorganizations, Roosevelt apparently dealt mainly with matters which were not very controversial and which did not require too much study and effort to accomplish. In this connection, Secretary of the Interior Harold L. Ickes recorded in his diary, on June 2, 1933: "We discussed somewhat at Cabinet meeting the matter of departmental reorganization. It is the present intention of the President to sign Executive Orders bringing about departmental changes about which there is no dispute, leaving debatable matters to be considered more carefully later." *The Secret Diary of Harold L. Ickes, The First Thousand Days*, 1933-1936 (New York: Simon and Schuster, 1953), p. 47.

14. Marshall E. Dimock and Gladys O. Dimock, *American Government in Action* (New York: Rinehart and Company, 1946), p. 583.

15. Good accounts of the developments of the "Hundred Days" are found in Ernest K. Lindley, *Half Way with Roosevelt* (New York: The Viking Press, 1937), pp. 85-280; Raymond Moley, *After Seven Years* (New York Harper and Brothers, 1939), pp. 162-195; and Frances Perkins, *The Roosevelt I Knew* (New York: The Viking Press, 1947), pp. 166-333.

16. It was apparently Roosevelt's conviction that his program had restored people's faith in the capitalistic system in the United States and had probably saved it from the imminent danger of revolution. In this connection it is interesting to note the account by Raymond Moley of "the unadulterated seriousness with which Roosevelt will explain to an old friend of the family that he has saved her from Revolution—

that, but for him, her well-coifed head would have been among the first to roll into the basket." Moley, *op. cit.*, p. 389.

17. *Public Papers*, 1933 Vol., pp. 11-16.

18. *Ibid.*, p. 15.

19. A preview of this policy could be seen during Roosevelt's term as Governor of New York when he overcame strong legislative opposition to create a new Temporary Emergency Relief Administration for the purpose of administering the relief program of the state, rather than placing it under the regular Department of Social Welfare. See *Public Papers*, 1928-1932 Vol., pp. 457-468; also Frank Freidel, *Franklin D. Roosevelt: The Triumph* (Boston: Little, Brown and Company, 1956), pp. 220-221. This agency was quickly labeled the T.E.R.A. by the newspapers, which made it the first of Roosevelt's many "alphabet agencies." "In forming this new agency," Robert E. Sherwood has written, "Roosevelt was setting a precedent for himself which he was to follow again and again in the New Deal and in the organization of the national effort to meet the demands of the Second World War: he was devising a new agency to meet a new problem rather than relying on the established department or bureau. . . ." Robert E. Sherwood, *Roosevelt and Hopkins* (New York: Harper and Brothers, 1948), pp. 31-32.

20. Good discussions of Roosevelt's views concerning the desirability of placing new functions in new agencies are found in Perkins, *op. cit.*, pp. 359-360, in Sherwood, *op. cit.*, pp. 158-159, and in Arthur M. Schlesinger, Jr., *The Age of Roosevelt: The Coming of the New Deal* (Boston: Houghton Mifflin Company, 1959), pp. 533-536. It appears, however, that in his early days as President, Roosevelt was somewhat concerned about establishing too many independent agencies outside the regular departments. In a Cabinet discussion in May, 1933, concerning how the government's public works program was to be administered, Perkins quotes Roosevelt as saying, "I am against so many independent agencies. We ought not to create any more if we can help it," and he decided to place public works under Secretary of the Interior Ickes. Perkins, *op. cit.*, p. 275.

21. James A. Farley, *Behind the Ballots* (New York: Harcourt, Brace and Company, 1938), pp. 223-238.

22. Leonard D. White, "Franklin Roosevelt and the Public Service," *Public Personnel Review*, 6:140, July, 1945.

23. Schlesinger, *op. cit.*, p. 534.

24. Civil Service Assembly, *News Letter*, 1:2, December, 1935.

25. *Public Papers*, 1935 Vol., pp. 367-368.

26. *Ibid.*, pp. 368-369.

27. White, *op. cit.*, p. 139.

28. George Fort Milton, *The Use of Presidential Power* (Boston: Little, Brown and Company, 1944), p. 259.

29. *Public Papers*, 1933 Vol., pp. 222-223.

30. *The Public Papers and Addresses of Franklin D. Roosevelt*, Samuel I. Rosenman, editor (New York: The Macmillan Company, 1941), 1939 Vol., p. 498. (The first five volumes of the *Public Papers*, covering the period through 1936, were published in 1938 by Random House; the next four volumes, covering the period through 1940, were published in 1941 by Macmillan.)

31. Raymond Moley, "The Issue Is Administration," *Newsweek*, Vol. 32, p. 80, September 6, 1948.

CHAPTER IV

1. Raymond Moley, "The Issue Is Administration," *Newsweek*, Vol. 32, September 6, 1948, p. 80.

2. Good accounts of Roosevelt's routine work schedule are found in Grace Tully, *F.D.R., My Boss* (New York: Charles Scribner's Sons, 1949), pp. 76-80; Samuel I. Rosenman, *Working with Roosevelt* (New York: Harper and Brothers, 1952), pp. 37-38; Robert E. Sherwood, *Roosevelt and Hopkins* (New York: Harper and Brothers, 1948), pp. 209-219; and in an interesting article by Drew Pearson and Robert S. Allen, "How the President Works," *Harpers*, Vol. 173, June, 1936, pp. 1-14. As President, Roosevelt followed practically the same work routine that he had developed as Governor of New York, as can be seen from the description of his schedule as Governor contained in Ernest K. Lindley, *Franklin D. Roosevelt* (New York: Blue Ribbon Books, Inc., 1931), pp. 31-34. John Gunther has commented that as Governor, Roosevelt "evolved most of the working techniques that were to be so useful to him as President, and the executive routine of his day became fixed; how he arranged his appointments and so on in the White House exactly duplicated the system he set up in Albany." John Gunther, *Roosevelt in Retrospect* (New York: Harper and Brothers, 1950), pp. 260-261.

3. Harold L. Ickes, *The Secret Diary of Harold L. Ickes*, Vol. 1, *The First Thousand Days, 1933-1936* (New York: Simon and Schuster, 1953), pp. 421-422. (Cited hereafter as Ickes I.)

4. Sherwood has commented: "Grace Tully points out that frequently when his baskets were piled up with letters, memoranda, reports, etc., he would sit up until well after midnight with her and perhaps a relay of secretaries to get through this tiresome work. It was always amazing to me to watch him at work with these baskets; his patience seemed infinite." Sherwood, *op. cit.*, p. 943. And Samuel Rosenman has described Roosevelt's routine evenings as follows: "After dinner—except for a rare social evening—he was wheeled into his study, where he continued to work on papers, speeches, bills; he even carried memoranda and reports to bed; frequently he continued to discuss business with me or others after getting into bed. And he always had to read several late newspapers before finally turning out the light. There were exceptions, of course, to this routine, but they were rare." Rosenman, *op. cit.*, p. 38.

5. Gunther, *op. cit.*, p. 63. Rosenman has said, "I never saw a man who worked harder. The loss of the full use of his legs deprived him of many of the diversions and amusements of other persons; the time he might so have spent he put largely into work. . . . I doubt whether—from the time he was first nominated for Governor until his death—a single day ever passed without some part of it being devoted to public affairs." Rosenman, *op. cit.*, pp. 37-38.

6. A statement by Roosevelt concerning the number of appointments which he usually kept each day before World War II is found in *The Public Papers and Addresses of Franklin D. Roosevelt*, Samuel I. Rosenman, editor (New York: Harper and Brothers, 1950), 1943 Vol., p. 126. (The first five volumes of the *Public Papers*, covering the period through 1936, were published in 1938 by Random House; the next four volumes, covering the period through 1940, were published in 1941 by Macmillan; the last four volumes were published in 1950 by Harper and Brothers. The various volumes will be cited hereafter as *Public Papers*, with a notation of the

particular yearly volume referred to.) On December 19, 1933, at the first meeting of the National Emergency Council, Roosevelt stated that, when Congress was in session, he had "probably on the average between three or four hours a day of conferences with congressional leaders," and as a result was not able to devote enough time to the administrative end of government. Arthur M. Schlesinger, Jr., *The Age of Roosevelt: The Coming of the New Deal* (Boston: Houghton Mifflin Company, 1959), pp. 545-546.

7. Gunther has written, "He did a great deal of business on the telephone; perhaps a quarter of his working day was spent telephoning. About a hundred people had the privilege of being put through to him without the intermediation of a secretary. . . ." Gunther, *op. cit.*, p. 125. In an interview with the writer on May 5, 1959, Louis Brownlow said that Roosevelt once told him that about 125 people could get the President directly on the telephone. Frances Perkins also says, "He was always easy to get on the phone and willing to interrupt whatever he was doing to talk to one of his associates." Frances Perkins, *The Roosevelt I Knew* (New York: The Viking Press, 1946), p. 131.

8. Rosenman, *op. cit.*, p. 17.   9. Perkins, *op. cit.*, p. 21.

10. *Public Papers*, 1943 Vol., p. 126.

11. Cordell Hull, *The Memoirs of Cordell Hull*, Vol. I (New York: Macmillan, 1948), p. 205. Henry L. Stimson also related this story in his memoirs, and added that Hull's remark "met with great applause from all the members of the Cabinet." Henry L. Stimson and McGeorge Bundy, *On Active Service in Peace and War* (New York: Harper and Brothers, 1948), pp. 561-562.

12. His personal physician, Admiral Ross McIntire, has written: "At the outset I learned the uselessness of trying to cut down on his list of daily visitors. Never at any time one disposed to solitude or reticence, but one of the most companionable men that ever lived, the President loved the give-and-take of conversation. The trouble was . . . he gave more than he took . . . People, however, were as necessary to him as meat and drink. . . . Try as I might, I could not keep him from crowding his days." Ross T. McIntire, *White House Physician* (New York: G. P. Putnam's Sons, 1946), p. 79.

13. "First Marvin McIntyre and then Pa Watson wore themselves out trying to cut down on the daily list of visitors, not to mention the job of getting them out after they got in. And always it was FDR who protracted the interviews, his interest caught by something that had been said." *Ibid.*, pp. 79-80. Also see Tully, *op. cit.*, pp. 77-78.

14. *Public Papers*, 1936 Vol., p. 60.   15. Tully, *op. cit.*, p. 141.

16. It is possible that his long-time political aide and confidant, Louis McHenry Howe, might well have tried to assume such a role if his activities had not been curtailed by a severe illness which began shortly after Roosevelt's inaugural and continued until Howe's death in 1936.

17. Although relatively unpublicized, compared with other leading figures of the New Deal, Walker was to remain one of Roosevelt's most valuable associates throughout his years as President. He eventually became Postmaster General from 1940 to 1945.

18. Tully writes, "It was through Justice Frankfurter and during Mr. Roosevelt's first term in the White House that Tommy Corcoran . . . became a 'leg man' for the Boss. . . . Frankfurter was concerned early in the Roosevelt term with the personal

and physical burden assumed by the Chief Executive. . . . He . . . wrote him a friendly and persuasive letter . . . that the assistance of an intelligent and energetic younger man as a 'trouble-shooter' and all-around aide would be of great service to the President, his Administration, and to those needing to do business with the White House. If the President agreed, he knew the 'right young man, brilliant and energetic' and would the Boss see him? The Boss would and did and took him." Tully, op. cit., p. 141.

19. Harold L. Ickes, *The Secret Diary of Harold L. Ickes*, Vol. II, *The Inside Struggle, 1936-1939* (New York: Simon and Schuster, 1954), p. 175. (Cited hereafter as Ickes II.)

20. The services of the "brain trust" are fully documented in Raymond Moley, *After Seven Years* (New York: Harper and Brothers, 1939), *passim*.

21. Rosenman, op. cit., pp. 87-88.

22. Moley became an Assistant Secretary of State and Tugwell, Assistant Secretary of Agriculture. Berle turned down a regular job in Washington, but he averaged about half of every week there during the first year of the Roosevelt administration and held an appointment as Special Counsel in the Reconstruction Finance Corporation. Schlesinger, op. cit., p. 182.

23. Moley, *After Seven Years*, op. cit., pp. 138-400.

24. Moley's own detailed version of the break with Roosevelt is given in *After Seven Years*, pp. 315-349. Rosenman has written that Roosevelt "felt that Moley's political and economic views were no longer close enough to his own. He thought that Moley had swung too far and too definitely to the right." Rosenman, op. cit., pp. 104-105.

25. Corcoran was officially on the legal staff of the Reconstruction Finance Corporation and Cohen on the legal staff of the Public Works Administration during these years.

26. Ickes' diary provides many examples of the services of Corcoran and Cohen during this period. See especially Ickes I, pp. 341-342, et passim.

27. Rosenman, op. cit., pp. 114-117. Rosenman himself, who had done much work of this sort when Roosevelt was Governor, remained throughout this period in New York where Roosevelt had appointed him to the State Supreme Court; consequently, he played no major part in the events of Roosevelt's first two terms, except for assistance in speech-drafting, though he was later to come to Washington to serve as one of Roosevelt's most trusted and valuable aides and "trouble shooters" during World War II.

28. Congress had raised the number of secretaries from one to three at the request of President Hoover. One writer has observed that this was "a fact that won the acid compliment of Franklin D. Roosevelt, who said it was the finest accomplishment of the Hoover administration." Sidney Hyman, *The American President* (New York: Harper and Brothers, 1954), p. 328. Roosevelt appointed as his three original secretaries Stephen Early for press relations, Marvin McIntyre for appointments, and the ailing Louis M. Howe. Moley has written of these appointments, "It was characteristic of F.D.R.'s way of doing things that McIntyre and, I believe, Early did not learn until they received their commissions that the Hoover arrangement—three secretaries with equal rank—had been discarded, and that they were to be assistant secretaries, with Louis enjoying the exclusive right to the title of Secretary to the President." Moley, *After Seven Years*, p. 80.

29. *Public Papers*, 1936 Vol., p. 671 and p. 675.

30. Sixty-sixth Congress, 1st Session, House of Representatives Select Committee on Budget, *Hearings* (Washington, 1919), pp. 649-677.

31. See Frank Freidel, *Franklin D. Roosevelt: The Ordeal* (Boston: Little, Brown and Company, 1954), pp. 33-34.

32. Rexford G. Tugwell, "The Sources of New Deal Reformism," *Ethics*, 64:272-273, July, 1954.

33. In describing his daily routine in 1933, Moley wrote: "9:00 In the President's bedroom to discuss the business of the day. The half hour between 9:00 and 9:30 was shared with Lew Douglas. He and I'd agreed in the beginning that each was to have fifteen minutes of that time, but one of us was likely to stay through the other's session." Moley, *After Seven Years*, p. 166.

34. Edward H. Hobbs, *Behind the President* (Washington: Public Affairs Press, 1954), p. 52.

35. During his first fifteen months in office, Roosevelt issued 674 executive orders, and a total of 2,538 in his first seven years as President. Caleb Perry Patterson, *Presidential Government in the United States* (Chapel Hill, North Carolina: The University of North Carolina Press, 1947), p. 146.

36. Nevertheless, the confusion resulting from inadequate information of this sort was such in the early days of the New Deal that, according to a story related by George Fort Milton, the "Petroleum Administration had jailed one J. W. Smith for violating a section of an order that actually had been stricken from a preliminary draft and so didn't exist." George Fort Milton, *The Use of Presidential Power* (Boston: Little, Brown and Company, 1944), p. 277. In an effort to eliminate such confusion by providing for coordinated dissemination of the many rules contained in executive orders, Roosevelt suggested in 1935 that all such orders should be issued in one publication so that their provisions would be readily available to all interested parties, both within and without the government. In the Federal Register Act (49 *Stat.* 500), enacted in July, 1935, Congress set up a Division of the Federal Register in the National Archives to publish a daily *Federal Register*, which would contain all executive orders, Presidential proclamations, and other regulations, rules, etc., having general applicability and regulatory effect. In Executive Order 7298, issued in February, 1936, Roosevelt sought to standardize and clarify the procedure of issuing executive orders further by requiring that all orders were to be cleared through the Director of the Register for uniform styling, form, titling, etc., before submission to the President. John M. Pfiffner, *Public Administration* (New York: The Ronald Press Co., 1946), p. 493 and p. 497; Hobbs, *op. cit.*, pp. 52-53.

37. At the same time, Roosevelt required that drafts of all other bills were to be submitted to the President through the Executive Director of the National Emergency Council, Frank Walker. With the decline in importance of the National Emergency Council, Roosevelt in 1937 vested in the Budget Bureau the authority for clearance of all legislative proposals, as well as all reports to be submitted to Congress and testimony prepared for Congressional hearings, and made the Budget Bureau completely responsible for determining if the position taken by an administrative agency on a particular measure was consistent with the President's program. Hobbs, *op. cit.*, pp. 57-58.

38. *Ibid.*, p. 58.

39. In commenting on Douglas's influence on Roosevelt in 1933, Perkins has said,

"I knew that Douglas saw him morning, noon, and night at the White House." Perkins, *op. cit.*, p. 272.

40. *Ibid.*, p. 270.

41. Both Moley and Ickes have reported that when Roosevelt decided to leave the gold standard, Douglas exclaimed, "This means the end of Western civilization." Moley, *After Seven Years*, p. 160; Ickes I, p. 659.

42. Ickes I, p. 174 and p. 194.

43. Following Douglas's resignation, "to Morgenthau's horror, Roosevelt asked him what he thought of Tom Corcoran as Douglas's successor. Morgenthau replied that this was out of the question: Corcoran was far too much of an operator. The Secretary, fearing more presidential bright ideas, quickly proposed as Acting Director Daniel W. Bell, a veteran civil servant who had entered the Treasury Department twenty-three years before . . . and had risen to be Commissioner of Accounts and Deposits. Roosevelt welcomed the suggestion. . . ." Schlesinger, *op. cit.*, p. 292.

44. By serving as Acting Director of the Budget on a temporary basis, Bell was able to retain his Civil Service status and seniority which he did not wish to sacrifice in order to take such a politically expendable job as Director of the Budget.

45. Harold D. Smith, "The Bureau of the Budget," *Public Administration Review*, 1:109, Winter, 1941.

46. Hobbs, *op. cit.*, p. 28.

47. Smith, *op. cit.*, p. 109 and p. 115. A trenchant summary of the Bureau's early inadequacies has been written by Arthur N. Holcombe:

"The Bureau came into existence at a time when the emphasis at Washington was placed strongly upon retrenchment and thrift. By example as well as by precept the early budget directors sought to give impetus and direction to the spirit of the time. The management of the Bureau itself was transmuted into parsimony, and the larger issues of administrative efficiency in the general business of government were obscured by the pursuit of petty savings in the budget-process. To balance the budget year by year, were the objectives which budget directors set themselves, regardless of the relations between public finance and the general welfare." Arthur N. Holcombe, "Over-all Financial Planning Through the Bureau of the Budget." *Public Administration Review*, 1:225, Spring, 1941.

48. Charles G. Dawes, *The First Year of the Budget of the United States* (New York: Harper and Brothers, 1923), p. 50 and p. 63.

49. For example, Ickes refers in several places to Acting Budget Director Bell's attendance at meetings as "representing the Treasury." Ickes I, p. 327 and p. 351. Arthur Schlesinger, Jr., has written that "Morgenthau, whose man Bell to some degree remained . . . now . . . felt he had . . . the Budget Bureau under his control. . . ." Schlesinger, *op. cit.*, p. 293.

50. Pendleton Herring, *Presidential Leadership* (New York: Farrar and Rinehart, 1940), p. 100.

51. Louis Brownlow, *The President and the Presidency* (Chicago: Public Administration Service, 1949), p. 100.

52. Paul H. Appleby, "Organizing Around the Head of a Large Federal Department," *Public Administration Review*, 6:205, Summer, 1946.

53. Harold L. Ickes was the other. During the twelve years, Roosevelt made a total of twenty-five appointments to the ten Cabinet positions; this involved only twenty-four individuals, however, as Henry Wallace served at different times as Secretary of Agriculture and Secretary of Commerce.

54. Statement by Miss Perkins to the writer, April 30, 1953. Other views attributed to Miss Perkins in the remainder of this paragraph are based on this interview.

55. It is Perkins' recollection that this was in 1941, shortly before Pearl Harbor, on the question of whether the United States Navy should try to defend Singapore if it was attacked by the Japanese fleet. In this connection, Cordell Hull has written: "The nearest the Cabinet came to formal voting on matters submitted to it by the President or any members was in the meeting of November 7, 1941, when I made a full report on the imminent danger of attack by Japan and Mr. Roosevelt asked each member his opinion on the gravity of the situation. Ordinarily the Cabinet did not take up a regular agenda of questions, debate them out, and at the end of the discussion have a show of hands or make any definite decision except to the extent that the comments of the members might indicate the trend of their opinion." Hull, *op. cit.*, p. 203.

56. After joining Roosevelt's Cabinet in 1940, Henry L. Stimson wrote, "The Roosevelt Cabinets are really a solo performance by the President interspersed with some questions and very few debates." Stimson and Bundy, *op. cit.*, p. 562.

57. Perkins, *op. cit.*, p. 377.

58. Jesse H. Jones, *Fifty Billion Dollars* (New York: The Macmillan Company, 1951), p. 303.

59. Roosevelt attributed most of the "leaks" to Vice President John N. Garner, whom he had invited to attend the meetings of the Cabinet. Perkins, *op. cit.*, pp. 133-134.

60. Ickes I, p. 308.

CHAPTER V

1. Harold L. Ickes, *The Secret Diary of Harold L. Ickes*, Vol. I, *The First Thousand Days, 1933-1936* (New York: Simon and Schuster, 1953), p. 50. (Cited hereafter as Ickes I.)

2. Established by Executive Order 6202A, issued on July 11, 1933. *The Public Papers and Addresses of Franklin D. Roosevelt*, Samuel I. Rosenman, editor (New York: Random House, 1938), 1933 Vol., pp. 279-280. (The volumes of this set will be cited hereafter as *Public Papers*, with a notation of the particular yearly volume referred to.)

3. *Ibid.*, p. 280.   4. *Ibid.*, p. 279 and p. 281.   5. *Ibid.*, p. 280.   6. *Ibid.*

7. The National Emergency Council was established by Executive Order 6433A, issued on November 17, 1933. *Public Papers*, 1933 Vol., pp. 487-489.

8. *Public Papers*, 1936 Vol., p. 58.

9. The Civil Works Administration was created by Executive Order 6420B, issued on November 9, 1933. *Public Papers*, 1933 Vol., pp. 456-457.

10. 48 *Stat.* 195. Public Law 67, 73rd Congress, enacted on June 16, 1933.

11. *Public Papers*, 1933 Vol., p. 488.   12. *Ibid.*, pp. 487-488.

13. *Ibid.*, p. 514.   14. *Ibid.*, p. 515.

15. Executive Order 6513, issued on December 19, 1933. *Ibid.*, pp. 530-532.

16. Arthur M. Schlesinger, Jr., *The Age of Roosevelt: The Coming of the New Deal* (Boston: Houghton Mifflin Company, 1959), pp. 545-546.

17. Executive Order 6889A, issued on October 31, 1934. *Public Papers*, 1934 Vol., pp. 441-444.

18. *Public Papers*, 1933 Vol., p. 531.

19. James MacGregor Burns, *Roosevelt: The Lion and the Fox* (New York: Harcourt, Brace and Company, 1956), p. 174.

20. The Industrial Emergency Committee was established by Executive Order 6770, issued on June 30, 1934. *Public Papers*, 1934 Vol. pp. 333-334.

21. Ickes I, p. 198; Donald R. Richberg, *The Rainbow* (Garden City, New York: Doubleday, Doran and Company, 1936), p. 82 and p. 183.

22. *Public Papers*, 1934 Vol., pp. 333-334.   23. *Ibid.*, p. 334.

24. Richberg, *op. cit.*, p. 186; Ickes I, p. 198.   25. Richberg, *op. cit.*, p. 82.

26. *Public Papers*, 1934 Vol., p. 442.

27. The members of the National Emergency Council under the new arrangement were: The President, the heads of the ten Cabinet departments, the Director of the Budget, the Secretary to the President, the Assistant Secretary of the Treasury, the Administrator of Agricultural Adjustment, the Administrator of Federal Emergency Relief, the Chairman of the Board of Reconstruction Finance Corporation, the Chairman of the Board of the Tennessee Valley Authority, the Chairman of the Federal Home Loan Bank Board, the Chairman of the Federal Trade Commission, the Director of Emergency Conservation Work, the Federal Coordinator of Transportation, the Governor of the Farm Credit Administration, the Adviser on Consumer Problems, the Chairman of the National Industrial Recovery Board, the Chairman of the Federal Alcohol Control Administration, the Federal Housing Administrator, the President of the Export-Import Banks, the Chairman of the Federal Deposit Insurance Corporation, the Chairman of the Federal Power Commission, the Chairman of the Federal Communications Commission, the Chairman of the Securities and Exchange Commission, the Governor of the Federal Reserve Board, and the Executive Director. *Ibid.*, pp. 441-442.

28. W. Y. Elliott, *The Need for Constitutional Reform* (New York: Whittlesey House, 1935), p. 97.

29. *Public Papers*, 1934 Vol., p. 442.   30. *Ibid.*, p. 443.

31. Richberg, *op. cit.*, pp. 183-184.   32. Ickes I, pp. 242-243.

33. *Ibid.*, pp. 220-221. Following the *New York Times* story, Roosevelt, who was always jealous of his Presidential prerogatives, exploded to Stephen Early in a memorandum of November 3, 1934: "Get hold of Krock and tell him . . . that this kind of thing is not only a lie but that it is a deception and a fraud on the public. It is merely a continuation of previous lies such as the headlines that Moley was running the government; next that Baruch was Acting President; next that Johnson was the man in power; next that Frankfurter had been put over the Cabinet and now that Richberg has been put over the Cabinet. . . . This whole story is made out of whole cloth and illustrates why the public is believing less and less the alleged news columns of the newspapers." Schlesinger, *op. cit.*, pp. 546-547.

34. Ickes recorded in his diary on October 2, 1934: "One interesting remark made by the President when he and Hopkins and I were alone was that the way the Government is being run now there is an inner Cabinet. He said the members of this inner Cabinet were Morgenthau, Cummings, myself, Miss Perkins, Wallace, Hopkins, Davis of the AAA and the man who would head up NRA." Ickes I, p. 201. It is significant that Roosevelt did not include Richberg as Executive Director of the National Emergency Council. Richberg did eventually become "the man who would

head up NRA," but not until much later, on March 22, 1935, when he was appointed NRA chairman. Richberg, *op. cit.*, p. 214.

35. For example, in a jurisdictional dispute between Ickes and Wallace concerning the transfer of some functions between the Departments of the Interior and Agriculture, Ickes noted in his diary that he wrote to Wallace "that while I was perfectly willing to discuss with him and the President matters of organization as between our Departments, I was not willing to refer the matter to Richberg since, so far as I was aware, he had neither the experience nor the special attainments that qualified him to pass judgment upon such a matter." Ickes I, p. 259.

36. Richberg wrote: "I asked the President to relieve me of responsibility as executive director of the National Emergency Council. There were physical limits to the amount of work which one man could perform at one time. The President persuaded my predecessor Frank Walker to resume his former position; and I managed to devote several full days to preparation for the argument of the Schechter case." Richberg, *op. cit.*, pp. 219-220.

37. Ickes I, p. 348. Richberg remained in the government as chairman of the NRA until June, and then returned to private law practice. He remained on friendly terms with Roosevelt, however, and in 1937 served as one of the President's chief behind-the-scenes lieutenants in the fight over Roosevelt's Supreme Court reform plan. He also served occasionally as a speech writing assistant until 1937, but after that date was not called on for such assistance because, according to Rosenman, Roosevelt thought his views were becoming too conservative. Samuel I. Rosenman, *Working with Roosevelt* (New York: Harper and Brothers, 1952), p. 142, pp. 145-146, and p. 158.

38. Robert E. Sherwood, *Roosevelt and Hopkins* (New York: Harper and Brothers, 1948), p. 53. Rexford Tugwell has written of Walker: "Everyone trusted and liked him. He was one character in the New Deal cast without taint of self-interest, of ambition, or of vindictiveness." Rexford G. Tugwell, *The Democratic Roosevelt* (Garden City, N.Y.: Doubleday and Company, Inc., 1957), p. 380.

39. Executive Order 7034, issued on May 6, 1935. *Public Papers*, 1935 Vol., pp. 163-167.

40. Ickes I, p. 422.   41. Sherwood, *op. cit.*, p. 69.

42. *Ibid.*, p. 71. Ickes' diary contains numerous accounts of such disputes, of the role of Walker as mediator, and of a good many cases where either Ickes or Hopkins carried the matter to the President.

43. Louis Brownlow, *A Passion for Anonymity* (Chicago: The University of Chicago Press, 1958), pp. 323-325.

44. *Public Papers*, 1937 Vol., p. 356.   45. Brownlow, *op. cit.*, p. 321.

46. *Public Papers*, 1933 Vol., p. 515.   47. *Public Papers*, 1939 Vol., p. 309.

48. Executive Order 7709A, issued on September 16, 1937. *Public Papers*, 1937 Vol., p. 356.

49. *Ibid.*, p. 553.

50. Ickes described this move in his diary as follows: "The President has at last agreed to set up a propaganda unit. On Monday Lowell Mellett, to whom I offered a position recently, will take over the National Emergency Council, which will be revived, and he will run propaganda from that vantage point." Harold L. Ickes, *The Secret Diary of Harold L. Ickes*, Vol. II, *The Inside Struggle, 1936-1939* (New York: Simon and Schuster, 1954), p. 375.

51. For a full description of all the National Emergency Council's informational functions see *Public Papers*, 1939 Vol., pp. 316-317.

52. *Ibid.*, pp. 310-330.

53. The duties of the Office of Government Reports were set forth in Executive Order 8248, issued September 8, 1939. *Ibid.*, pp. 490-496. All of 'the functions of the National Emergency Council were placed under the Office of Government Reports except those of the United States Film Service and The Radio Division which Mellett had been developing. These were placed under the jurisdiction of the Office of Education in the new Federal Security Agency, for, Roosevelt wrote, "these are clearly a part of the educational activities of the Government and should be consolidated with similar activities already carried on in the Office of Education." *Ibid.*, p. 315 and p. 327. Also see Lowell Mellett, "The Office of Government Reports," *Public Administration Review*, 1:126-131, Winter, 1941.

54. *Public Papers*, 1939 Vol., pp. 316-317.   55. *Ibid.*, p. 316.

56. John Gunther, *Roosevelt in Retrospect* (New York: Harper and Brothers, 1950), p. 51.

57. Frances Perkins, *The Roosevelt I Knew* (New York: The Viking Press, 1946), p. 360.

58. Raymond Moley, "The Issue Is Administration," *Newsweek*, Vol. 32, August 30, 1948, p. 84 and September 6, 1948, p. 80.

59. *Ibid.*, p. 84.

60. Rosenman, *op. cit.*, p. 104. Perkins also commented on this trait as follows: "Roosevelt's cabinet advisory committee (for the NRA) was perhaps an example of the administrative duplication we were to see so many times in the future. I had never noticed this characteristic in the Albany days. My own duties had been well defined and segregated, and I had never heard complaints from heads of other departments that Roosevelt mixed up their work with other people's and caused confusion. That became a constant complaint in Washington." Perkins, *op. cit.*, p. 210.

61. Doris Fleeson, "Woodring's Role Recalled," syndicated column in the *Champaign-Urbana (Illinois) Courier*, August 6, 1954, p. 4.

62. Ickes I, p. 326.

63. James A. Farley, *Jim Farley's Story, the Roosevelt Years* (New York: McGraw-Hill Book Company, Inc., 1948), p. 233. In this connection, see also Cordell Hull, *The Memoirs of Cordell Hull*, Vol. I (New York: Macmillan, 1948), pp. 202-203.

64. Perkins, *op. cit.*, p. 211.   65. Burns, *op. cit.*, p. 373.

66. Gunther, *op. cit.*, p. 51.

67. Herbert A. Simon, Donald W. Smithburg, and Victor A. Thompson, *Public Administration* (New York: Alfred A. Knopf, 1950), p. 168.

68. Gunther, *op. cit.*, p. 129.

69. Arthur Schlesinger, Jr., "Curmudgeon's Confessions," *New Republic*, Vol. 129, December, 1953, pp. 14-15. For further amplification of these views by Schlesinger, see his *The Coming of the New Deal*, pp. 533-552. Roosevelt's method of testing his subordinates through competition led Elmer Davis to remark on one occasion that it seemed to him "that FDR imitated the farmer with a batch of newborn puppies—he took them out for a row, dumped them overboard, and then kept those who managed to swim back to shore." Gunther, *op. cit.*, p. 83.

CHAPTER VI

1. *The Public Papers and Addresses of Franklin D. Roosevelt*, Samuel I. Rosenman, editor (New York: The Macmillan Company, 1941), 1938 Vol., p. 183. (The first five volumes of the *Public Papers*, covering the period through 1936, were published in 1938 by Random House; the next four volumes, covering the period through 1940, were published in 1941 by Macmillan; the last four volumes were published in 1950 by Harper and Brothers. The various volumes will be cited hereafter as *Public Papers*, with a notation of the particular yearly volume referred to.)

2. *Public Papers*, 1939 Vol., pp. 498-499.

3. *Public Papers*, 1938 Vol., pp. 183-194. In connection with Roosevelt's views as expressed here, it is interesting to note what Wilfred E. Brinkley has reported concerning a statement which Roosevelt made following his first re-election to the effect that "he could have employed better campaign strategy than the Republicans did against him; he would have attacked the New Deal at its weakest point, its administration." Wilfred E. Brinkley, *President and Congress* (New York: Alfred A. Knopf, 1947), p. 236. Samuel I. Rosenman has related a somewhat similar remark which Roosevelt made during the 1936 campaign to some of his speech-wriitng assistants. According to Rosenman, "He said to us: 'You know, boys, I had a lovely thought last night. I thought what fun it would be if I could now be running against Franklin D. Roosevelt. I don't know whether I could have beaten him or not,' he hastened to add cautiously, 'but I certainly would have given him a close race—a darned sight closer than Landon is doing. . . . I would say: "I am for social security, work relief, etc., etc. But the Democrats cannot be entrusted with the administration of these fine ideals." I would cite chapter and verse on WPA inefficiency—and there's plenty of it—as there is bound to be in such a vast, emergency program.

" 'You know,' he added reflectively, almost longingly, 'the more I think about it, the more I think I could lick myself.' " Samuel I Rosenman, *Working with Roosevelt* (New York: Harper and Brothers, 1952), pp. 131-132.

4. *Humphrey's Executor v. United States*, 295 U.S. 602 (1935).

5. *Myers v. United States*, 272 U.S. 52 (1926).

6. Arthur M. Schlesinger, Jr., *The Age of Roosevelt: The Politics of Upheaval* (Boston: Houghton Mifflin Company, 1960), pp. 279-280.

7. *Humphrey's Executor v. United States*, 295 U.S. 602 (1935).

8. Harold L. Ickes, *The Secret Diary of Harold L. Ickes*, Vol. I, *The First Thousand Days*, 1933-1936 (New York: Simon and Schuster, 1953), p. 374. (Cited hereafter as Ickes I.)

9. Louis Brownlow, *A Passion for Anonymity* (Chicago: University of Chicago Press, 1958), p. 326. Brownlow's book provides the most comprehensive account of the steps leading to Roosevelt's appointment of the President's Committee on Administrative Management and of the Committee's subsequent activities. Mr. Brownlow also supplemented the information in his book in a lengthy interview with the writer on May 5, 1959. Also see 75th Congress, 1st Session, Joint Committee on Government Organization, *Hearings on Reorganization of the Executive Departments* (Washington, 1937), p. 1.

10. The National Resources Board, later to be named the National Resources Committee, was created by Executive Order 6777, dated June 30, 1934. It was composed of Secretary of the Interior Ickes as Chairman, Secretary of War Dern,

Secretary of Agriculture Wallace, Secretary of Commerce Roper, Secretary of Labor Perkins, Federal Emergency Relief Administrator Hopkins, and the three members of the Advisory Committee, Delano, Mitchell, and Merriam. The members of the Advisory Committee had originally been brought into the government on July 20, 1933, as the National Planning Board to assist Ickes in planning the activities of the public works program. *Public Papers,* 1934 Vol., pp. 335-338.

11. This memorandum is reproduced in full in Brownlow, *op. cit.,* pp. 327-328.

12. *Public Papers,* 1936 Vol., p. 144.   13. Brownlow, *op. cit.,* pp. 337-338.

14. *Ibid.,* p. 333. See also Herbert Emmerich, *Essays on Federal Reorganization* (University, Alabama: University of Alabama Press, 1950), p. 64.

15. *Public Papers,* 1936 Vol., p. 144.

16. Clinton L. Rossiter, "The Constitutional Significance of the Executive Office of the President," *The American Political Science Review,* 43:1206, December, 1949.

17. Senate Resolution 217, 74th Congress, 2nd Session.

18. The other members of the Senate advisory committee were Luther Gulick, Director of the National Institute of Public Administration, Harold W. Dodds, President of Princeton University, Tudor Gardiner, former Governor of Maine, and Professor John B. Clark of the University of Nebraska.

19. Brownlow, *op. cit.,* p. 334.

20. *Public Papers,* 1936 Vol., p. 145. The President's letter is also found in the *Congressional Record,* 74th Congress, 2nd Session (Washington, 1936), p. 4146.

21. *Ibid.,* p. 146.   22. House Resolution 460, 74th Congress, 2nd Session.

23. *Public Papers,* 1936 Vol. p. 145.

24. George Fort Milton relates an interesting, though somewhat apocryphal, story about Roosevelt's appointment of Brownlow as chairman of the President's Committee, using the story to illustrate that Roosevelt's remarkable memory was one of his most important assets.

According to Milton's story, Roosevelt remembered a debate which took place between Brownlow and Joseph E. Davies, later Ambassador to Russia, in a meeting of the Council Club to which all three men belonged during Wilson's first term. The debate was on the subject of how the national government should be organized to run efficiently. Roosevelt had made notes of the views of both men. In 1936, he got out his old Navy Department files, looked up the notes, called Brownlow to his office and told him he had "dug out that memo because the views you expressed in your fight with Joe represent my idea of how government should be organized. That's why I have sent for you now." George Fort Milton, *The Use of Presidential Power* (Boston: Little, Brown and Company, 1944), p. 280. Brownlow has confirmed to the writer that Roosevelt did get out his old Navy Department files, looked up the notes he had made on the Brownlow-Davies debate, and discussed the views expressed therein with Brownlow at the time of the appointment of the President's Committee. But of course, this hardly constituted the only reason for Brownlow's selection, as Milton's version infers.

25. The Committee first offered the appointment as Director of Research to Clarence A. Dykstra, then the city manager of Cincinnati and later president of the University of Wisconsin. As Dykstra replied that he could not undertake the position before June, the Committee appointed as temporary director a well-known political scientist, Joseph P. Harris, who was serving at the time as the Director of Research of the Committee on Public Administration of the Social Science Research Council. It later

developed that Dykstra never did assume the job and Harris carried it through to its conclusion. *Public Papers,* 1936 Vol., p. 681; Brownlow, *op. cit.,* pp. 345-346 and 350-351.

26. The Committee's report and all of the special studies are found in President's Committee on Administrative Management, *Report with Special Studies* (Washington: Government Printing Office, 1937), 382 pp.

27. Louis Brownlow, *The President and the Presidency* (Chicago: Public Administration Service, 1949), pp. 105-106.

28. Ickes I, p. 596.   29. Brownlow, *Passion for Anonymity,* p. 381.

30. Brownlow, *The President and the Presidency,* pp. 105-106.

31. Brownlow, *Passion for Anonymity,* p. 381.

32. Harold L. Ickes, *The Secret Diary of Harold L. Ickes,* Vol. II, *The Inside Struggle, 1936-1939* (New York: Simon and Schuster, 1954), p. 23. (Cited hereafter as Ickes II.)

33. Statement by Miss Perkins to the writer, April 30, 1953. The other views attributed to Miss Perkins in the remainder of this paragraph are based on this interview.

34. Miss Perkins never found out exactly why Roosevelt held up the release of the report, although she said it may have been because he sometimes liked to maintain "an air of mystery" about matters so there would be "an element of surprise" when his plans were announced.

35. Interview with Brownlow, May 5, 1959.

36. Brownlow, *Passion for Anonymity,* p. 384.

37. Those attending the meeting were Vice-President John N. Garner, William B. Bankhead, speaker of the House of Representatives, Robert L. Doughton, chairman of the House Ways and Means Committee, James Paul Buchanan, chairman of the House Appropriations Committee, Joseph Robinson, majority leader of the Senate, and Pat Harrison, chairman of the Senate Finance Committee. *Ibid.,* p. 387.

38. *Ibid.,* pp. 387-388.

39. After witnessing Roosevelt's performance at this meeting, Herbert Emmerich wrote in his diary that night, "The President in presenting the report jumped around like a cat, three steps ahead of everyone. Among the numerous branches of this complicated tree, he barely touched the branches which seemed to give slightly under his weight and rested securely on those which seemed to support him." *Ibid.,* pp. 391-392.

40. According to Brownlow, the President's message was drafted by Luther Gulick. *Ibid.,* pp. 388-389, and interview with Brownlow, May 5, 1959.

41. *Public Papers,* 1936 Vol., pp. 668-674. The President's message is also found at the outset of President's Committee on Administrative Management, *op. cit.,* pp. iii-v, as well as in the Congressional Record, 75th Congress, 1st Session (Washington, 1937), p. 187.

42. *Public Papers,* 1936 Vol., pp. 671-672. This summary is also found in President's Committee on Administrative Management, *op. cit.,* p. 52. The Committee's full discussion of these basic proposals is found in pp. 1-53.

43. *Public Papers,* 1936 Vol., pp. 672-674.

44. 75th Congress, 1st Session, Select Committee to Investigate the Executive Agencies, *Preliminary Report on Investigation of Executive Agencies of the Government,* Senate Report 1275 (Washington, 1937). The Brookings report made many

suggestions for consolidations and transfers. Probably the most significant among them were the following: To create a new Department of Welfare, which would include all existing activities in the fields of education, labor, public health, and relief; to consolidate the transportation activities of the government in either a new Department of Transportation or a Division of Transporation in the Department of Commerce; and to place the governmental electric power activities under a single agency, either the existing Federal Power Commission or a new Federal Power Administration. The advisability of establishing a new public works agency to supervise all governmental engineering and construction work was considered by the Brookings investigators but was rejected by them, contrary to the recommendations of the President's Committee on Administrative Management.

45. 50 *Stat.* 7.

46. 75th Congress, 1st Session, Joint Committee on Government Organization, *Hearings on Reorganization of the Executive Departments* (Washington: U.S. Government Printing Office, 1937), 414 pp., *passim.* The position of the Brookings Institution, as presented by Lewis Meriam and Daniel T. Selko, is to be found on pp. 275-361.

47. Brownlow, *Passion for Anonymity,* p. 392.   48 See Chapters I and III.

49. *F. D. R., His Personal Letters, 1928-1945,* Vol. I, Elliott Roosevelt, editor (New York: Duell, Sloan and Pearce, 1950), pp. 696-697.

50. *Public Papers,* 1937 Vol., pp. 434-435.   51. *Ibid.,* pp. 498-499.

52. Ickes II, p. 349.   53. S. 3331, 75th Congress, 3rd Session.

54. Ickes II, p. 354.   55. *Public Papers,* 1938 Vol., pp. 101-192.

56. *Ibid.,* pp. 179-181.

57. James MacGregor Burns, *Roosevelt: The Lion and the Fox* (New York: Harcourt, Brace and Company, 1956), p. 345.

58. *Congressional Record,* 75th Congress, 3rd Session (Washington, 1938), p. 5123.

59. Ickes II, pp. 356-357.   60. Brownlow, *Passion for Anonymity,* pp. 398-399.

61. Ickes II, p. 360.   62. *Ibid.,* pp. 359-360.   63. *Ibid.,* p. 358.

64. *Ibid.,* pp. 358 850.   65. *Ibid.,* p. 375.   66. *Ibid.,* p. 411.

67. 53 *Stat.* 561. The Act had passed the Senate on March 21 by the razor thin margin of only two votes. According to Ickes, the bill had been saved because "Senator Truman had flown on from Missouri, and Senator Chavez, of New Mexico, had switched his vote." Ickes II, pp. 602-603.

68. Emmerich, *op. cit.,* p. 84.

CHAPTER VII

1. 53 *Stat.* 561.

2. *The Public Papers and Addresses of Franklin D. Roosevelt,* Samuel I. Rosenman, editor (New York: The Macmillan Company, 1941), 1939 Vol., p. 248. (The various volumes will be cited hereafter as *Public Papers,* with a notation of the particular yearly volume referred to.)

3. Louis Brownlow, *A Passion for Anonymity* (Chicago: The University of Chicago Press, 1958), pp. 413-416; interview with Mr. Brownlow on May 5, 1959.

4. *Public Papers,* 1939 Vol., p. 247.   5. *Ibid.,* pp. 248-249.

6. *Ibid.,* pp. 249-250.   7. *Ibid.,* pp. 259-260.   8. *Ibid.,* p. 250.

9. *Ibid.,* p. 251.   10. *Ibid.,* p. 252.   11. Brownlow, *op. cit.,* pp. 417-418.

12. *Public Papers,* 1939 Vol., pp. 261-263.   13. *Ibid.,* p. 254.

14. *Ibid.,* pp. 265-268.   15. *Ibid.,* p. 256.   16. *Ibid.,* p. 271.

17. Brownlow, *op. cit.,* pp. 418-419.

18. *Ibid.,* p. 418. After a relatively brief existence, the Federal Loan Agency was abolished by Roosevelt on February 24, 1942. Some of its activities pertaining to the financing of housing were transferred to the new National Housing Agency which was created on that same date. The remainder of its component agencies and functions were vested in the Department of Commerce. Of this transfer, Brownlow has written: "There is an interesting tale of why the Federal Loan Agency was so short-lived. During the war the President, through his counsel, Sam Rosenman, decided to send up a plan for the establishment of a National Housing Administration. I was ill in the Hay-Adams House at the time. I hadn't seen the President in a long time, but Sam came over to see me and said the President would like to see my initials on the housing plan. I said, 'Sam, I'll make a trade. If he will send up another plan to throw the Federal Loan Agency back into the Department of Commerce where it belongs, I will initial this.'

'But how in the world can we do that?'

'It is very easy now,' I said. 'Jesse Jones is now the secretary of commerce.' It was done." *Ibid., pp.* 418-419. See also *Public Papers,* 1942 Vol., pp. 137-139 for Roosevelt's discussion of this matter in his eight hundred and seventh press conference.

19. *Public Papers,* 1939 Vol., p. 269.

20. Major changes were made by Plan No. II. The Foreign Commerce Service of the Department of Commerce and the Foreign Agriculture Service of the Department of Agriculture were transferred to the Department of State where they were consolidated with the Foreign Service; the independent Foreign Service Buildings Commission was placed under the Department of State; the Bureau of Lighthouses was transferred from the Department of Commerce to the Department of the Treasury and consolidated with the Coast Guard; the Office of the Director General of Railroads and the War Finance Administration were abolished and their functions transferred to the Secretary of the Treasury for termination; the National Training School for Boys and Federal Prison Industries, Inc., were both transferred to the Department of Justice.

In addition the National Bituminous Coal Commission was abolished and its functions transferred to the Secretary of the Interior; the Bureau of Insular Affairs in the War Department was transferred to the Department of Interior, to be consolidated with the Division of Territories and Island Possessions; the Bureau of Fisheries of the Department of Commerce and the Bureau of Biological Survey of the Department of Agriculture were transferred to the Department of Interior; the independent Rural Electrification Administration was placed under the Department of Agriculture; the Inland Waterways Corporation was transferred from the War Department to the Department of Commerce; the Radio Division and the United States Film Service of the National Emergency Council were transferred to the Federal Security Agency and placed under the Office of Education; all other functions of the National Emergency Council were transferred to the Executive Office of the President and the National Emergency Council was abolished. *Ibid.,* p. 311; pp. 320-330.

21. *Ibid.,* p. 319.   22. *Ibid.,* pp. 319-320.

23. Public Resolution 2, 76th Congress, 1st Session; approved June 7, 1939.

24. Brownlow, *op. cit.,* p. 428.

25. *Public Papers,* 1939 Vol., pp. 491-494.   26. *Ibid.,* p. 491.

27. Clinton L. Rossiter, "The Constitutional Significance of the Executive Office of the President," *American Political Science Review,* 43:1209, December, 1949.

28. *Brownlow, op. cit.,* pp. 428-429.

29. Roosevelt activated the Office for Emergency Management on May 25, 1940. *Public Papers,* 1940 Vol., pp. 693-694 and pp. 697-698.

30. *Public Papers,* 1939 Vol., pp. 488-489.

31. Robert E. Sherwood, *Roosevelt and Hopkins* (New York: Harper and Brothers, 1948), p. 210.

32. Wayne Coy, "Basic Problems," *American Political Science Review,* 40:1131-1133, December, 1946.

33. The following were the major internal adjustments made in various departments and agencies by Plan No. III: In the Treasury Department, the Office of the Commissioner of Accounts and Deposits, and the Public Debt Service were brought together in a new Fiscal Service, under the direction of a permanent Fiscal Assistant Secretary, so that all of the Department's financing and fiscal activities would be consolidated; the Federal Alcohol Administration was abolished and its functions transferred to the Department of the Treasury for administration through the Bureau of Internal Revenue; the Bureau of Fisheries and the Bureau of Biological Survey, transferred to the Department of Interior by Reorganization Plan No. II, were consolidated into a new Fish and Wildlife Service.

Moreover, the Division of Marketing and Marketing Agreements of the Agricultural Adjustment Administration and the Federal Surplus Commodities Corporation, both under the jurisdiction of the Department of Agriculture, were consolidated into a Surplus Marketing Administration; the offices of Commissioner of Immigration and the offices of District Commissioner of Immigration and Naturalization in the Department of Labor were abolished; and the relations of the Administrator of the Civil Aeronautics Authority and the five-member Board of the Civil Aeronautics Authority were defined so that the Administrator would be the chief administrative officer of the Authority in charge of all functions other than those relating to economic regulation and the other activities of a rule-making and adjudicative nature which were vested in the Board. *Public Papers,* 1940 Vol., pp. 117-123.

34. The more important changes made by Plan No. IV were: The Weather Bureau was transferred to the Department of Commerce from the Department of Agriculture, primarily because of its importance to the field of air transportation; the Food and Drug Administration was transferred to the Federal Security Agency from the Department of Agriculture; the functions of the Department of Interior relating to the administration and supervision of Saint Elizabeth's Hospital, Freedmen's Hospital, Howard University, and Columbia Institution for the Deaf were transferred to the Federal Security Agency; the functions of the Soil Conservation Service in the Department of Agriculture with respect to conservation on lands under the jurisdiction of the Department of Interior were transferred to the Department of Interior; the functions of the Secretary of the Interior and the Secretary of the Treasury relating to the enforcement of minimum wage provisions in contracts for Federal construction were transferred to the Secretary of Labor; the functions of regular inter-building messenger service and the transportation of mail between government agencies and the post office, which had been carried on in Washington independently

by many agencies, were transferred from such agencies and centralized under the Post Office Department; and the independent Civil Aeronautics Authority was placed in the Department of Commerce. *Ibid.*, pp. 145-152.

35. *Ibid.*, pp. 144-145.   36. *Ibid.*, pp. 223-225.   37. *Ibid.*, p. 223.

38. *Public Papers*, 1939 Vol., pp. 319-320.

39. *Public Papers*, 1940 Vol., p. 223.   40. *Ibid.*, p. 224.

CHAPTER VIII

1. Bureau of the Budget, *The United States at War* (Washington: Government Printing Office, 1946), p. 16; Herman Miles Somers, *Presidential Agency* (Cambridge: Harvard University Press, 1950), p. 6.

2. Harold L. Ickes, *The Secret Diary of Harold L. Ickes*, Vol. III, *The Lowering Clouds*, 1939-1941 (New York: Simon and Schuster, 1954), pp. 4-5. (Cited hereafter as Ickes III.)

3. See 76th Congress, 2nd Session, Senate Document No. 134, October 24, 1939.

4. Ickes III, p. 4.

5. *The Public Papers and Addresses of Franklin D. Roosevelt*, Samuel I. Rosenman, editor (New York: Macmillan, 1941), 1939 Vol., pp. 586-587.

6. Civilian Production Administration, *Industrial Mobilization for War* (Washington: Government Printing Office, 1947), pp. 8-11.

7. *The United States at War*, pp. 23-24; Somers, *op. cit.*, pp. 6-8; Edward H. Hobbs, *Behind the President* (Washington: Public Affairs Press, 1954), pp. 156-157; Louis Brownlow, *A Passion for Anonymity* (Chicago: University of Chicago Press, 1958), pp. 423-432.

8. Brownlow, *op. cit.*, pp. 424-427. In this connection, it should be noted that the Industrial Mobilization Plan of 1939 contained a provision that, "The personnel to fill positions of responsibility in the War Resources Administration should be obtained from the patriotic business leaders of the Nation." Fritz Morstein Marx, *The President and His Staff Services* (Chicago: Public Administration Service, 1947), p. 7.

9. Statement by Miss Perkins to the writer, April 30, 1953.

10. Ickes III, p. 195.   11. *Ibid.*, p. 207.

12. *New York Times*, May 23, 1940, p. 1.

13. Robert E. Sherwood, *Roosevelt and Hopkins* (New York: Harper and Brothers, 1948), p. 159.

14. Statement by Miss Perkins to the writer, April 30, 1953.

15. Wayne Coy, "Basic Problems," *The American Political Science Review*, 40:1127, December, 1946.

16. Samuel I. Rosenman, *Woking with Roosevelt* (New York: Harper and Brothers, 1952), p. 190.

17. Ickes III, p. 8.   18. Brownlow, *op. cit.*, pp. 434-436.

19. *Ibid.*, p. 436.   20. Ickes III, p. 93.

21. *Ibid.*, p. 93; p. 181; pp. 186-187.

22. An interesting and detailed account of some of the behind the scenes activities pertaining to the appointments of Stimson and Knox is found in Brownlow, *op. cit.*, pp. 433-455. See also Ickes III, pp. 214-215; Sherwood, *op. cit.*, pp. 162-164; and Henry L. Stimson and McGeorge Bundy, *On Active Service in Peace and War* (New York: Harper and Brothers, 1948), pp. 323-331.

23. Concerning the appointment of Republicans to the war agencies, Robert Sherwood has written an amusing and revealing anecdote about Roosevelt and William S. Knudsen, the President of General Motors, whom Roosevelt placed in a high position of leadership in the defense program. According to Sherwood, "Roosevelt loved to tell a story of how, in the spring of 1941, Knudsen had sent him a list of some twenty names of prominent businessmen for appointment to executive positions in the Office of Production Management. Needless to say, most of the important men in this agency were Republicans. Having inspected this new list, Roosevelt said to Knudsen, 'There must be some mistake here, Bill. One of the men on this list is a Democrat.' Knudsen laughed and said, 'It's all right, Mr. President—I have checked on this man and found out that last year he voted for Willkie.'" Sherwood, *op. cit.*, p. 494.

24. *5 Federal Register*, p. 2109.   25. *Public Papers*, 1940 Vol., p. 697.

26. Somers, *op. cit.*, p. 43.

27. Joseph P. Harris, "Wartime Currents and Peacetime Trends," *The American Political Science Review*, 40:1137-1142, December, 1946.

28. Brownlow, *op. cit.*, p. 424.   29. Coy, *op. cit.*, p. 1132.

30. National Archives, *Federal Records of World War II*, Vol. 1, *Civilian Agencies* (Washington: Government Printing Office, 1950), p. 106.

31. Louis Brownlow had suggested McRenolds for such a position in the long August 1939 conversation with Roosevelt referred to above, after refusing Roosevelt's offer to place Brownlow in the post. Statement by Brownlow to the writer, May 5, 1959; Brownlow, *op. cit.*, p. 426.

32. *Federal Records of World War II*, p. 106; pp. 126-127; Marx, *op. cit.*, p. 21.

33. 39 *Stat.* 872.

34. Concerning the appointment of Miss Elliott, Louis Brownlow has written that "the President told me that 'Frances and the two Eleanors are after me to be sure to put a woman on the board.' 'Frances,' of course, was Miss Perkins, Secretary of Labor, and the two Eleanors were 'Eleanor'—Mrs. Roosevelt, and 'Elinor'—Mrs. Henry Morgenthau, Jr." Brownlow, *op. cit.*, p. 430.

35. 39 *Stat.*, 649; *Federal Records of World War II*, p. 126.

36. *Public Papers*, 1940 Vol., p. 243.   37. Ickes III, p. 104.

38. Sherwood, *op. cit.*, p. 162.

39. Donald M. Nelson, *Arsenal of Democracy, The Story of American War Production* (New York: Harcourt, Brace and Company, 1946), p. 89; *The United States at War*, p. 23; Somers, *op. cit.*, p. 11.

40. Sherwood, *op. cit.*, p. 162.   41. *Public Papers*, 1940 Vol., pp. 242-243.

42. George Fort Milton, *The Use of Presidential Power* (Boston: Little, Brown and Company, 1944), p. 292.

43. *Public Papers*, 1940 Vol., pp. 244-245.   44. *Ibid.*, p. 325.

45. *Ibid.*, p. 695.   46. Ickes III, p. 194.   47. Marx, *op. cit.*, p. 14.

48. *Federal Records of World War II*, p. 127; Somers, *op. cit.*, p. 13.

49. Ickes III, p. 194; Statement by Brownlow to the writer, May 5, 1959.

50. Nelson, *op cit.*, p. 87.   51. Ickes III, p. 194.

52. Nelson, *op. cit.*, pp. 82-83.   53. *Public Papers*, 1940 Vol., p. 245.

54. *Ibid.*, pp. 249-250.

55. Roosevelt described McReynolds' job as follows: "McReynolds will act as secretary to this body and be a clearinghouse, in a sense, himself. For example, this

list of factories and sites, et cetera and so on, would go right to Mac as the secretary of this group of seven; and he would give a copy of each of the things to each of the group of seven so that we could avail ourselves of the offers that have been made in case the group of seven finds we need it. In the same way, the people who have offered their personal services, all of these letters would go over to Mac. They would be listed and turned over to these people who would have to set up certain machinery with new personnel." *Ibid.*, p. 248.

56. Somers, *op. cit.*, p. 43.   57. Ickes III, p. 195.

58. *The United States at War*, p. 25.

59. See Herbert Emmerich, "Some Notes on Wartime Federal Administration," *Public Administration Review*, 5:55-61, Winter, 1945.

CHAPTER IX

1. Bureau of the Budget, *The United States at War* (Washington: Government Printing Office, 1946), p. 52.

2. *The Public Papers and Addresses of Franklin D. Roosevelt*, Samuel I. Rosenman, editor (New York: Macmillan, 1941), pp. 623-624. (The first five volumes of the *Public Papers*, covering the period through 1936, were published in 1938 by Random House; the next four volumes, covering the period through 1940, were published in 1941 by Macmillan; the last four volumes were published in 1950 by Harper and Brothers. The various volumes will be cited hereafter as *Public Papers*, with a notation of the particular yearly volume referred to.)

3. *Ibid.*, p. 625.   4. *Ibid.*, p. 630.

5. Donald M. Nelson, *Arsenal of Democracy, the Story of American War Production* (New York: Harcourt, Brace and Company, 1946), p. 117.

6. *Public Papers*, 1940 Vol., p. 691; *The United States at War*, pp. 53-54.

7. Executive Order 8629, 6 *Federal Register* 191; *Public Papers*, 1940 Vol., pp. 689-692.

8. *Public Papers*, 1940 Vol., pp. 683-685.

9. Harold L. Ickes, *The Secret Diary of Harold L. Ickes*, Vol. III, *The Lowering Clouds*, 1939-1941 (New York: Simon and Schuster, 1954), pp. 397-398. (Cited hereafter as Ickes III.)

10. *Ibid.*, p. 433.   11. *Public Papers*, 1940 Vol., pp. 690-691.

12. *Ibid.*, p. 692   13. *Ibid.*, p. 685.

14. Administrative Order of May 25, 1940. 5 *Federal Register* 2109.

15. *Public Papers*, 1940 Vol., pp. 693-694.

16. Herman Miles Somers, *Presidential Agency* (Cambridge: Harvard University Press, 1950), p. 20.

17. Nelson, *op. cit.*, pp. 125-126.   18. 55 *Stat.* 31.

19. Executive Order 8875, August 28, 1941. *Public Papers*, 1941 Vol., pp. 349-353.

20. On the steps of the White House, after a discussion with the President, Baruch told the press that the establishment of the Supply Priorities and Allocations Board was a "faltering step in the right direction." He continued: "You have seven excellent men there, any one of whom is capable of doing a swell job, but none has the final word." Ickes III, p. 614; Somers, *op. cit.*, pp. 21-22.

21. Somers, *op. cit.*, p. 21.   22. Nelson, *op. cit.*, p. 156.

23. Ickes III, pp. 544-545; pp. 614-615; pp. 617-618.

24. Robert E. Sherwood, *Roosevelt and Hopkins* (New York: Harper and Brothers, 1948), p. 475.

25. Executive Order 9024, January 16, 1942, 7 *Federal Register* 329; *Public Papers,* 1942 Vol., pp. 54-56.

26. In a memorandum placed in his files on January 14, 1942, concerning Nelson's appointment, Harry Hopkins wrote: "The amusing part of the whole business was that everybody was a candidate. Wallace, I am sure, hoped the President would ask him. Bernie Baruch was in a hotel room in Washington spreading propaganda for himself. A great many of my friends were pushing Bill Douglas. Morgenthau wanted it worse than anything in the world. So did Jesse Jones and, of course, Knudsen." Sherwood, *op. cit.*, p. 476.

27. Nelson, *op. cit.*, pp. xi-xii.

28. Discussing such disputes, one of Roosevelt's closest advisers, Judge Samuel Rosenman, has written: "The more serious . . . had to be settled by the President himself. I have seen him spend many hours, and often many days, deciding such disputes between the Army and the W.P.B." *Public Papers,* 1942 Vol., p. 57.

29. *Ibid.*, pp. 331-333.

30. Executive Order 9250, October 3, 1942, *Public Papers,* 1942 Vol., pp. 396-404.

31. James F. Byrnes, *Speaking Frankly* (New York: Harper and Brothers, 1947), p. 18.

32. Established as Economic Defense Board by Executive Order No. 8839, July 30, 1941. *Public Papers,* 1941 Vol., pp. 290-293. Following Pearl Harbor, the name was changed to Board of Economic Warfare by Executive Order No. 8982, December 17, 1941. *Ibid.*, pp. 294-297.

33. *New York Times*, December 17, 1942.

34. *Congressional Record*, Vol. 89, part 5, p. 7260.

35. *The United States at War*, p. 422.   36. *Ibid.*, p. 425.

37. Somers, *op. cit.*, pp. 33-40; *The United States at War*, pp. 421-428; pp. 296-297; pp. 445-447.

38. 78th Congress, 1st Session, Senate Special Committee Investigating the National Defense Program, *Report No. 10*, pp. 4-5; Somers, *op. cit.*, p. 37.

39. 78th Congress, 1st Session, Senate Subcommittee on War Mobilization, *Report to the Committee on Military Affairs*, May 13, 1943; Somers, *op. cit.*, p. 37.

40. Edward H. Hobbs, *Behind the President* (Washington: Public Affairs Press, 1954), pp. 187-192.

41. Byrnes resigned on April 2, 1945, and was succeeded by Fred M. Vinson who had been a long-time member of Congress from Kentucky, a Federal Judge, Director of the Office of Economic Stabilization, and Federal Loan Administrator before his appointment to the Office of War Mobilization and Reconversion. Vinson's designation was the last major appointment made by Roosevelt, a little less than two weeks before his death.

42. 78th Congress, 2nd Session, *Public Law 458*, October 3, 1944.

CHAPTER X

1. Caleb Perry Patterson, *Presidential Government in the United States* (Chapel Hill, North Carolina: The University of North Carolina Press, 1947), p. 146.

2. John H. Ferguson and Dean E. McHenry, *The American System of Govern-*

ment (New York: McGraw-Hill Book Company, 1950), p. 463.

3. The number of agencies and functions consolidated, transferred, or abolished during Roosevelt's Administration from 1933 to 1945 totals over 300. These were accomplished in almost all cases by Presidential action. *United States Government Manual, 1945* (Washington: Government Printing Office, 1945), pp. 590-622; Joseph P. Harris, "Wartime Currents and Peacetime Trends," *The American Political Science Review*, 40:1150, December, 1946.

4. Arthur M. Schlesinger, Jr., *The Coming of the New Deal* (Boston: Houghton Mifflin Company, 1959), p. 521.

5. Wayne Coy, "Basic Problems,"*The American Political Science Review*, 40:1131, December, 1946.

6. George A. Graham, "The Presidency and the Executive Office of the President," *Journal of Politics*, 12:599, November, 1950.

7. The Commission on Organization of the Executive Branch of the Government, *General Management of the Executive Branch* (Washington: Government Printing Office, 1949), pp. 1-51.

8. Clinton Rossiter, *The American Presidency* (New York: Harcourt, Brace and Co., 1956), p. 101; same author, "The Constitutional Significance of the Executive Office of the President," *The American Political Science Review*, 43:1209, December, 1949.

9. Herman Miles Somers, *Presidential Agency* (Cambridge: Harvard University Press, 1950), pp. 208-209; Graham, *op. cit.*, p. 603; and Fritz Morstein Marx, *The President and His Staff Services* (Chicago: Public Administration Service, 1947), p. 15.

10. Edward H. Hobbs, *Behind the President* (Washington: Public Affairs Press, 1954), pp. 84-85; Marx, *op. cit.*, p. 11.

11. *The Public Papers and Addresses of Franklin D. Roosevelt*, Samuel I. Rosenman, editor (New York: Macmillan, 1941), 1939 Vol., p. 250.

12. *General Management of the Executive Branch, op. cit.*, pp. 25-27.

13. *Public Papers*, 1939 Vol., pp. 498-499.

14. Harold D. Smith, "The Bureau of the Budget," *Public Administration Review*, 1:114, Winter, 1941.

15. Arthur N. Holcombe, "Over-all Financial Planning Through the Bureau of the Budget," *Public Administration Review*, 1:225-230, Spring, 1941; Hobbs, *op. cit.*, p. 29.

16. Louis Brownlow, *A Passion for Anonymity* (Chicago: The University of Chicago Press, 1958), p. 423. Brownlow's account of his own highly important part in this action is related in pp. 423-432.

17. *Ibid.*, pp. 426-427; p. 457.

18. Secretary of the Interior Harold Ickes reported in his diary on December 21, 1940: "The President also indicated that he was going to offer Fiorello LaGuardia one of his Executive Assistantships with the idea of making him liaison man between himself and the new setup. . . . I learned later that when the President suggested this to the Stimson, Knox, Knudsen, Hillman group, he met with almost unanimous opposition. The theme was that LaGuardia would not work with the team but would run all over the field with the ball." Harold L. Ickes, *The Secret Diary of Harold L. Ickes*, Vol. III, *The Lowering Clouds, 1939-1941* (New York: Simon and Schuster, 1954), p. 398.

19. Herman Miles Somers, "The President as Administrator," *The Annals of the American Academy of Political and Social Science,* September, 1952, p. 111.

20. Robert E. Sherwood, *Roosevelt and Hopkins* (New York: Harper and Brothers, 1948), p. 72.

21. *Ibid.,* pp. 72-73.

22. Rossiter, *The American Presidency, op. cit.,* pp. 117-118.

INDEX

216

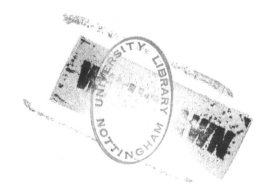